# Pagan Theology

# Pagan Theology

*Paganism as a World Religion*

Michael York

NEW YORK UNIVERSITY PRESS

*New York and London*

NEW YORK UNIVERSITY PRESS
New York and London

Library of Congress Cataloging-in-Publication Data
York, Michael, 1939–
Pagan theology : paganism as a world religion / Michael York.
p.   cm.
Includes bibliographical references.
ISBN 0-8147-9702-4 (alk. paper)
1. Religions.  2. Paganism.    I. Title.
BL85 .Y67  2003
299—dc21                        2002151073

New York University Press books are printed on acid-free paper,
and their binding materials are chosen for strength and durability.

Manufactured in the United States of America
10 9 8 7 6 5 4 3 2 1

# Contents

# Preface

Witches and neopagans are increasingly becoming fixtures on American campuses, especially the contemporary liberal university alleged to foster "destructive experimentation with personal identity." The associate provost of Boston University, Peter Wood, for example, does not find neopagans particularly dangerous but simply confused, deluded, frivolous, and devoid of intellectual seriousness. "Little inanities that once would have been brushed aside [by campus clergy] now settle in as opportunistic infections."[1] For critics like Wood, paganism is little more than a jumble of magical formulas and invocations to miscellaneous gods and goddesses that should be distinguished from the ethical guidance offered by Christianity, Judaism, Islam, and Buddhism. In Wood's view, contemporary paganism is a movement that disdains any goal of intellectual coherence, and he questions its position in a university community.

In a vote at Boston University among "legitimate campus religious groups, . . . the witches were cast out," allowing Wood to feel that in this case simple piety triumphed over the "idol of Diversity" that is otherwise increasingly becoming the prevailing politically correct ideology.[2] But despite the Boston University clergy's retroaction, paganism is frequently cited as one of the fastest-growing spiritual orientations, at least in the West. While many reasons may be furnished as to why this is so (the ecological threat to the planet, a popular emergence of antiauthoritarian spirituality, or part of the information revolution itself), the question remains whether paganism can be in any way considered serious religion.

The answer to this question is the purpose of this book. Part of the answer is to situate paganism as a world religion, that is, as a legitimate spiritual perspective that already exists globally. While the numbers of people who adhere to pagan religion may not be as numerically significant as those who follow the teachings of Christ, Muhammad, or Gautama Buddha, their numbers are still impressive. Although many, if not most, of them do not use the word *pagan* to describe their beliefs or practices, I contend that they hold an identifiable position of common characteristics and understandings for which the label *pagan* is feasible and debatably accurate.

Besides examining these particular "pagan" religiosities, I also explore paganism as a general form of religious behavior. To this end, I survey some of the other major world religions to identify the kind of spontaneous ritual veneration that can be interpreted as pagan. My aim is to show the pagan affinity of spiritual behavior that might be seen as integral to human nature. I then conclude with a theological analysis that distinguishes between paganism and gnosticism as essential spiritual ideal types that differentiate most religious activity. This means that I examine paganism as, successively, a religion, behavior, and theology.

To situate paganism as a theological religion and a religious behavior, we must first understand what religion is. This question is a vexing and contentious one. Despite the complexities and disagreements that the issue raises, it still is a necessary question to ask when considering whether any spiritual practice or affirmation is actually religious or whether its expression constitutes a religion. Here I contend that paganism represents what I term a *root religion* and that historically all other religions are offshoots and/or counterdevelopments of the root religion. Consequently, if we wish to understand any religion, we must also understand paganism as the root from which it grew. The irony in this understanding is that it precludes recognizing a root religion as being religious.

In chapter 1, I examine some of the world's living indigenous religions as constituents of a pagan religiosity that represents a major world religion. What are the shared characteristics of these practices and between them and classical and Indo-European paganisms? After initially concentrating on the "pagan religions," in chapter 2 I look at vernacular pagan behavior: the activities of cultic response found in other, nonpagan religions. Finally, in chapter 3, I conclude with a delineation of generic paganism from a theological perspective. I hope in this endeavor to establish the concept of paganism as a useful designation for an important religious perspective. In so doing, the advantage is not only the recognition of a marginal position but also the authentication of the basic differences among the religions themselves. My reason for doing this is not to create a religious threat to established world religions but to make clearer the integral self-sufficiency of each religion.

I would like to make clear that this book is in no way meant to be an encyclopedic presentation of religions. Rather, it is aimed at developing an understanding of what paganism is or at least could be understood to be. To this end, the book is part confessional, part apologetic, and part sociological. If I had to name my own denominational predilection, I would say that I am a "religionist." I believe in religion itself and its central role in expanding human consciousness above and beyond immediate daily concerns. In its overall, collective sense, I see religion as an ongoing dialogue that questions the purpose of life and our terrestrial incarnations. In my own pursuit and love of religion as religion, I have been particularly attracted to paganism not only as the source and origin of all religion but also as an organic alternative to the institutionalized authority and parochial insularity that much religious expression has become.

With regard to religions more globally, much of my direct experience of faiths beyond the Judeo-Christian tradition has been in the Far East: in India, Nepal, Thailand, China, and Japan. It is for this reason that my investigation into formulating an understanding of paganism draws particularly from these areas. In regard to other areas on which I have drawn for this book, my direct observation has been more limited. I recognize that this portends a deficiency from the start, but here I am searching for salient features that might support my thesis. These areas are, therefore, supplemental and not intended to be exhaustive. For tribal religions and especially for an awareness of Islam, I am more dependent on secondary sources, although I have nevertheless been able to benefit to some extent from direct experience in Muslim countries through visits to Morocco, Turkey, Pakistan, Bangladesh, Egypt, and India (which contains the world's second largest Muslim population).

I also have been involved in Native American studies since 1960. But with regard to sub-Saharan Africa, I am confined at present to two visits to South Africa, in 1999 and 2000. Consequently, I am particularly indebted to my colleagues in the Department for the Study of Religions at Bath Spa University College, namely, Richard Hoskins for suggestions concerning anthropological studies of African religion and Jo Backus for Aboriginal and Maori studies. Denise Cush and Mahinda Degale have assisted in the area of Buddhism; Catherine Robinson, in that of Hinduism. I would also like to acknowledge and thank my many colleagues who contribute regularly to the Nature Religions Scholars list: Chas Clifton, Bron Taylor, Jeff Kaplan, Wendy Griffin, Macha Nightmare, Tanice Folz, Gus diZerega, Barbara A. McGraw, Christiellen White, Fritz Muntean, Grant Potts, Doug Ezzy, Lucie DuFresne, Vivianne Crowley, Shawn Arthur, Cat Chapin-Bishop, Kirk White, Sian Reid, Barb Davy, Adrian Ivakhiv, Adrian

Harris, Jenny Blain, MJ Patterson, Jo Pearson, Shelley Rabinovitch, Eric Jette, Francine Nicholson, Jone Salomonsen, Sheri Morton Stanley, Laura A. Wildman, Dave Green, Brendan Cathbad Myers, Sarah Pike, Morgan S. Davis, Craig S. Strobel, Eylon Israeli, Marilyn R. Pukkila, John Bauman, Grove Harris, Nancy Ramsey Tosh, and Michael Strmiska, to name only the barest few.

Other people who have rendered assistance or inspiration or both include Phoebe Wray, Cara-Marguerite-Drusilla, Ian Elliott, Keishin Inaba, Lois Drake, Kenneth Jay Wilson, Caroline Robertson, Deborah Light, Melinda and Aidan Kelly, Melissa Ellen Penn, Jonas Trinkunas, Vilius Dundzila, Selena Fox, Dennis Carpenter, and David Nelson. This enterprise could not have reached completion without the assistance and suggestions furnished to me by Jennifer Hammer and Despina Papazoglou Gimbel of New York University Press. Finally, a special round of thanks are to be extended to my parents Otto H. York and Myrth Brooks York, to my wife Nancy York, my sister Myrth York, and to my dear friend Richard Lee Switzler.

# Pagan Theology

# Introduction

I believe in the supernatural, but I cannot demonstrate its existence. It is, by definition, beyond the empirical dimension of factual truths. Thomas Aquinas coined the term to refer to what is thought to be privileged *above* the agency and laws of nature, but I prefer the term *preternatural* as encompassing whatever is other than the ordinary, explicable, and natural. If we accept the preternatural as simply what is miraculously other than the natural or empirical, it carries the general understanding of what we mean by the supernatural but without connotations of hierarchy, that is, as something "better" than the natural. It is in this sense that I use the term *supernatural*, as a nonhierarchical preternatural reality.

The path between the supernatural and humanity is one way. We cannot approach it or interact with the supernatural as we can with the world itself; at best we can only prepare ourselves for its possible intrusion. The supernatural reveals itself to us, but we are unable to measure it and appraise it with our laboratory methods of science. It is "beyond" them and "beyond" our reliable means of control.

Religion, however we wish to define it, is a compilation of suggestions and techniques by which we might become receptive to the supernatural and encourage or discourage its operation within our lives. Some religions might dismiss it altogether; others, like Theravada Buddhism, devalue the supernatural without denying its reality. But other religions incorporate various understandings of the supernatural into their formulations of what is meaningful or valuable in the human enterprise, either individually or collectively.

My own understanding of religion is as a shared apprehension of the world, humanity, and the supernatural and their interrelation. Each religion formulates a comprehension of what these three poles of existence are in ways that provide significance and the location of value for its respective adherents. Some dismiss or devalue the supernatural; some dismiss or devalue

1

the world—but they all have a position on empirical and superempirical realities and their relationships to humanity. Those things that are accepted as valuable and meaningful within any given religious framework become its foci. This includes delineating the scope of possibility.

Perhaps an advantageous approach to understanding religion is to think of each individual religion as functioning like a map. There are many different ways of constructing a map, different features to be emphasized or ignored, different areas to be covered, and different ways of using the map. Maps can be complex or simple, out-of-date or useful for the given place and time at hand, accurate or misleading. But each map is recognized by its focus and range of emphases.

The use of a map depends in part on the authority that has constructed it. One might be drawn by an explorer into a new territory. Another might be compiled by the National Geographic Society. If we do not respect the map drawer, however, as presenting either an accurate or useful likeness, the map at best becomes something of idiosyncratic and antiquarian interest and not something to be used to find our local supermarket or the direction to Kathmandu.

A religion, like a map, depends on the authority we invest in it. If we have little or no respect for whoever has formulated the religion, its mapmaker so to speak, we will have little occasion to consult its schematization from the vantage point of a user. Christians respect the authority of Jesus Christ, his disciples, the church fathers, and the clergy. Muslims respect Muhammad, the Qur'an, and perhaps the imams or jurists. Confucians accept Confucius and Mencius as authorities who drew and legitimated the Confucian map. Scientologists turn to L. Ron Hubbard; Sannyasins to Osho; The Family to Moses David Berg, the Bible, and institutional directives; the Church Universal and Triumphant to Elizabeth Claire Prophet and her conveyance of messages from the "ascended masters"; and so forth. Each identifiable religion has a tradition or canon that it accepts as its prevailing authority.

In our modern world, however, with its growing questioning of all authority and its ever emerging cosmopolitan encounter with other traditions and different maps, there is a growing tendency for the individual to draw from within as well as from a range of available external resources to construct his or her own map. In this process, much of the individual's spiritual journey is achieved through a trial-and-error methodology of experimentation and innovation. But the individual is emerging as his or her own authority, perhaps one that is then invested in some other authority, such as the Buddha, a Tibetan lama, a rabbi, a charismatic healer or channeler, or perhaps one that is left with the self alone. Part of our contemporary intellectual and emotional ferment springs from the plethora of spiritual maps now available as well as the growing confidence for a do-it-yourself undertaking in cartographic construction of one's personal worldview.

The most obvious aspect of religion and maps is that they are representations and are not the territory itself. The map is not Banaras or Bath or Aix-en-Provence but a tool for finding one's way within those particular places. They are drawings and not the Ganges River or the thermal spring of Sulis Minerva.

The same thing applies to religions. They are formulations meant to help the individual navigate the intricacies of the world, nonempirical influence, and human life. They are not these things in themselves.

In the development of cartography, modern improvements have refined our mapmaking propensities with newer methods of data collecting, information analysis, and construction. To keep up with contemporary sociocultural changes, religious maps must evolve as well. The increasing disquiet and internal dialogue within the world's major religions as well as the continual emergence of new religious movements may be reflections of the current need for revised blueprints in the development of more suitably commensurate spiritual frameworks for our complicated times.

If religions are to be seen as unfolding maps of greater degrees of complexity, they can still be only as valid as the authority that is invested in them. The atheist and agnostic disinvest credible authority concerning spiritual validity, but for the world majority, traditional ecclesiastical institutions—church, synagogue, mosque, or temple, and their established clergies and prophets—still retain legitimacy. Nevertheless, as mainstream religion continues to lose its former public role vis-à-vis society as a whole, many in today's pluralistic and consumeristic social milieus have felt comfortable investing their trust in a guru or charismatic leader. In these cases, authority has been transferred from the traditional institution to an innovative particularity.

This growth in sectarianism is perhaps balanced by one in individual exegesis. In the great turn-of-the-millennium proliferation of spiritual authority, the locus of religious mapping credibility now extends from the established church to include, for followings of varying sizes, the self-proclaimed saint or revered prophet as well as, in many cases, simply the individual consumer herself or himself with little or no socioreligious connections to others or allegiance to any exterior figure or institution. In this way, religions are simply the different plans that different people find accurate or at least useful in determining their relationships with one another, the world in which they live, and the nonempirical as a possibly additional factor.

The point I wish to stress here is that each religious orientation has a right to legitimacy to the degree that its respective adherents so choose. Mind control or brainwashing by sinister manipulators is another matter, but what may look to be unfair coercion, intimidation, or duping from the outside can often be seen from an entirely different perspective from inside. Every religion has means for indoctrinating or acculturating its members, and some are more successful than others. But in every case, at some point the individual invests in the perceived legitimacy of the respective faith. As the Dalai Lama put it, we all are different, and therefore we need different kinds of religions. At the bottom line, a map is only as good as its user considers it to be, and just as many of us employ different kinds of maps for different reasons, so too many of us subscribe to different religions for various reasons—reasons that vary from having been born into a particular religion to those shaped by our developmental history and events in our life. Religious choice becomes something we judge for ourselves and in general refrain from judging for others.

As both a pagan practitioner and a religious studies academic, I am interested in paganism both personally and objectively. Since the advent of Christianity, paganism has generally been dismissed as a travesty of religion. This dismissal is, of course, a historical development that has little foundation beyond the built-in prejudices of a rival perspective. The attitude I take in this book is that paganism *is* a religion. It is not a parody but a legitimate, albeit different and distinctive, form of belief. The crux of the problem is how we define religion, any religion. From the layperson's perspective, there are doubtless many answers to this question. But scholars themselves are no more in agreement over what constitutes it. Indeed, academics provide not only an enormous range of conflicting understandings but also various breakdowns concerning the various kinds of religion. In order to understand paganism as a world religion, therefore, we must tease apart our understandings of religion itself as a broad category of human experience. If we can discern the nature and types of religion, we can then understand paganism as simply a particular form of religion.

The phenomenologist of religion Ninian Smart (1996) argued that there are two primary kinds of religion: that of *bhakti* and that of *dhyana*. The former involves worshiping the personhood of its focus. It tends to be theistic and involves a numinous or awe-inspiring experience. *Dhyana*, by contrast, is usually less theistic, concentrates on contemplation, and involves experiencing a mystical consciousness. The reality of religions, however, is that these two forms do not exist as completely separate categories but as two poles of a continuum along which different religions can be located—from nontheistic through idealistic and realistic forms of quasi monism and idealistic, theistic, and realistic forms of monism to personalistic theism. While Smart regards both polytheism and secular atheism as additional systems beyond the scope of this continuum, he considers shamanism as possibly the ancestor of both the *bhakti* and *dhyana* religious experiences. He also assesses the *panenhenic* experience (Zaehner 1957) as yet another type whose emphasis is on the dramatic experience of the individual's oneness with the cosmos. Unlike the necessary duality and numinousness of *bhakti* and the nontheistic contemplation of Theravada and Mahayana Buddhism, the panenhenic is centered on union with an ultimate.

Smart (1996) has little or nothing to say about paganism per se, and the word *pagan* is completely absent from John Hinnells's *A Handbook of Living Religions* (1984). Paganism gets only a mention in *The World's Religions* (1988), edited by Stewart Sutherland and others, in connection with William Frend's history, "Christianity in the First Five Centuries," and with Hugh Wybrew's exposition of Russian Orthodox Christianity. In both cases, the term refers to non-Christian targets to be converted. The designations *pagan* and *paganism* also find no place in Keith Crim's *Abingdon Dictionary of Living Religions* (1981) and Hendrik Kraemer's *World Cultures and World Religions* (1960). In John Bowker's *The Oxford Dictionary of World Religions* (1997) we find three brief entries, "Neo-Paganism," the "Pagan Pathfinders," and "Witchcraft." While Smart discusses the earliest religions; the Indian South Asia, China, Japan, Polynesian and Melanesian religions; the ancient Near Eastern religions; and the classical African religions in his *The World's Religions* (1989), paganism is mentioned only in his discussion "The Greek and Roman World" and then only infrequently.

Part of this problem is one of terminology. There is a reluctance to consider various indigenous religions as pagan despite the ostensible similarities they often have with the pre-Christian practices of Europe. A brief exception to this general tendency is found in William Young's *The World's*

*Religions* (1995), in which he recognizes Christian missionaries' use of the term *paganism* to refer to the indigenous religion of American Indians. In fact, Young claims that this pejorative term came to be applied to any indigenous population untouched by the Christian gospel, and he sees *neo-paganism* as a deliberate attempt to revive the earlier beliefs and practices. Young also continues the traditional understanding of the term *pagan* as a Roman reference to the "countryside," explaining the rural populace as the last to be converted to the new religion that first took root in the urban centers of the Roman Empire. Ronald Hutton, however, disputes this etymology and claims instead that the term derives from *paganus*, or "civilian," in contrast to early Christians who considered themselves as "soldiers of Christ." But Pierre Chuvin claims that this understanding fell into disuse before *paganus* entered the vernacular in the sense of pagan. He argues instead that *pagani* were simply "people of the place" who preserved their local traditions.[1]

While Ninian Smart's analytic is helpful for the study of religions, no religion is presented as nontheistic liberationism, quasi monism, realistic monism, personalistic theism, and so forth but instead as Christianity, Judaism, Hinduism, Buddhism, and the like or some form thereof. Among the broad sweep of world religions, a designation is required for the competing perspective encompassing or delineated by animism, polytheism, pantheism, and shamanism. One objection to using the term *pagan* is that it represents a Eurocentric imperialism that denies indigenous peoples their separate identities. Some would have the term *pagan* used solely for the pre-Christian European traditions.

There are two objections to using the term in this narrower sense. The first is a boundary-drawing question: what inherently distinguishes the European traditions from the Indo-European complex from which they descend other than the accident of geographic location? If the ancient European civilizations were pagan, why would not the related Indian and Iranian civilizations in their earliest expression be pagan also? If the line is arbitrary in the first place, it can just as easily be drawn elsewhere and more inclusively if need be. Second, I maintain that subsuming primal religiosities under a Eurocentric label is not "politically incorrect" but an ethnocentric blinder that prevents us from being able to appreciate the natural kinship between indigenous tribal religion and European paganism. Although Christian missionaries used the term *pagan* pejoratively, they at least recognized the similarities among the faiths to which they were opposed. My argument is essentially that if they can do it, we can do it too. In other words, as a general designation in today's more cosmopolitan world, it is time to rescue paganism from its historically negative connotations to be a useful and more affirmative endorsement of a neglected practice and marginalized worldview.

# 1

## Paganism as Religion

The difficulty in comprehending paganism as a world religion was made clear on the Nature Religions electronic discussion list after its participants failed to achieve official recognition in the American Academy of Religion. Part of the ensuing debate involved whether any future bid ought to be made again in the name of nature religion(s) or that of paganism. What emerged in the discussion of this question was the narrow understanding of paganism of many on the list. Most thought that the term referred only to modern, Western neopaganism.

The purpose of this book is to expand the concept of paganism. Western neopaganism is an important new development and can be considered an aspect of paganism more generally. But at the same time, it represents numerically but the merest fraction of those we can accept as pagans in the broader sense of the term.

I believe the most productive perspective is a global one. Despite its date, David Barrett's 1982 *World Christian Encyclopedia* provides the most detailed and comprehensive population figures for the world's various religions.[1] This work includes projections for 2000 as well. Extrapolating from Barrett, approximately 6 percent of the religiosity of the world's population is considered pagan. While the results concerning paganism, Christianity, Hinduism, and the like are rough estimates at best, at the same time the completed picture allows us to assess the relative numerical strengths of the world's broad religious traditions. When we speak of Christianity, Islam, and Judaism as world religions, how does the world divide them? What are the general positions of the various worldviews vis-à-vis one another?

To think again in cartographic terms, the religious maps of more than half the planet's population may be described as theistic and centering on a transcendent personality as their creator. Despite the overwhelming differentiation even here, broadly speaking one-third of the world is Christian and another fifth is Muslim. In the present venture to develop a global perspective, the many varieties of Christianity and Islam are secondary. It is enough at this point to recognize that half the planet or more affiliates with one or the other of these two religious identities and/or options.

The next largest "block" in the world arena is actually nonreligious, due to the historic influence of Marxism, scientific rationalism, and the growth of secular thinking. However, using Tillich's term, Barrett considers a category of "quasi religions"[2] consisting of secular movements that in part or whole can be regarded as religions, including both "antireligious quasi religions" and "nonreligious quasi religions." Atheism, communism, dialectical materialism, Leninism, Maoism, Marxism, scientific materialism, and Stalinism all are examples of quasi religions that are antireligious, while nonreligious quasi religions comprise various forms of agnosticism, fascism, humanism, liberal humanism, nationalism, and Nazism. They also, according to Barrett, include some kinds of nonreligious secularists, such as freethinkers, liberal thinkers, nonreligious humanists, postreligionists, materialists, and post-Christians as well as those who are indifferent to both religion and atheism.

Barrett describes humanism as a philosophy based on agnosticism and/or the rejection of supernaturalism. Both philosophies regard the human being as a natural object.[3] Essentially, whether naturalistic or scientific, humanism exalts the intrinsic dignity of the human individual and his or her ability to achieve self-realization through reason and scientific inquiry. However, this understanding leaves open the possibility of there also being a "religious humanism." This we can recognize as not only a strain of thought in Christianity but also an important theological perspective that is part of a pagan worldview. But if Christianity and Islam represent roughly half the world's population and if secularism (both atheism and nonreligious agnosticism) applies to slightly more than one-fifth of the global population, the Hindu-Buddhist orientation is the third largest with just under another fifth of the world's population. These people identify with either Hinduism or Buddhism as their primary religious affiliation. The vast majority of Hindus are Vaishnavite (70%), centering on the god Vishnu or his incarnations such as Rama and Krishna. A smaller number, fewer than half the Vaishnavites, are Shaivite or devotees of the god Shiva (25%). The third most significant Hindu tradition (approximately 3%) is described as Shaktite, the worshipers of Shakti or the female manifestation of divinity. Hinduism also includes various reformist movements (e.g., Arya Samaj), neo-Hindu sects, and modern Hindu movements. Buddhism, in many respects a "Protestant" form of Hinduism, is divided among the Mahayana,

Theravada, and Vajrayana traditions. Barrett places into a separate category the followers of Asiatic new religions, new religious movements, or syncretistic mass religions.[4] These spiritualities represent major innovations since 1800 and mostly since 1945 that remain distinct from the world's traditional religions. They include Japanese new religious movements developing from Buddhism or Shintoism as well as the syncretistic faiths emerging in such places as Korea, China, Vietnam, and Indonesia. Together, these new religions comprise about 2 percent of the world's population.

What is interesting about these *World Christian Encyclopedia* figures is the relative position of a traditional world religion like Judaism. Excluding those orientations that we can identify as pagan, the followers of Judaism as well as Sikhism, Jainism, Bahai, and all other remaining religions (e.g., Gnostic, Masonic, Occult, Mystic) constitute together *less* than 1 percent of the number of total global inhabitants. In other words, the religious profile of humanity in broad terms breaks down into six general categories: Christian/Islamic (50%), nonreligious/atheist (21%), Hindu-Buddhist (19%), new religious (2%), other (1%), with, allowing for a 1-percent margin of error, pagan as a sixth grouping (5% to 6%). It is to these animist, spiritist, and/or polytheist traditions we shall turn now.

The *World Christian Encyclopedia* projects world estimates for both mid-1985 and 2000 as follows: Chinese folk religionists (3.9/2.5%), tribal religionists (1.9/1.6%), shamanists (0.3/0.2%), Confucianists (0.1/0.09%), spiritists (0.14/0.19%), and Shintoists (0.07/0.04%). Barrett considers Confucianism to represent non-Chinese followers of Confucius and Confucianism.[5] The more than five million Confucianists estimated for 1985 are mostly Korean and found in Korea. Barrett recognizes six elements in the followers of traditional Chinese religion: local deities; ancestor worship; Confucian ethics; Chinese universism, divination, and magic; and some Buddhist elements. For tribal religionists, including shamanists, Barrett estimates 103,296,200 individuals in 1985 who would claim this orientation as their primary religious affiliation.[6] This category includes what are variously called primal or primitive religions, animism, spirit worship, shamanism, ancestor veneration, polytheism, pantheism, African traditionalism, and local or tribal folk religions. The Chinese are excluded as a special case. Barrett also uses such government census terms as *pagan*, *heathen*, *fetishist*, and *without religion* in compiling this category.[7] He includes adherents of revived or new paganism (e.g., the neopagans of Iceland) as well as non-Christian local or tribal syncretistic or nativistic movements (e.g., cargo cults, witchcraft eradication sects, tribal messianic movements, and possession-healing movements). The unifying element of this classification is the tribal or local association of the religiosity, one not open to all peoples but belonging to essentially a single tribe or people.

Tribal religiosity contrasts, therefore, with "universal" spiritism, whether "high" or "low." For Barrett, high spiritists are non-Christian and concentrate on the institution of the medium. They can be described as spiritists, spiritualists, and/or thaumaturgicalists and can be distinguished from "low," or Afro-American, spiritism.[8] This last is a syncretization of Catholicism with African and Amerindian animisim. It includes followers of Afro-Brazilian, Afro-Cuban, Afro-Haitian, and other African religious survivals in the Americas. It differs from "high" spiritism in its incorporation of Christian elements.[9]

The pre-Christian religions of Europe, especially those of the Greco-Roman world, constitute the paradigm of paganism. Before evaluating the Chinese folk, Shinto, tribal, and spiritist religions in terms of their pagan affinities and identities, I will therefore first examine the classical traditions, including the religions of the ancient Near East and Egypt and the European hinterlands, in order to gauge what might be considered salient features of these faiths. In this project, we do not possess the advantage of established properties, as ancient paganisms were living practices rather than defining dogmas or doctrines. We have little in the way of authoritative creeds and must approach pagan religiosity essentially as anthropologists in determining what might set this orientation apart from the Christianity that replaced it. We will therefore first consider the ancient paganisms of the Roman Empire and its neighbors before we examine kinship with other pre-Christian indigenous traditions and the living pagan orientations in the world of today.

In the multicultural cosmopolitanism of the Roman Empire, numerous mystery cults came to compete with the indigenous animistic religion of ancient Rome, a religion that had already been modified through both Etruscan and Greek influence. Particularly as the Roman state expanded to the East, mystery religions were imported into the capital. These included initiatory rites of the Anatolian Magna Mater-Cybele, Ma from Comana, the Egyptian Isis and Osiris, Sabazius from Asia Minor, the Syrian Heliopolitanus, and the Persian or Cappadocian Mithras. Along with these Eastern imports came Christianity, a religion that shared with its competitors the quest for salvation and likewise provided an emotional bonding for its fellowship of adherents. Membership in all these new religions rested with the voluntary choice of the individual, as opposed to an affiliation determined by either locality or family inheritance, but unlike the others, Christianity countenanced no compromise with other faiths, and eventually, with Constantine's recognition in 313 C.E., it became the state religion.

For the Romans, the term *paganus* referred to a "person of the place," whether town or country, who preserved the native customs of his or her locality. The pagan contrasted with the *alienus*, the "person from elsewhere," who increasingly was Christian and out of touch with indigenous expressions of polytheism.[10] While the term *paganus* acquired the additional connotation of "peasant," the alternative Eastern designation for *pagan*—the Greek *Hellene*—suggests that the pagan could be equally urban and cultured. Consequently, whether rural or cosmopolitan, the pagan is someone with intimate connections to his or her immediate locality who respects the gods of the city-state. As Chuvin points out, rituals conducted in honor of the local manifestations of deity were the key issue, taking precedence over faith.[11] Paganism was not a practice of professing dogma and doctrine but instead was the performance of cult acts. In a more modern context, this predilection of paganism was described by Margot Adler (1986) as contemporary paganism's concern with what is done rather than with what is believed. Paganism is experiential and not a religion of creeds and faith affirmations. Christianity came in large part to define itself in contrast to the indigenous paganisms it encountered. One approach to reunderstanding classical paganism, therefore, is to evaluate its contrasts with Christianity. Foremost, of course, is the polytheistic orientation of Greco-Roman religion as well as that of the Germanic, Celtic, Egyptian, and Near Eastern peoples. In contrast to the monotheism of the Judeo-Christian tradition, ancient paganism centers on a pantheonic understanding of the godhead, whether it includes the Roman Jupiter, Juno, Minerva, Mars, and Quirinus; the Greek Zeus, Hera, Athena, Apollo, and Dionysus; the Norse Thor, Frigg, Freya, Frey, and Tyr; the Gallic Taranis, Rosmerta, Epona, Teutates, and Cernunnos; the Egyptian Osiris, Isis, Nephthys, Horus, and Set; the Akkadian Enlil, Ninlil, Ninhursag, Ea, and Ishkur; or any of a countless additional enumeration of gods and goddesses in these and other traditions. In these pagan understandings, a particular deity was generally seen to possess certain functions and specialties rather than being an all-comprehensive, omnipotent, and omniscient figure. In other words, the range of cosmic being was apportioned and individually personified.

This pluralistic concept of divinity would appear to be typical of pagan identity. But this polytheistic bias does not preclude the possibility of a monistic understanding of the sacred cosmos. What ultimately distinguishes paganism from Christianity is not the number of its gods but the nature of its deity. Whereas the Christian God is transcendent, the pagan godhead is immanent. Spirituality for the pagan is corporeal or at least includes the physical. The pagan god is not "wholly other" (*ganz andere*), as is the Christian God. Consequently, paganism's corpospirituality allows for perception of the divine in nature, for idolatry, for appreciation of the sacredness of place, for contact with the divine through both local geodynamics and pilgrimage to revered holy centers, and for multiplicity of manifestation. Its deities are in some sense corporeal, whether through metaphorical bodies or venerated physical representations.

In a profound sense, pagan gods are human. Their superhuman qualities, whatever they may be or symbolize, are secondary to their essential human nature. It is through this anthropomorphic understanding of the godhead that paganism affirms its recognition of the fundamental affinity between humanity and its gods. The human being and the divine are intimately related to the extent of sharing a mutually kindred nature. This relationship, along with the distinction between mortality and immortality, translates into the ubiquitous pagan concept of soul duality (the Egyptian *ka* and *ba*, the Greek *thymos* and *psyche*, the Roman *genius-juno* and *animus-anima*) which conceives of the individual's free—or dream—soul as separate from the body—or life—soul (Hultkrantz 1953).

We will explore all these concepts in more detail as we find them in individualized, local, and ethnic pagan expression. We would be hard-pressed, however, to draw up a definitive list of necessary characteristics for any given practice to be assessed as pagan. At best, we can determine a range of possibilities that we might expect to find in any bona fide pagan example. These include polytheism, animism, idolatry, corpospirituality, local emphasis, recognitions of geosacred concentrations, perceptions of soul duality, and either nature worship or nature as a chief metaphorical register expressive of the divine. If paganism is humanistic in essence, it is simultaneously never far from exalting the natural cycle of birth-death-rebirth. Dying-rising deities (Ninlil, Osiris, Dionysus) are one metaphor for this cyclical understanding of the cosmic dynamic; phallicism is another. Consequently, despite its often underlying gnostic or transcendental philosophy, ancient Egyptian religion with its phallic god Min, its resurrected god Osiris, its pantheon, and its understanding of the individual's two souls, is pagan.

In comparing classical and related pre-Christian paganisms with Christianity, we find that paganism includes (1) a number of both male and female gods, (2) magical practice, (3) emphasis on ritual efficacy, (4) corpospirituality, and (5) an understanding of gods and humans as codependent and related. Paganism has no belief in historic revelation. Instead, this world and the otherworld are intimately interrelated, and while the myths and stories about the gods are chiefly to be understood as metaphors, the divine itself is to be experienced directly. Individual pagan religions furnish frameworks and techniques for encouraging experiential encounters with the godhead for both improving one's welfare in this world and exploring the otherworld in search of spiritual renewal. In other words, they provide hermeneutical tools for interpreting the world and the supernatural and humanity's relationship to both.

The traditional contemporary understanding of pagan refers to a person who is not Christian, Jewish, or Muslim. It is also a term applied to someone who is irreligious. Finally, it refers to an adherent to a modern revival of an ancient religion. All three usages, however, are unsatisfactory: the first for being too inclusive, the last for being too restrictive, and the middle for being inaccurate. Paganism represents a theological perspective and consequent practice that, despite its plethora of micro and local expressions, is a viable and distinguishable religiospiritual position, one that is today found, for example, as Chinese folk religion, Shinto, primal tribal religions, and spiritism as well as contemporary neo-, reco-, and geopagan new religions in the West. Let us, therefore, now examine these living traditions to assess how and why they are to be considered pagan.

## Chinese Folk Religion

The traditional religion of the Chinese people is often described as a blend of Taoism, Buddhism, and Confucianism. However, Fung Yu-lan (1960) claims that there is really a fourth element or tradition, which he labels *classical*.[12] The folk religion of China is the traditional worship of local deities, including both Buddhist and Taoist figures; the veneration of ancestors; a Confucian ethical system; a particular cosmological worldview; and the practice of magic and divination.[13]

The basis of Chinese folk religion is animistic, focusing on natural ob-

jects such as rocks, trees, springs, rivers, and mountains.[14] The autochthonous or indigenous deities associated with nature consequently form a
substratum for all other forms of veneration that extend to ancestors and
the provinces of home, family, clan, farm, harvest, community, city, and
cosmos. These fundamental beliefs in the powers of natural phenomena
occur against an understanding of the universe as the product of the two
cosmological forces of *yang*, "male," and *yin*, "female," the five elements
(wood, fire, earth, metal, water), and a hierarchical bureaucracy of celestial
agents.[15] Behind the macrocosm, calendar, city, temple, and family house
is the concept of the Lo Shu magic square in which south (placed at the
top) represents summer and life; north (at the bottom), winter and death;
east, spring and harmony; and west, autumn and harmony. This complex
understanding and its superimposition onto all human habitation form
the basis of Chinese geomancy (*feng-shui*), earth-based divination.[16]

Chinese folk religion is premised on the assumption that the spirit
world can influence the course of human events. "The whole structure of
the Chinese world of the supernatural [is] a complex interrelationship of
the occult and the everyday."[17] This is a pragmatic transactional faith
based on proper offerings and auspiciousness of timing rather than on the
degree of ardor and quality of devotional sentiment. "Harmony is, in the
Chinese worldview, primarily a this-worldly phenomenon."[18] The goals
are social and familial stability and prosperity as well as a pleasant afterlife. From a traditional Chinese perspective, maintaining good relationships with the invisible spirit world is part of ordinary behavior. This
world is variously understood to be another dimension embodied in the
visible world or a place to be found in either the north or heaven. Chinese
spirituality as a whole maintains a tripartite comprehension of the universe with its associated numinous forces: the earth and the *ch'i* (immanent powers), heaven and the *shen* (spirits), and humanity and the *kuei*
(ghosts). Each broad category requires propitiation for a balanced individual and communal state of being.

As with any pagan religion, the Chinese tradition reveals idiosyncratic
and individualistic characteristics. It has its own pantheon of deities; a peculiar perception of the relationship among humanity, the world, and the
supernatural; and its own mode of relating to the invisible. In the present
enterprise, we are looking for those particular features that render Chinese
folk religion a pagan form of spirituality. Others have argued that because
the various indigenous religions are separately tribal, ethnic, and/or territorially narrow, there is no such thing as a panpagan spirituality. Instead,

we have a series of radically different religions. I wish to argue, by contrast, that it is this intense locality of focus that is part of the universal quality that all forms of paganism share. The earth and nature constitute the seminal and unifying sacred text for the various localized expressions of what can be identified as pagan religions.

Earth by its very nature is known through the immediacy of local vicinity. If we look for a moment at the widespread Indo-European cultures, we find shared cognitive theonyms (etymologically related deity names) for the "bright sky" and the "dawn" but not for the "earth." Instead, names for the earth tend more often than not to be drawn from local associations, poetic metaphor inspired by the local region, and the terminology bequeathed by earlier local inhabitants. Despite consideration of a supreme and essentially transcendent "superior emperor" (*shang ti*), the Chinese also venerate the *t'u ti*, or local earth gods.[19] These are frequently represented by a stone block situated at a village entrance where joss sticks (incense) are offered. Jonathan Chamberlain found that both the philosopher Confucius (551–479 B.C.E.) and the earth gods operate territorially and that Confucius could now well be "the earth God of the state."[20] Unlike most other gods and goddesses who are depicted in anthropomorphic form, Confucius and the earth gods, as well as the ancestors and the leading Taoist deity, the Jade Emperor, are generally represented in plaque form. The local city god often functions as the earth god of the locality and serves as the link between the official religion and that of the people. As Chamberlain puts it, the city god is the "lowest Heavenly operative and highest Earth God."[21] Deborah Somme informs us that traditionally "at the state level, earth received sacrifices second in importance only to those of heaven."[22] The terrestrial cult involves not only the *ch'i* powers inherent in the earth or mountain peaks and other natural formations but also the respective powers of both the land and the growing crops.[23] Originally, these cults were practiced at state as well as regional and local levels. In the domestic and community domains, these earth figures are frequently associated with the ubiquitously popular gods of *fu* (happiness), *lu* (high rank), and *shou* (long life), the same three gods that one can often find in the window of, or on a shelf in, Chinese restaurants throughout the world. The earth gods are occasionally designated the "True Gods of Good Fortune and Virtue."[24]

Chinese animism is complex and involves a highly nuanced gradation of animistically charged or numinous spirits ranging from powers (*ch'i*) inherent in the sun, moon, forests, rivers, and lakes to those designated as *shen* that reside in the individual and in some other aspects of nature.[25] Those who die prematurely or violently may become *li* or "wraiths," which are considered dangerous. If, however, the *li* are provided with a "spirit place" (*shen wei*) where sacrifices in their honor can be made, they are given a sense of direction and cease to be "wraiths" or "hungry ghosts." These altars used to be found on both state and local levels. The domestic ancestor worship is part of this same transformative process in which the human soul and ghost are mollified and encouraged to be propitious to their living descendants. Offerings directed to departed ancestors form a central aspect of Chinese religious expression.[26]

The cult of ancestral spirits in which sacrificial offerings are made by blood descendants is distinguished from the worship of "public" spirits, the spirits of culture heroes, great teachers, virtuous individuals, and other people significant to the human enterprise. Formerly, rites to these last could be made only by high-ranking officials, whose influence likewise extended beyond that of their immediate kin. While anyone could communicate with his or her own ancestral spirits, it was considered inauspicious for ordinary folk to sacrifice to the higher powers, and no blessings would follow.

Popular worship today by Chinese folk religionists extends to a range of deities, both the spirits of natural powers and the deified spirits of once-living human beings.[27] As Somme indicates, "no unified pantheon or categorization of spiritual powers existed in China throughout antiquity,"[28] and this situation is essentially the same today. Virtually all "canonized" human beings, the Chinese bureaucracy of deities was recognized and elevated through imperial edict, though in reality the emperor generally acknowledged those figures who were already revered in popular sentiment.[29] In popular worship, apart from the special cases of Kuan Yin and Confucius, the most venerated and powerful deities are the Jade Emperor (subsequent personification of the supreme god of heaven, Shang Ti), Kuan Ti (a war god), and Tin Hau (queen of Heaven)—the latter two, if not Shang Ti as well, being mortals who have been deified.

Kuan Yin, the female manifestation of Avalokita, the all-compassionate aspect of the Buddha, is, like Monkey (Hanuman) and Na Cha (Vajrapani), a Buddhist development. She is nevertheless almost wholly a Chinese creation. In her propensity to absorb the properties of virtually all other goddesses as her manifestations, Kuan Yin belongs to a category of what I term *supergods*. Such figures as the Hebrew Yahweh, the Hindu Shiva and Vishnu, and the Roman Fortuna also appear to be similar developments. These supergods constitute a later, usually artificial, creation of supernatural powers that superseded the rudimentary animistic powers of nature and the apotheosized souls of humans. From a pagan perspective, they belong, at best, to a marginal realm between paganism and transcendentalism. Some supergods may be pagan, such as Fortuna; some are not, for example, Yahweh or Ahura Mazda.

The Chinese Tin Hau (or Ma-tzu, maternal grandmother) is an apotheosized virgin who is one of the few Sinitic goddesses to have successfully resisted absorption into the Kuan Yin hypostasis. She was born in Fukien Province and lived possibly during the tenth century C.E. She is worshiped today as protectress of travelers, especially seafarers. Her representations tend to depict her with a black face, as either a sign of impartiality or a connection through her aquatic associations with the direction of north, whose color is black. Chamberlain sees her as possibly a personification of the earth "in whose realm lie the Yellow Springs—source of water and of life."[30] She is sometimes associated with the goddess of measure, Tou Mou, an officiant of funerals, who herself may have derived from the Hindu Marici, goddess of the dawn.

Kuan Ti, or Kuan Kung, the red-faced god of war, is acknowledged as the most powerful of the Chinese gods. He is the god who defends the state, civilization, and morality. He is the patron of literature, restaurants, pawnshops, money changers, and secret societies. Originally, he was a virtuous general by the name of Kuan Yu, or Yun-chang, born in 162 C.E. He was captured and beheaded in 220 during the struggles that marked the end of the Han dynasty. His posthumous cult developed to the point of being adopted by the Buddhists in the seventh century. Later, the Taoists convinced the Sung emperor to grant Kuan Ti the title of duke in 1102. He was subsequently raised to prince and emperor and eventually accorded honors equal to those of Confucius in 1813. His image is placed today in Chinese homes facing the front door to prevent malevolent spirits from gaining entry.

Yu Huang, or the Jade Emperor, first appeared to the Sung emperor Chen Tsung (998–1023) in dreams, although it is claimed that he had had an earthly existence as the son of a much earlier emperor, Ch'ing Ti. As a result of retaining Heaven's imperial mandate, Chen Tsung began the process of granting titles to Yu Huang until, in 1115 C.E., he was identified with the supreme Shang Ti, the Superior Emperor, the highest of all the gods. Having gained his place on the "celestial throne," Yu Huang is now considered the successor of the more shadowy Shang Ti and, in this capacity, has become part of the supreme triad consisting of Shang Ti, Yu Huang, and his future successor, "The Heaven Honored One of the Dawn of Jade of the Golden Gate."[31] Shang Ti and Yu Huang, along with Tin Hau, Tou Mou, and the god of literature (K'uei Hsing), reside in the still center of the celestial heavens: either the North Star (the "purple planet") or the proximate constellation of Ursa Major. The Jade Emperor does not receive much direct popular worship, which is instead given to such deities as Tin Hau, Kuan Ti, and the wealth god Tsai Shen. The door or earth god, represented by a plaque of wood or tin placed at the foot of the door, is another relatively ubiquitous figure. There is also the stove or kitchen god who presides over the welfare of the household and reports on the family at the end of the year to the Jade Emperor in heaven.

Chinese worship is ritualistic. This means that it is essentially a matter of conducting the proper external forms rather than the internal maintenance of a particular attitude of reverence or devotion. This last is not precluded, but it is also not the central concern. The worshiper is interested in drawing the propitiated spirit near in order to ward off negative influences, ask for future blessings, or give thanks for favors already received. According to Overmyer, "The chief values in Chinese popular religion are health, a full lifespan, prosperity, family harmony, continuation of the family line, and protection from calamity."[32] The gods are usually offered incense, paper talismans, and comestible foodstuffs. Only Kuan Yin is not offered wine or meat, which is deemed inappropriate for this feminine form of the Buddhist bodhisattva Avalokitesvara (embodiment of mercy and compassion).

Since the invisible world is conceived as virtuous by nature, those desiring to communicate with spirits are expected also to be in a state of moral correctness and ritual purity. In describing Confucius' presacrificial vigils preceding communication with spirits and numinous powers, Somme cites the *Analects* 7.12, 10.7, and 10.8.10, which describe him as wearing immaculately clean clothing, altering his diet (eating only soup and vegetables), and changing the place where he commonly sat. "He thus removed himself from everyday existence in preparation for access to another dimension."[33] She also explains Confucian spirituality as not experiential transcendence but the more mundane "experience of connection and communication with people and beneficent forces both seen and unseen." Despite the transcendent emphases of Buddhism and Taoism, this Confucian approach is the more typical of Chinese folk religion in general.[34]

In the basics of Chinese religion, there is what Chamberlain refers to as

an "incurious acceptance of divinities": "They are, they have their special-
izations and they are to be worshipped."[35] Everything else becomes gratu-
itous and superfluous. Nevertheless, the "Chinese in relation to their gods
are rather like consumers determined to get the best value for their
money. Otherwise they will shop elsewhere."[36] The prime purpose of temple worship is the acquisition of good fortune in terms of wealth. While
some people visit merely to pay their respects, most are seeking help from
the gods in what is conceived of as an ongoing, mutually interdependent
relationship. Much of Chinese religious expression, therefore, is connected
with divination and falls under the aegis of such wealth gods as Chao
Kung and Pak Tai. The experience of the otherworld through spiritual invocation in the Chinese context, however, is in general oriented toward
family, regional, or political welfare rather than for the personal edifica-
tion of the individual sacrificer himself or herself.

Chinese folk religion has become essentially disestablished and no
longer receives imperial endorsement or support. In the People's Republic
of China, in fact, folk practice and belief are classified as superstitious
rather than religious behavior. Confucianism, too, has been relegated to
the status of philosophy, and during the Cultural Revolution, the Confucian temple found in virtually every town was destroyed. This leaves Taoism alone as the only pagan or pagan-type religion that is legally sanctioned today in mainland China.

Throughout the surviving folk practices both within and beyond mainland China, we can detect in religious lore, institutional expression, and ritual behavior various elements of polytheistic, animistic, and naturistic/nat-
uralistic religiosity. This pagan orientation cannot be separated from either
Confucianism or Taoism which, inasmuch as they constitute independent
religions in themselves, may be seen as offshoots from or even sectarian
developments of the broader-based vernacularism. As a pagan religion,
Chinese spirituality clearly reveals its organic interweaving of humanism,
naturism, and supernaturalism or magical practice. We find deified mountains, rivers, rocks, trees, and springs; honored guardians of home, community, city, and profession; human concerns like childbirth, health, wealth
and status; the ongoing interchange between the living and the dead; patrons of the weather; and particular meteorological aspects (e.g., rain, thunder, lightning); and apotheosized paradigms of virtue and civic contribution. We also find the wilder, less tamed, or even malefic personifications
within the Sinitic worldview, those very forces that proper ritual and efficacious deities and ancestors are believed to keep under control.

Chinese religion as such also includes Buddhism, and while Buddhism itself is not a pagan religion, in China it has adopted many pagan aspects and, at the same time, has been considerably incorporated into pagan vernacular religiosity. The Chinese pantheon is as likely to include Buddha, Kuan Yin, and (the military hero and Hindu-Buddhist derivative) Na Cha as it is not, reflecting a universal pagan urge to worship or venerate via an iconographic or idolatrous structural mode. Worship itself consists primarily of the ritualized expressions of wishing or thanking.

Much of Chinese devotion involves ordinary or daily concerns. This is, above all, a this-worldly religion. But apart from interest with the mundane and in contrast to the Mahayana emphasis on bodhisattvahood[37] and eventually nirvana, Chinese religion seeks immortality and, in exceptional circumstances, apotheosis. While the soul of the individual may disintegrate with the body, the spirit lives on.[38] This fluid understanding of the continuation of human identity, emotion, and consciousness becomes the foundation of Chinese veneration of the dead. In fact, as Bloomfield puts it, "There can be few other people in the world who are as involved with the dead as the Chinese."[39] With the typical pagan recognition of the thin line between the world of the living and that of the departed, the propitiation of ancestors becomes an easy consequence, as does the possibility of influence on the living by the deceased. A fundamental pagan attitude, which Chinese folk religiosity fully expresses, is one that considers the possibility of active exchange between this world and the otherworld.

Another aspect of Chinese religion is its basic nonpriestly character. According to Bloomfield, "Chinese society has always lacked a priestly caste."[40] Generally, shrines and temples as well as religious activities are maintained by the laity. Priestly supervision is often minimal if it exists at all. The function of the traditional Chinese priest, the *wu*, is predominantly as shaman and diviner rather than administrator. Whereas formerly such concerns as the vernal and autumn sacrifices, temple fairs, and religious festivals were conducted by local officials, these are now performed and supervised by the people themselves.

Chinese religion is also much involved with divination.[41] Whether through consultation of the *I Ching* (*Book of Changes*) or the casting of lots before a temple altar, the Chinese often seek to know the future. The practice of sortilege (foretelling the future by drawing lots) is once again something we find in classical paganism that is also associated with many of the pagan or quasi-pagan activities of today. Divination, however, may, in the final analysis, appear to be less concerned with ascertaining things to come per se as it is with divining the present and understanding the current influences for good or ill. It becomes therefore an attempt to act propitiously in the here and now and to achieve a more illumined state of effective decision making.

Divination, apotheosis, polytheism, and animism are constituent features of Chinese folk religion, along with venerational practice, festival celebration, geomancy, this-world/otherworld interaction, soul duality, and naturism. In other words, the traditional religiosity of the Chinese people encompasses the same characteristics that we find for the pre-Christian religions of the Greco-Roman world. The possibility that humans can achieve deification—whether in Egypt, the Near East, Greece or Rome, or China—is a pagan affirmation of the essential link if not identity between the divine and the human. The profile of Sinitic religiosity also confirms the pagan understanding of the sacred as fundamentally immanent, as opposed to transcendent. The Chinese pantheonic hierarchy refers to its administrative capacity and is not an ideological statement denying either ultimate reality or value to matter. T'ien or Shang Ti is resident in the North Star or Ursa Major and is not something "wholly other." He is, in fact, the son of the original mother T'ai Yüan, presumably the embodiment of yin and matter. All in all, Chinese religion—that of the folk as well as both Confucianism and Taoism—retains no nonpagan world weariness and world rejection. Even the Taoist attainment of the most ethereal form of *hsien*-ship, or immortality, is one of admittance to the "land of fairy." It is the same kind of fairyland that has become a ubiquitous depiction of the otherworld in the West; for both China and the West, it represents a transformation of the physical, not a renunciation of it.

## Japanese Shinto

The Japanese situation is highly reminiscent of the Chinese in that it consists of a national religiosity identity that blends together nominally distinct traditions.[42] The term *shimbutsu shūgō* describes Japanese Buddhist-Shinto fusion. However, with the Meiji reforms of the late nineteenth century, a *shimbutsu bunri*, or dissociation of Shinto and Buddhist divinities, was enforced.[43] For several Western as well as Japanese scholars, the creation of Shinto as an independent religion was an artificial and political development of the 1868 edicts. But even though Shinto ranges from imperial worship to shrine worship and sect worship, it also includes folk worship, which in many respects informs its basic underlying tenor. While the term *Shinto* itself emerged only in the sixth century c.e. as a response to Buddhism, as in China "popular or folk religion in Japan, which reaches back into prehistoric times, has always included divination, inspired healings, ancestor veneration, spirit possession, and the worship of other deities and spirits."[44]

The *minkan shinkō*, or "folk religion" of Japan, comprises an indigenous form of primitive religion to which elements of Buddhism, Taoism, Confucianism, and yin-yang dualism have been added.[45] Nevertheless, Shinto appears to be the base of folk religiosity. A typical *minkan shinkō* pantheon includes ancestral spirits, or *kami*; the Shinto deities Hachiman, Kumano, and Tenjin, respectively, the gods of war, the mountain, and learning; the Buddhist Kannon, Fudō, and Jizō, respectively, the goddess of mercy, the bodhisattva who destroys evil, and the protector of the otherwise unaided spirits of dead children; and the Taoist sun, moon, and stars.[46] The "seven lucky gods" of Japan—reminiscent of the Mongolian "seven old men" save for the inclusion of Benten or Benzaiten, the Japanese designations of the Hindu goddess of the arts and learning, Sarasvati—are popular figures who represent an assemblage of Indian, Chinese, and indigenous divinities having folk religion appeal.[47]

Consequently, Shintoism possesses a wide range of divergent expressions.[48] On one end of the spectrum, we find the imperial cult, drawing from the mythohistorical political digests of the *Kojiki* (*Record of Ancient Matters*) and the *Nihongi* (*Chronicles of Japan*), and the formerly state-regulated "Shrine Shinto" comprising most of the shrines found throughout Japan. What is known as "Sect Shinto" includes thirteen specific religious groups that came into being at the end of the Edo period (1600–1868) and the beginning of the Meiji period (1868–1912) and that gained governmental recognition as offshoots of Shinto but as something separate from official Shrine or State Shinto.[49] Beneath all three Shinto forms lies the loosely defined amalgam of folk practice, superstitious behavior, and magicoreligious rites with their emphasis on efficacious rituals and the use of charms and talismans. Japanese folk religion is closely tied to the cycle of annual festivals, observation of rites of passage, performance of exorcism, and even various ceremonial executions of cursing. In describing folk or popular Shinto as the common elements of Shinto worship that are peripheral to the other sects, Nigosian claims that "superstition, occult practices, and devotion to innumerable deities whose images or symbols dot the countryside are its most common features."[50]

The Japanese custom of having Shinto marriages but Buddhist funerals may be considered a development of this same fluid and adoptive perception characteristic of folk belief. Consequently, in Japan, veneration remains veneration, and whether it is performed in front of the domestic *kamidana* (Shinto altar) or the *butsudan* (Buddhist altar),[51] the household or kinship group shrines, the *dōsojin* or *sai no kami* stone pillar guarding the community's entrance, or the village hall, it transcends sectarian compartmentalizing. It is involved with what the Japanese call *majinai*, or positive magic, which largely has such typical this-worldly aims as happiness, protection, and exorcism.

As in China, Buddhism in Japan is colored with indigenous pagan elements. The interaction between Buddhism and Shinto has been constant and of long duration, despite their radically different theological emphases. Assimilative procedures of Buddhism in Japan include not only the identity of old folk deities as Buddhist deities but also the development of the *jingū-ji* (shrine temple) constructed within Shinto precincts as a place in which Buddhist priests may perform ceremonies—including the chanting of sutras—with the aim of securing the enlightenment of the *kami*.[52] Moreover, various Buddhist-Shinto syncretic sects came into being, such as Ryōbu Shinto, Sannō Shinto, and Yoshida Shinto. The first two took root in the philosophical concept of *honji-suijaku*, in which the *kami* came to be considered secondary manifestations of certain Buddhas or bodhisattvas as the primary entities. The Japanese term for the incarnation of a Buddha or Buddhist divinity as a Shinto deity is *gongen*, a word also used to describe a Shinto sanctuary style that developed during the Edo period when Shinto shrine types were strongly influenced by Buddhist architecture. Yoshida Shinto stresses that the *kami* are the fundamental phenomena from which the Buddhistic beings are outgrowths.[53]

As with animism in general, Japanese Shinto and *minkan shinkō* do not break down into neat classifications but are a heterogeneous conglomeration of ideas, feelings, and perceptions of unseen activities and living vitalities. The basic life force, or *tama*, animating the human body as well as the deity body of the *kami*, is a supernatural power capable of being simultaneously both male and female.[54] As Blacker explains, "The *tama* is an entity which resides in some host, to which it imparts life and vitality."[55] In Japan, it has provided the impetus for a religiocultural positivistic tradition comprising belief in enjoyment, achievement, gratitude, renewal, and purity.

As a religion, Shinto is focused on the *kami*. The scholar Motoori Norinaga (1730–1801), the famed Shinto restorationist, considered that the *kami* refer to anything that inspires a feeling of awe.[56] As Harris explains, "The *kami* themselves defy exact description and exist in an altogether different world while making their presence felt in the works of nature and of humans."[57] These are the spirits that dwell in the shrines, the gods and goddesses of heaven and earth. They constitute the proper objects of veneration. They may be found in trees, plants, rocks, mountains, oceans, springs, animals, birds, or human beings. But in all cases, they are perceived of as special and extraordinary.

In general, the *kami* are purely local. Some belong to nature or the soil, and some are concerned with fertility.[58] The evolution of the Shinto shrine itself parallels the developing perception of the *kami*. The earliest sanctuaries were simply specific areas marked off as separate—often by a ring of stakes, trees, rocks, or ropes of pleated straw. The *kami*'s physical presence remains today as either a consecrated flat and empty area or a sacred pile of rocks.[59] Other abodes of deity could be plots of land or even a sacred mountain.

In time, however, the *shinden* complex developed.[60] These are generally wooden buildings of which the *honden* serves as the main sanctuary, the seat of the deity. It is characteristically recognized by an elaborately latched pair of doors. The *honden* contains an inner sanctum that houses the sacred object (*shintai*) in which the *kami*'s divine spirit is believed to dwell.[61] "Sequestered within the innermost sanctuary, the shintai (referred to by priests with the honorific prefix *go-*) is a material object that is a shrine's 'holy of holies' because the Kami invest it with their presence during rituals."[62] According to Harris, the *shintai* is literally the "kami body."[63] The *shintai* might be a mirror, sword, spearhead, bow and arrow, bronze bell, magic box, fan, or scroll. It could also be the ritual purification wand, a folded cloth, a phallic elder or willow rod, or a baton to which paper strips are attached.[64]

The more permanent *honden* is an evolutionary development from the purely and often earlier natural setting of rocks, trees, or stake rings.[65] It has been thought to be a response to Buddhism and its impressive temples. Buddhist architecture is occasionally cited as the influence for the typical curved gables and roof edges of the *shinden* as well as the complexity of the emerging floor plan. The *honden* itself is often too small to allow physical entry. Instead, a worship hall is frequently found in front of the *honden*, sometimes connected with a covered passageway. The entire *shinden* complex is generally surrounded by one or more fences. A two-story gate provides the central access to the complex. This gate in turn is pre-ceded by the distinctive *torii*, or archway, indicating the approach to the shrine arrangement.[66]

But whether the more rudimentary sacred pile of rocks and ringed-off area or the more elaborate *shinden*, the notion of divinity as physically present and immanent in the tangible remains a perennial feature of Shinto religiosity. With nature itself stressed as a *kami* symbol, the natural is virtually always present in Shinto worship. "Shintō is essentially the rela-tionship of people to nature, and its rites express requests, gratitude and propitiation."[67] It is therefore through nature and the various icons as res-idences of the *kami* that one attains communion with deity. Even in the urban environment, this natural orientation is maintained and repre-sented in the shrine by a landscape garden with miniature replicas of mountains, rocks, ponds, and winding pathways meandering through the re-creation.

The animistic tradition of Shinto is rich and varied. Many of the *kami* are anthropomorphic. Some are taken from the *Kojiki* and the *Nihongi*; others are clan ancestors or renowned historical figures who have been apotheosized. The nonhuman spirits (*mi*), august spirits (*goryō*), demons (*mono*), and quasi-personified calamitous influences (*tatarigami*) remain beyond the range of specific shrine worship.[68] Although the Shinto pan-theon includes various cosmogonic deities, it is the local *kami* along with such figures as the sun goddess Amaterasu, her brother the storm god Susa-no-o, the war god Hachiman, and the *kami* directly concerned with food production that are the foci of popular cult.[69]

The fertility expression of Shinto animism blends into phallicism.[70] Penis icons are frequently encountered in shrines, temple, and roadside chapels. The principal phallic deities are the *dōsojin*, which are typically represented as a male-female couple: sometimes as a Buddhist monk and nun, frequently as an affectionate husband-and-wife pair, and occasionally even in the act of coition. As earth (or road) ancestor deities, they are be-lieved to ensure fertility and fecundity in animal, vegetable, and human life; to protect the community from illness and malevolent influences; and to safeguard the road and the traveler. The *dōsojin* may descend from the Jōmon period of Japanese prehistory (12,500–300 B.C.E.) during which erect stones, stone circles, or stones arranged in holes most likely indicated ritual spots or graves. The upright stones developed into phallic stone clubs. Early ones tended to be small, but a large stone club from the Ōzakai cave in Toyama Prefecture, dating to the Middle Jōmon period

(2500–1500 B.C.E.), both depicts the phallus and contains "raised lines and a carving of circle and tripartite lines symbolizing female organs." As Harris explains, "Such motifs consisting of male and female symbols sometimes appear in the decoration of clay pots and figurines."[71] These stone clubs, containing combinations of male and female symbols, were established not only at sacred spots but also at building entrances, more than likely being antecedent to the more ubiquitous *dōsojin* of today.

*Dōsojin* are generally found in the countryside, often at crossroads leading from a town or toward the rice fields. In rural communities, they may be seen as adjuncts to the shrine of the tutelary deity or, alone, at the village center or adjacent to the town hall where public notices are posted. These deities are variously identified. They may be understood as a god of happiness (Sai-no-Kami), as a "road-blocking deity" (Sae-no-Kami), or as the procreative divine couple Izanagi and Izanami.[72] More frequently, however, a *dōsojin* is regarded as the phallic deity Saruta-hiko (monkey rice field prince) or the divine shamaness Ame-no-Uzume (heaven-alarming female, the goddess of sexual attraction) or as both these figures. Sometimes a *dōsojin* represents a triad composed of Saruta, Uzume, and the popular cereal goddess Ugadama (Toyouke).[73]

The composite nature of significant *kami* is a recurring feature in Shinto. Beside the *dōsojin* and the war god Hachiman, there is the highly popular rice deity, Inari-sama. Harris considers that approximately one-third of the 100,000 listed shrines of Japan are dedicated to this deity of rice production.[74] Worshiped throughout Japan and especially at Kyoto's Fushimi-Inari shrine complex, Inari represents Saruta-hiko, Uzume, Onamochi, and Ugadama.[75] The composite yet singular Inari-sama typifies the *kami* of food and productivity that lie closer to the root level of Shinto and were too important to folk worship not to be included in the political formation of a state pantheon. We can also recognize the fluid pantheonic interplay among many of the figures of popular cult. Both the *dōsojin* and Inari include the *kami* of Saruta, Uzume, and Ugadama.[76]

The Grand Shrine of Ise, dedicated to Amaterasu and Toyouke (Ugadama) in Mie Prefecture fronting the Pacific Ocean, is perhaps the most revered spot in Japan. Another grand shrine pilgrimage center, that of Izumo Taisha and dedicated to the *kami* of fishing and sericulture, is found on the Japan Sea side of the country in Shimane Prefecture. But while Ise is sacrosanct, distancing, and exclusive, and Okuni-nushi's shrine of Izumo is openly austere, the Fushimi-Inari Shrine in Kyoto contains the more familiar elements of popular cult. With its *nagare-zukuri*–style *honden, romon,* and various additional buildings painted in striking white and vermilion lacquer, Fushimi-Inari occupies a three-pronged hill or small mountain in the southeastern corner of Kyoto. The area is full of small shrines guarded by statues of foxes, the messengers of Inari. Sexual symbolism abounds. The Shoichi kuniyo dai-myōjin tree, whose two main roots suggest the kteis or female genitalia, is a highly venerated pine tree at the Kyoto shrine. It is, however, the *torii* (temple gateways) and *otsuka* (sacred stones) that chiefly characterize the Fushimi-Inari cult center. The entire mountain is laced with stone pathways forming corridors beneath the vermilion-lacquered sacred gates erected by pious devotees. There are thought to be ten thousand *torii* and more than twenty thousand *otsuka*.

Fushimi-Inari and the ubiquitous roadside *dōsojin* shrines typically express the cultivation of numinous presence and aura in both Japanese Shinto and paganism more universally. A particular form of *dōsojin* is the *korin-seki* or *yogo* stones found along roadsides: natural stones, one set on top of the other and identified through the presence of straw ropes, paper strips, and other cult vestiges.[77] The venerative act performed by those seeking safety while traveling or successful matchmaking consists of raising the upper stone and carrying it around the lower one while praying and imitating male and female behavior. More commonly found, however, are the stone sculptures of the *dōsojin* couple of which it is often possible to distinguish the male figure from the female partner only with great difficulty if at all. This nondifferentiation of such an earth-oriented fertility deity is characteristic, and with this singular deity, we find one of the clearest expressions of *anima-animus* veneration as a unified but dualistic principle. The animistic identity of Shinto retains many aspects in common with venerative cults found throughout Asia. Aside from the more strictly shamanic and phallic tendencies, such correspondences include the *jichin-sai* ceremony in which the land *kami* of a construction site, river, or mountain are propitiated with offerings of saké, rice, money, and strips of cloth.[78]

Shinto also includes the same idea of apotheosis as found in the religious expression of China. The god of learning Tenjin represents the deification of Sugawara no Michizane (845–903). At the lovely Tōshōgū shrine of Nikkō are enshrined the spirits of three of Japan's most famous shoguns: Minamoto Yoritomo (1147–1199), Toyotomi Hideyoshi (1537–1598), and Tokugawa Ieyasu (1543–1616). This last, the founder of the Tokugawa shogunate of Edo (Tokyo) which ruled the country from 1603 until 1867, was granted the honorific title of Gongen sama (the incarnated one). The deification process, of course, extends to emperors but also includes many local heroes, illustrious personages, or provincial warriors. These may be identified with the locally venerated *dōsojin* or considered as august spirits (*goryō* or *goryō-shin*) and *arahito-gami* (rough man god) and are honored as neighborhood protectors. It is perhaps the this-worldly orientation of Shinto, however, that more than anything else links it with pagan veneration. The preoccupation is with this life rather than with the world-to-come. This, coupled with a belief in the oneness of god and humans, divinity and humanity, has produced a positivistic expression stressing gratitude and renewal as well as simplicity, purity, honesty, endeavor, and selflessness.

Shinto is rooted in a perception of *kami* that are generally believed to reside during the winter in the mountains but descend to the cultivated areas in the springtime as deities of the fields.[79] With the coming of each new year, the *kami* are revitalized. They may be petitioned for tangible blessings, or one may seek an inner mystical experience, that is, internal communion with the *kami*. Shinto, and especially the Folk Shinto *dōsojin* corpus of belief and custom, merges into folk religion more collectively with its magicoreligious emphasis that stresses efficacious rituals and the use of charms and talismans. It is closely tied to the cycle of annual festivals and observes rites of passage as well as those of exorcism and even various ceremonial forms of cursing. Shinto, however, is unusual among the different forms of paganism in its largely aniconic or image-free character. True enough, the gods may be representationally depicted, especially in such roadside protectors and fertility figures as the *dōsojin*, but the typical Shinto shrine displays no plastic or anthropoid image.[80] Instead, it is in the Buddhist temple that Japanese idolatry finds its chief expression.

It is the naturalistic orientation of the *kami* that is the cornerstone of Shinto. This includes ancestor worship and spreads into the areas of shamanism and phallicism. Veneration of the phallus and *kteis*, like that of the Indian *lingam* and *yoni*, rests on the dual aspects of these symbols as both procreative and preventive or protective powers. The cult of stones as having magical capabilities—particularly those of phallic or ktenic shape —is found across Japan. Round stones are specifically associated with the female, while phalli are found throughout the shrines or roadside chapels as either natural or carved stones or as reproduced in wood.

Shinto also is infused with shamanic practices. These have many features in common with Korean forms, but unlike the case in Korea, it is almost exclusively the female shaman or shamaness that presides in Japan, as the *miko* or *kuchiyose*. Male magicians and practitioners also can be found. The primary function of the Japanese shaman is that of the *asobi-be*, the person who invokes the *mitama* or *shinrei*—the spirit or emanation of the *kami*—and mandates its ceremonial presence. The principal female shaman is considered to be the erotic goddess Uzume.

Finding a root inspiration through ancestor worship—the revering of *sosenshin* (ancestral *kami*) and *ujigami* (*kami* of the kin group)—folk religion rests on a fundamental animism and frequently resorts to a shamanist approach to a pervasive world of life and spirit. *Kami* are of all kinds, but predominant are those belonging to nature and agriculture and involved with fertility. Like humankind, they delineate the human soul.[81]

When the postmortem human soul receives proper commemoration over a period of time, it is believed to join the *sosenshin* capable of bringing blessing to its descendants or worshipers at large. Neglected souls, however, may evolve into vengeful *goryō*. Even malevolent *kami* and spirits as well as animal spirits can become, through propitiation and rites of honor, not only deflected from inflicting harm but also won over as powerful protectors, that is, as community-guarding *goryō*, clan-defending *wakamiya*, or bodhisattva-sheltering attendants.[82]

In the Japanese perception, however, the *tama*, or life force, does not become a *kami* per se but is something that both the human being and the *kami* possess or emanate in common, once again suggesting the divine-human link definitive of paganism. The deific spirit of the *kami* is more correctly known as the *shinrei*. Otherwise, the deity is considered to have four souls: the "rough soul," the "gentle soul," the "luck soul," and the "wondrous soul."[83] These four souls are implicit in human beings as well. Since the blessing-bestowing "luck soul" and the mysterious transformation-causing "wondrous soul" are considered the two aspects of the gentle and pacifying soul, there is really an understanding of soul duality.[84] While the *tama* is the agent animating an object or entity and giving it life and vitality, the coarser and more violent "rough soul" may be thought of as the body soul. The "gentle soul" corresponds then to the free soul.

In Japan, the word *matsuri* refers to both "worship," especially that relating to individuals and their daily life, and "communal festival," in which food, drink, music, *norito* (prayers), and sacred *kagura* dances are offered to the deities. The general pattern of the Shinto *matsuri* at a shrine begins with an overall purification of both the area and the items to be used as well as the performers themselves. Only then does the invocation occur, followed by the presentation of the offerings, recitation of the *norito*, presentation of the *shintai*, offering of music and dance, and a culminating divination. At the conclusion, the offerings are withdrawn for a final feast which takes place after the divine spirit is invited to depart.[85] Japan is a country of perpetual festivals. Every community celebrates its festival in honor of the local *kami*, and each shrine also holds commemorations for its enshrined deity. Many celebrate in particular the various stages in the growing of rice—irrigation, sowing, transplanting, protection, harvest, and thanksgiving.[86]

All in all, we can see in Japanese Shinto some differences but at the same time many similarities with the immanent, this-worldly, polytheistic religiosity of China. In both nations, there has been a historical fusion of indigenous ideologies with Buddhism, though again with both peoples, pagan assumptions can be distinguished from Buddhist theology. While the respective pantheons are different and essentially culturally local, in broad outline and range of departmental focus, they remain generically similar.

Terminologies differ, but the basic outline of soul-duality beliefs is detectable among both the Chinese and Japanese peoples. In the religious orientation we are delineating, the quest for an afterlife of extinction or oblivion is absent. Whether a permanent destination or a domain of sojourn between terrestrial lives, the otherworld plays a role in Chinese and Japanese pagan beliefs. This otherworld is invariably modeled on a concept of the earthly paradise. It is a place of delight, a fairyland, which is sensual even when ethereal. The pagan concept of the afterworld may include an understanding of a vapid, gloomy Hades in which insubstantial shades dwell, but even this spectral dimension is usually complemented by the more joyous land of enchantment and ecstasy, the natural home of the gods.

At the same time, this otherworld is never something wholly other. It intersects with the empirical world of time and space and is immanent within the here-and-now of reality. Particular physical places are thought to be where the otherworld and this world are especially bridgeable, and these geographic areas become revered shrines and foci of pilgrimage. But as the world of mundane concerns and the world of spiritual reality are thought to interconnect, so too in both the folk religion of China and the Shinto of Japan are the human and the divine approached as interrelated phenomena rather than unbridgeable and forever separate identities. Human apotheosis is an occurrence and an open possibility in paganism as a whole. But apart from the ultimate translation of humanity into the godhead, the Sino-Japanese perception entertains the understanding that the core of the human is already divine. The difference between humankind and godkind is not fixed and absolute. Instead it is malleable, flexible, and shifting. The one leads into the other and vice versa.

There are many points of comparison between the native practices and formulations of China and Japan, whether polytheism, shamanism, animism, cult behaviors, festival practices, worldviews, or ancestor veneration. But rather than explore the parallel resemblances at this point, we will now turn to the tribal religiosity found in the South Seas, Africa, and elsewhere to look for similar elements. The folk religion of China and the *minkan* and Shinto of Japan provide significant expressions of pagan identity despite their amalgamation with the imported religion of Buddhism. Buddhism in both China and Japan has been deeply colored by indigenous spiritualities, but the non-Buddhist propensity of both peoples is clearly detectable and distinguishable as a self-contained religious perception with identifiable characteristics and practices. In the world-denying religions of Hinduism and Buddhism, the returning cycle becomes a curse or at least something to escape. Paganism, by contrast, has an invariable salience of regeneration. Whether in the Chinese lunar new year or the Japanese adaptation of the Gregorian year, the celebration of life is typified in the resurgence symbolized by the new year. It is this revivification, drawing its sources from both the world of nature and the otherworld of mythology, which emerges as the characteristic of pagan identity and what we find in the spiritualities of both China and Japan.

## Primal Tribal Religions

Indigenous tribal religions are found in most parts of the world,[87] stretching from the Aboriginals of Australia to the northern tribes of the Lapps, Samoyeds, Tungus, Chukchees, Ainus, and Inuits. They flourish among the Indian peoples of the Amazon and the Andes. We find them as well across Asia and Oceania: from the Konds of India, the Senoi of Malaysia, the native peoples of Sumatra and the Celebes, to the Maori of New Zealand and the followers of *huna* in Hawaii.[88] Along with the many and countless regional variations, at the same time these religions have some general features that allow the individual ethnic expressions to be recognized as conforming to the sort of paradigmatic religiosity discussed earlier in the introduction. According to Clifford Geertz, this is "a system of symbols which acts to establish powerful, pervasive, and long-lasting moods and motivations in men by formulating conceptions of a general order of existence and clothing these conceptions with an aura of factuality that the moods and motivations seem uniquely realistic."[89]

Despite the missionizing inroads made by both Christianity and Islam, the number of sub-Saharan Africans following traditional religions is variously estimated from between 30 to 50 percent of the African population as a whole. Within this segment there are extraordinary contrasts among tribes and even within tribes in terms of individual practices, mythology, and tangible forms. But there are also general similarities, and according to Olupona, despite the diversity in traditional African ethnic religion, "it maintains a unity, as certain themes run all through the religious traditions irrespective of where they may be found."[90] These generalities, in fact, are identifiable across the whole global spectrum of indigenous religions.[91]

On this level we are almost invariably speaking of oral traditions.[92] Primal peoples do not have scripture or written records such as we find among Jews, Christians, Muslims, Hindus, or Buddhists. While the Confucianism and Taoism of China and the Shinto of Japan may be assessed as pagan, they differ from the tribal peoples and their religions by possessing sacred texts. This is not to say that the word is not important to indigenous peoples. It is almost the opposite. The name for the African carries and conveys a power to whomever it is given. It is not just a symbol or referent but often the very means by which the ancestor lives on through the namesake.[93] In a postmodern sense, the oral tradition is itself a text that forms and informs its users. It is simply not a written text.

Again among the Africans, the individual is secondary to the community.[94] This primary emphasis on the tribe, family, or clan over individual behavior and expression appears to be the most significant feature of all indigenous or tribal religious identity. As we shall see, this is perhaps the greatest contrast between local ethnic traditions and the contemporary paganisms of the West. Difference is not an asset, and willful individual behavior that conflicts with the group's interests and communal welfare is condemned. Amerindians likewise demonstrate an adherence to community and its welfare as a preoccupation that takes precedence over the interests of a single person. As Guy Cooper explains in connection with Navajo culture, difficulties inevitably arise in that "individuality requires mechanisms of integration into a cultural whole, whereas collectivism must allow space for individual expression."[95] In this particular case, such mechanisms involve traditional ceremonies (as well as peyotism, Christianity, and Western medicine) for the successful resolution of the tensions that increasingly arise between individualism and the necessities of cultural resilience. As they are for the Navajo, traditional primal systems of order in general are usually embodied in a well-defined body of knowledge and practice.

In other words, and most often, the tribal individual is habitually significant only in relation to the degree that he or she is part of the community. Uniqueness is alien to collective identity and harmony. All rites of passage from birth, naming, adult initiation, marriage, death, and burial are oriented toward integrating the human being into the community.[96] Funeral rites ensure that the dead person becomes a benevolent ancestral spirit. The Baluba of the southern Congo (Zaire) are typical of African tribals in regarding people who have no children or who die from particular diseases or far from home or, last, who are witches as those who become malevolent ghosts rather than regularly propitiated guardians. Whereas a sorcerer is someone who deliberately seeks to harm others, a witch is someone who has the same capabilities but is simply not cognizant of them. But to be unmindful of oneself as the cause of evil influence is no excuse, and any and all actions inimical to the communal welfare are judged to be anticommunity and, hence, antireligious.[97]

According to Ray, "one of the most fundamental features of traditional African life [is] the relation between the living and the dead."[98] But for Africans, death is not understood as originally part of the human scenario.[99] Formerly, men and women moved freely back and forth between this world and the other. Usually by some accident, this link between the worlds was broken. But death is still not considered as natural except as a consequence of extreme old age or certain diseases like smallpox or when one is struck by lightning.[100] Otherwise, death is the result of the interventions of a sorcerer, witch, or negative spirit. In this context, African religions often resort to the counterinfluence of a medicine person, shaman, or priest to diminish and expose the workings of the evildoer. Health and general welfare are protected and augmented by ancestral, territorial, and nature spirits and the gods of superhuman potency. The shaman or so-called witch doctor is often the medium who secures supernatural assistance, especially in difficult or critical situations. Otherwise, regular communal and family offerings to the invisible powers are made to effect divine-human harmony.

American Indians likewise incorporate the religious specialist into their ideological framework and practice.[101] Native American medicine men and women are expected to perform religious ceremonies, to prophesy, to cure both mental and physical illnesses, to exorcise malevolent influences, and to instruct adolescents in vision questing and initiate them into adulthood. Sometimes these various rites are undertaken privately or in the context of a small group only; at other times these are large-scale ceremonies involving most if not all the tribe. Beside being the primary custodian of the tribal sacred pipe as the key ceremonial artifact, the medicine person is the chief participant in the sacred dancing ceremonies, often in masked costume.

In the animistic framework of tribal religion, vitality is universally immanent.[102] This is undoubtedly one of the typical features of pagan identity. Unlike the Abrahamic division between the spiritual and the physical or the Hindu consideration of the material as *maya*, or "illusion," life and hence spirituality dwell in everything. The purpose of human activity, therefore, is to live communally within a spiritual equilibrium as reflected through the rhythms and patterns of the universe. For instance, in African spiritual experience, "the sacred and the profane tend to be symmetrical."[103] All error and falsehood are simply the forgetting of the natural balance that exists between this world and the divine. For the primal traditionalist, with the sacred omnipresent, every activity in itself becomes a holy ritual. The closer we get to the indigenous perspective, the less the purely mundane appears to exist.

A primary force is at the center of the Amerindian and African animating forces composing both the natural and the supernatural. The Sioux refer to this as *wakan*; the Algonquins call this *orenda*; and the Hawaiians designate sacred power as *mana*.[104] But whatever the local terminology, it is this dynamic power that legitimates religious and magical rituals. As an ambivalent force, it can be used for positive or negative purposes, and it is often the vital energy believed or perceived to reside in ritual objects as well as the Oceanic totem, the Native American visual representation of a god or spirit, and the African idol.[105]

The ubiquity of the sacred, however, does not preclude magic but becomes instead the pretext for it. While everything partakes of divinity, there is still a primus inter pares possibility that some things are more charged and hence more taboo than others. Primal religiosity is full of sacred objects, talismans, restricted behaviors, divination, and magic. Ritual implements are used to ward off negative influence, for healing and to increase welfare. They become part of the corpus of religious ceremony designed for these same ends. When the concentration of *mana* adheres to a tree, pond, spring, rock, or carved object, the vehicle of containment often becomes a *locus religiosus* or shrine. This is the *tirtha*, the place where the ingress and egress between the worlds is the easiest.[106]

Sacred places and objects must be approached and handled with due caution and preparation. *Mana*, numinous or divine power, is described as akin to electricity. One of its chief metaphors is that of fire. It is powerful and hence useful, but it is also dangerous and hence potentially lethal. Consequently, the animistic framework entails the corresponding possibility of pollution or contamination. This in turn involves various sets of procedures or systems for the efficacious removal of ritual impurity.[107] Often the ceremonial means employ the use of water, fire, or smoke. Whether we are concerned with Shinto ablutions, vernacular Hindu bathings, Hawaiian *huna* seclusions, American Indian sweat lodges, or African fire dances, the emphasis on ritual purity and its restoration is a fundamental feature of animistic religiosity, regardless of the particular form in which it is undertaken.

One essential feature of most if not all tribal religions is a belief in a number of gods.[108] These often include the earth as, for most American Indians, the mother of all. With all of nature regarded as spiritually alive, spirits include animals, natural phenomena, and the dead. Spirits may be friendly or dangerous or even just plain nuisances. They may be territorial and inhabit a specific domain, or they may be itinerant as wandering entities. When they become gods, they tend to rule over a particular activity such as thunder, metalworking, war, or learning.[109]

As we have seen, behind the plurality of gods is a primary animating force that is sometimes personified as a high god, and one peculiarity among many tribal peoples is the persistence of belief in a supreme being.[110] The Maoris call this entity Io; the American Indian refer to the "Great Spirit" (the Pawnee call it Tirana; the Lakota, Wakan Tanka); the African Baluba speak of Vidye Mukulu; the Bantu, of Ngai. This supreme god is invariably the creator of the world, though sometimes the earth is recognized as his female counterpart. In both African and Amerindian instances, there may have been derivative influences from the Judeo-Christian God. But the tribal supreme being is most often remote from everyday life and human concerns. If the mythology surrounding the high god has him originally active on the terrestrial plane, he has since departed and deals with the human community now only through intermediaries like the human shaman or the panoply of divine departmental beings. While "in some African religions the concept of a supreme God operates as a principle of ultimacy that gives an underlying multiplicity of deities and spirits [in which the] many powers are understood to be aspects of, or intermediaries for, the One God," Benjamin Ray explains that this concept of ultimacy is always contextual and depends on the perspective of the individual.[111] Usually the supreme being is associated with the sky, sometimes the sun. Of more immediate concern for the people today are the "culture hero" who brought civilization to humanity and the trickster who tests the limits of social convention.

By being at heart a preliterate civilization, indigenous culture has, as such, no written history. As has been mentioned, primal culture is largely an oral tradition. Thus it also differs from the universal religions in having no revelation *through* history. Whereas the gods and spirits interact with humanity and the shaman enters their world through trance, encounter with the godhead becomes direct and experiential; it is not disclosure from a wholly other and transcendental realm. For instance, for Africans, traditional "religion, as an experiential phenomenon, is essentially pretheoretical and does not begin as an intellectual enterprise."[112]

In the Western transcendental context, in fact, the godhead is, in principle, beyond the sway of human effect and petition. Such is not the case among most indigenous peoples. Instead, gods and spirits may be reached and influenced through ritual behavior. In other words, sacrifice, ritual, and even magic are believed to be efficacious. In one sense, then, magic and religion interconnect, because occultism is understood to be able to cause real changes in the material world. These changes are believed to occur through the mediumship of the supernatural.[113] It is, therefore, this intermixing of religion and magic and the foundational belief that ceremony produces tangible results that constitute salient features of tribal religion and that distinguish it as paganism. What applies to African traditional religion, namely, that "there is always the sustained and insatiable demand for magical benefits, the elimination of evil agents, a sense of access to power, protection, the enhancement of status, health, increase in prosperity, and relief from both physical and mental anguish in day-to-day life,"[114] generally applies to indigenous spirituality wherever it is encountered.

In primal religiosity, whether found among the ancient and perhaps still surviving Bön religion of Tibet or practiced by the Kondhs (Kui) in Orissa; the Bontocs, Kalingas, and Aëtas-Negritoes in the Philippines; the Senoi and Semang-Negritoes in Malaysia; the Toradja in the Celebes; the

Melpa and Foe in Papua New Guinea; the Aborigines in Australia; the Shona, Sotho-Tswana, and Bantu in Africa; the Inuit in Canada; or the Quechuas and Aymaras in the mountainous regions of Ecuador, Peru, and Bolivia, there is an organic perception of the world, the supernatural, and humanity in which gods and humans are seen as interrelated components of a single cosmic system. The sacred is not separate from secular time and place. There is instead a mutual dependence between gods and humans. Consequently, the paganism of indigenous tribal religions is detectable in the absences of doctrines of monotheistic worship, a creation *ex nihilo*, a morally predetermined godhead, and salvific redemptionism. Instead, there is an intimacy with nature and its inhabitation by mysterious powers. Because the level of technological development among the peoples of oral traditions renders them more vulnerable to the vagaries of nature and the environment, they seem to have a greater sensitivity to the superhuman and invisible powers in the world and a more identifiable attempt to access and accommodate the supernatural alliance.

## Shamanism

Much of what can be identified as paganism involves shamanistic practices. Shamanism in itself, however, is not necessarily intrinsic to paganism, although it nevertheless is frequently found as an associated institution and belief system.[115] The term as we know it comes from the Tungus Ewenk peoples of Siberia and refers to an ecstatic priest-magician. *Shamanists*, by contrast, refer to followers of a usually animistic religion in which a shaman plays a pivotal role. Whatever the history and origin of the term,[116] the shaman refers to the medium who in a trance state communes with the spirits, and this designation has come to be applied to similar practices among non-Siberian peoples, for example, the Amerindian medicine person, the Korean *mudang*, and the African witch doctor.

The shaman is a religiotechnical specialist who knows the traditional rites of his or her community, is skilled in medicinal practice, and is often adept in clairvoyance or divination.[117] As an ecstatic healer-priest in traditional primal society, the shaman possesses a clearly defined social role. The Western understanding of the nature of shamanism has differed over whether the key function of shamans is their attainment of ecstasy or ability to commune with spirits.[118] Shamans' propensity for "out-of-body' experiences allows their experience of the mediumistic dimension and supposed encounter with supernatural forces or entities. The theology or quasi theology that develops around such people who are believed to make contact with animistic powers and either control them or at least acquire information from them is a form of spiritualism.

A key feature in all forms of indigenous shamanism is the role played by the community. Indeed, all traditional paganisms are intricately related to locality in one sense or another.[119] In the context of shamanism, the local community serves a vital function for the shaman's own viability. Inasmuch as the shamanic specialist explores the invisible world of spirit, from a rationalistic, mundane perspective, he or she moves among mental constructs and/or fantasies that are essentially deranged. As long as the shamanic excursion is temporary, this mental imbalance is of limited duration. But a permanent state of trance would be the equivalent of schizophrenia or madness.[120] Properly, trance in itself is transient, a temporary "crossing over," and it is the community that provides an important rationale or anchor for the shaman's flight of mind to return to the everyday, pragmatic world of this-worldly life. In other words, it is the shaman's social duties or responsibilities in providing health and welfare to the community that provides the means or necessity for his or her return from the otherworld. This "return" is the corollary of the shaman's fundamental "mission to ensure that the spiritual equilibrium of the entire society is maintained."[121]

While sometimes the shamanic profession is hereditary, it is almost always preceded by a call in the form of a crisis or physical or mental illness.[122] In the hereditary context of indigenous shamanisms, Eliade is unequivocal: "The illness is only a sign of election, and proves to be temporary."[123] Most traditional societies do not seclude the "mentally ill" but attempt to integrate them as much as possible into the normal rhythms of community life. It is common for most people who experience what the Westerner might call schizophrenia to recover fully after a period of usually six to nine months. Those who do not regain a state of mental balance or who have demonstrated unusual propensities during their illness are often selected for special training. Richard Noll likens shamanism to the Western occult traditions of alchemy and ceremonial magic "in that they, too, cultivate mental imagery in order to contact imaginal beings."[124]

Shamanic apprenticeship can be an arduous and prolonged education.[125] Shamans must learn about medicinal herbs and "power plants" and become familiar with the local terrain and its sacred geography. Much of their training may take place in seclusion or isolation. The novice undergoes various ordeals, perhaps even physical mutilation. The experience of these as well as exposure to the raw extremes of climate constitute part of the apprentice's physical and mental conditioning. In describing the extremely painful ordeals that some, though not all, initiates undergo, Rutherford claims, "Beatings, burning with fire, slashing with knives, suspension often upside down from a tree for hours or even days, ascending a ladder of upturned sword blades are all to be found."[126] The Yaminawa of the Peruvian rain forest employ ants to bite the neophyte. Apprenticeship culminates with initiation.

Despite the great geographic range of shamanic practice, the initiatory experience exhibits a surprising uniformity with regard to the theme of death, dismemberment, and reconstitution. Skeletalization is a commonly recurring element.[127] The process appears to be designed to free the initiate from the fear of death and the extreme pain often associated with it. As the shaman's province is journeying to the afterlife worlds, the initiatory death ritual prepares him or her for this function. Eliade finds that the reduction of "oneself to the skeleton condition is equivalent to re-entering the womb of this primordial life, that is, to a complete renewal, a mystical rebirth."[128] The candidate may acquire a "spirit animal" at this time that will become the person's vehicle or familiar for accessing the otherworld.[129]

Shamans are often known by their distinctive dress: robes, kafkans, headgear, and footware. They usually have a special drum, rattle, and/or staff.[130] Baldick describes the shaman's drum of the Altai Turks enveloped by the smoke of the ceremonial fire as the intermediary summons the spirits to gather in the drum.[131] The shamanic performance, during which the shaman may dance to an incessant drumbeat, is in some sense a reliving of the initial experience of initiation. But because the shaman is an adept at entering a trance state, the purpose of the ceremonial rite is to encourage "soul travel" in which the shaman's dream soul leaves for the invisible worlds of the heavens or the nether regions to effect change, acquire information, and often rescue the lost soul of an ill person.[132] Consequently, shamanism as a quasi theology or ideology is intimately connected to the doctrine of soul duality.[133] While the ordinary person experiences the otherworld only through the dream soul, which departs the body in its sleeping state, the shaman sends forth the same at will. The use of ritual, sleep deprivation, various physical austerities including fasting, and psychotropic substances help induce the desired alternative state of consciousness within which the shaman operates. "The function of the . . . shaman, throughout Asia, as in China, Japan, Korea and South-East Asia, is to descend to the underworld . . . to inquire about the needs of the unattended or sickness-causing soul."[134]

The shaman is healer, diviner, prophet, and ritual specialist.[135] In the case of illness resulting from "soul loss," the shaman travels to the otherworld in search of the person's missing soul and tries to rescue it. But if sickness is the result of witchcraft intrusion into a person's physical being, the shaman cures through sucking to remove the harmful object.[136] Another shamanic duty is to escort the soul of a deceased person to the otherworld.[137] Beside this role as psychopomp, the shaman also seeks to acquire information relevant to his or her community: divining future weather conditions, controlling the weather, finding lost objects or persons, harming enemies, or engaging in spiritual battle. It is through the acquired ability to transcend ordinary human limitations that shamans achieve their goal. The shaman's superhuman powers may be demonstrated by such feats as walking through fire, immersing a limb in boiling water, piercing or cutting open the flesh, and releasing from bonds.

There is obviously a degree of the sham in shamanism. In referring to the Norse Loki, Rutherford employs the term *shaman-trickster*.[138] The shaman is a magician in both senses of the term: one who can operate through tricks and deceit and one who can change consciousness at will. The shaman is a sorcerer but one who relates magical ability to the communal welfare as the primary objective. The shamanic stocks-in-trade are the abilities to fly and to become invisible. Sometimes the specialist is proficient in bilocation, the ability to appear in more than one place simultaneously. Other shamanic "virtues" include a developed aptitude for heightened vigilance as well as the cultivation of multiple perspectives. But whereas sometimes these attributes are intended to be literal accomplishments, the line between the metaphorical and the actual is rarely clearly drawn.

This clouding of boundaries is a hallmark not only of shamanism but also of paganism as a whole. Both paganism and shamanism as a type of paganism are locality oriented. There is a constant demarcation of centers and borders and, in the case of shamanism in particular, subsequent boundary transgression. The shaman's very raison d'être is his or her expertise in crossing from this world to the next—and back. The liminal zone through which this movement occurs is the boundary region itself; it constitutes the very bridge between this world and the other, between the inner and outer, between the literal and symbolic.[139] A shaman's propensity to reach the other depends on his or her expertise in traversing the liminal. It is this realm between the worlds, this edge between chaos and order, in which the kind of spiritual innovations central to paganism and shamanism are most likely to emerge.

Often the shamanic excursion takes place against an understanding of a tripartite cosmos: either the heavens above and the underworld below or a concentric understanding of the earth containing the netherworld and surrounded by the celestial.[140] The link among these three worlds is the *axis mundi*, often understood as a cosmic pillar, a world tree, or a sacred mountain.[141] In the shamanic ritual this central axis is usually symbolically present and represents the means by which the shaman's soul travels to the other dimensions. The cosmology implicit or explicit in shamanism suggests, via the axial communication link if not a blurring of boundaries between the worlds, at least the possibility of interaction and mutual influence from one dimension to the next. The basic assumption in shamanism is that spirits on all three levels have the capacity to influence the course of human life on the terrestrial plane. In other words, the human soul or life essence is subject to the actions of agents in the invisible world of spirits, deities, sorcerers, demons, and ghosts.

In indigenous shamanic communities, the spiritual specialist is both revered and feared as someone who has mastery over the spirits. Consequently, the shaman is often socially isolated to a degree, and vis-à-vis the community as a whole, he or she is nearly a social outcast. So while the shaman is the person who is figuratively preoccupied with boundaries, he or she is often someone who literally dwells at the community's borders as well. In many traditional settings, the shaman is someone with sexually deviant preferences, and sometimes transvestite dress becomes characteristic of the shaman's differences.[142] Nevertheless, unlike the Western and contemporary scenario in which the "marginalized other" struggles to find a voice; in indigenous primal societies, while shamans may be excluded from the norm, they possess strong "voices" in their community affairs.

Almost invariably, native shamanisms are found among polytheistic peoples. The shaman as a specialist who is adept at communicating with gods and spirits has developed a capacity to encounter the divine as an internal experience. The religious framework in which this experiential engagement takes place typically ranges between animism and the more developed pantheonic conceptions of definitive gods and goddesses. While shamanism as a technique of ecstasy may have wider applications, it finds its original and most common home among pagan systems of belief and practice.

Regardless of the universal features found throughout shamanic practices, the notion of shamanism is a Western construct. In their indigenous contexts across the Arctic Circle, throughout the Americas, in Africa, in Southeast Asia, and in Oceania, "techniques of ecstasy" and healing through spirit communication are individually local and tribal. This projection of a single designation onto local idiosyncrasies is an artificial development but one that nevertheless helps us delineate a particular range of religious behavior, one that we can identify as pagan.

In the contemporary West, thanks originally to Carlos Castaneda and his "documentary novels" beginning in 1968 with *The Teachings of Don Juan*, a form of neoshamanism has increasingly grown in popularity. Michael Harner (1986) developed what he refers to as "core shamanism," reputedly based on his South American ethnographic research but that conforms to no particular tribal practice.[143] By and large, contemporary Western shamanism has a New Age flavor, and much of it has been "appropriated" from Amerindian practices, often without the latter's blessings.[144] But inasmuch as shamanism in its wider manifestations is highly flexible and innovative, modern urban and nonindigenous developments may represent an expression and adaptation of a natural shamanic impulse.[145]

In a retroactive sense, Mircea Eliade's *Shamanism: Archaic Techniques of Ecstasy*, first published in French in 1951 and translated in 1972, has also played a role in the emergence of neoshamanism. This emergence differs in certain respects from the indigenous shamanisms. First, it is less community based and focuses instead on the individual. There is also less emphasis on shamanism as a rigorous training of the specialist and more on techniques and orientations available to the religious seeker. By itself, shamanism has little if any ethical inclination apart from the well-being of its host community. Traditional shamanisms entertain the existence of both positive and negative spirits, and the shaman's endeavor may include attempts to destroy or "kill" the latter. Neoshamanism, by contrast, tends to regard spirit simply as spirit and honors the integrity of each individual spirit, including those of illness. If evil is a construct largely absent from paganism in general, it is even more absent from New Age formulations of shamanism.

The question may ultimately be one of asking to what degree neoshamanism is still pagan. Or it may be indicative of the adaptability of ancient techniques of ecstasy to contemporary society, including the modern urban environment. The answer to the question will ultimately rest on which shamanic features are considered essential or intrinsic and which are local and idiosyncratic. The contemporary shaman may not, perhaps, follow the initiatory trajectory of death and dismemberment, and his or her community may be more figurative and inventive, but the specialist may still be shamanic and pursue a shamanic path of orientation. The question of the legitimacy of neoshamanism relates to the broader question concerning the authenticity of contemporary Western paganism, one to which we shall return later.

For the present, it is enough to recognize a particular spiritual orientation that we are calling shamanism, one that has both tribal and, now, urban manifestations.[146] This is an orientation that focuses on healing through techniques of ecstasy and almost invariably takes place within a cosmological framework that we are designating as pagan. It is animistic and polytheistic and rests largely on an implied or explicit doctrine of soul duality. It is also, despite its interest in otherworldly or spiritual dimensions, this-worldly in its fundamental orientation. Within its worldview perception, tangible reality is animate and immanent with the divine. It takes a basically magical stance vis-à-vis the world, humanity, and the supernatural.

## American Indian Spirituality

American Indians' religious practices may also be described as largely shamanic. While direct access to the godhead is not denied to the ordinary individual and, indeed, in many American primal traditions, is even encouraged, there exists all the same an understanding that certain people have a greater ability to communicate with the otherworld. These people are variously referred to as shamans, medicine persons, "bear doctors," or mediums. Each may exhibit different ways of accessing the supernatural, but in general they reveal supernormal powers or capabilities not available to the ordinary tribal member. Among the Eskimo, the acquisition of spiritual powers or spirit helpers often involves maiming or psychic/symbolic dismembering.[147] Shamanic initiations in other regions may be similar. Spirit animals range variously and according to local environment: bears, elk, jaguars, eagles, ravens, hawks, seals, frogs, mosquitoes, and so forth.

While Amerindian spirituality may properly belong in the section on primal tribal religion, I am treating it separately because, like the Australian Aboriginal peoples to some extent, it also is found in industrialized Western society. Whether or not it wishes to, American Indian culture must interact—and survive—in areas that are becoming increasingly urban or at least are increasingly confronting the dominant secular culture of the West. Consequently, the very survival of Native American peoples, their cultures, and their religions has become an issue in itself.[148] At the same time, Amerindianism in its different forms and expressions is the most direct exposure that many Westerners may have to what could be broadly assessed as indigenous pagan religion, however controversial and contested this classification might be by the holders of these particular faiths.[149]

As with shamans elsewhere, the main purpose of Amerindian spiritual activity is healing. This activity is usually carried out in a ceremony that involves drumming, chanting, dancing, trance induction, and visions.[150] According to Vogel, "Indian medical treatment is . . . seen as a combination of rational and religious practices, differing from the usual white practice in that *both are performed by the same functionary* among the Indians."[151] In this context, the shaman seeks to flatter, implore, and outmaneuver demonic spirits. Auxiliary functions exercised by Native American shamans often relate to tribal welfare and assistance with hunting, fishing, or agricultural matters.

Beside shamanic ritual, however, the ceremonial format is also used for key rites of passage, to avert a particular misfortune, to prepare for a special occasion, to seek renewal, and to offer thanksgiving.[152] For the Amerindian, ritual purification is frequently undertaken in a sweat lodge—sometimes as a preparation for other ceremonies or a major endeavor, sometimes as a complete ceremony in itself—either to petition the gods or to offer them gratitude for good fortune or a manifest favor. But once again, the "sweat bath was more than a sanitary device; it was also a panacea for all diseases."[153] Other important ritual undertakings for American Indians include the vision quest, ceremonies for the dead, participation in the great cycles of nature, world renewal rites, interpersonal bonding, and puberty rituals preparing boys and girls for adulthood.[154]

Akin to indigenous primals in Africa, Asia, Oceania, and Siberia, Amerindian religiosity reveals similar common patterns. According to Amanda Porterfield,

> The universally agreed-upon tenets of American Indian spirituality include condemnation of American exploitation of nature and mistreatment of Indians, regard to precolonial America as a sacred place where nature and humanity lived in plentiful harmony, certainty that American

Indian attitudes are opposite to those of American culture and morally superior on every count, and an underlying belief that American Indian attitudes toward nature are a means of revitalizing American culture.[155]

Foremost is the shared understanding that all of nature is alive.[156] According to Morgan, the works of nature constitute the foundation not only of the Amerindian religious system but also for inducing collective belief in a Great Spirit as an invisible but omnipresent deity.[157] This comprehension of nature's inherent vitality or fundamental animism is what distinguishes paganism or paganisms from nonpagan transcendental or gnostic religions such as the God-is-wholly-other comprehension of Christianity and Judaism or the matter-is-an-illusion belief of Hinduism. It is also the natural home or orientation for shamanic trance and the interaction of ecstatic consciousness with the plethora of spirit and animistic presences.[158]

This ubiquitousness of life corresponds to an understanding that sacrality imbues all things. With the perception that everything is sacred and alive comes the notion that all is interdependent and connected. Primal Native American animisms lead directly to their shared organic or holistic worldview. Spirit and matter are not considered separate but interrelated parts of the whole. Consequently, the primal American spiritual-physical worldview includes concepts of space and time that are expressed by and for Amerindians through characteristically distinctive symbols. The sweat lodge and conical-framed wigwam or *tipi* or Navajo *hogan,* for example, represent both the cosmos and, microcosmically, the human being.[159] This complete integration of life and the sacred further reflected, or enhanced through architecture and ritual, allows that there is no term in any of the Amerindian languages that designates "religion" as a category independent of or separate from other cultural elements.

Space is variously conceived in terms of direction and approached as dual (e.g., upstream and downstream, right and left), quadral (east, south, west, and north), pentadic (cardinal directions plus the intercardial center), or heptadic (cardinal plus up, down, and middle). These sanctified directions become the basic units from which the religious worldview is constructed. Tribal distinctiveness rests in part on which numeric framework is used and which color is assigned to the various directions. For instance, Creeks, Hopis, Navajos, and Zunis symbolically express east with the color white, but for Apaches and Cherokees this color designates the south, and for Cheyennes, the north. Red is linked to the east by the Cherokees and Lakotas, to the south by the Hopis and Zunis, to the west by the Cheyennes, and, along with yellow, to the north by the Creeks. These particular color differentiations help foster tribal cultural identities.[160] Apart from the Mayas and Aztecs, who developed elaborate "chrono-theistic" calendars, space rather than time appears to be the element stressed in most Amerindian cultures.[161]

Despite the spatial emphasis in worldview construction, American Indians celebrate the passing seasons and other calendrical rituals. Apart from those answering an immediate critical need such as doctoring, life-cycle rites, or threat of war, many ceremonies are regular annual celebrations, either lunar and/or solar determinations or key hunting/harvesting aspects of subsistence. Regularly recurring rites on the tribal calendar are invariably socially directed to the clan, moiety, village, or tribe as a whole. The popular annual intertribal powwow of today is still directed toward group welfare, in this case, that of the combined tribes represented or on behalf of the Indian community as a whole. What distinguishes Amerindian understandings of time from the progressively linear perception in Western secularism is the cyclical and reciprocal nature of temporal movement.

Amerindian ceremony and shamanism involves a world understanding that is both animistic and polytheistic. There are many gods and goddess as well as spirits, and while a concept of a supreme god or creator may be present, this figure is invariably associated with a variety of deific beings: elemental personifications, local presences, or full mythological deities. Among these, we find Water-Woman, White Buffalo Calf Woman, Old Man White Oak Acorn, Mother Earth, Wind, Sun, Thunder, and/or Coyote. The Apaches honor Sun Boy, the Creator-of-All, and First Goddess. The Aztecs, following the Mayas, worshiped an array of calendrical deities, including the rain god Tlaloc, the spring god Xipe Totec, and the feathered-serpent Quetzalcoatl.[162] The Inuit have no High God but consider an omnipotent goddess Sedna as the ruler of all sea life; a Great Master or Keeper, the sovereign responsible for the various spirits of land animals; and the personified figure of the Great Meat Dish representing the unity of all living beings.[163]

The high god is usually thought of as a creator. Sometimes he becomes the original culture hero as well, though often this last function is attributed to, or at least shared with, the antihero or trickster figure: Coyote, Rabbit, or Raven.[164] Among the Northwest Coast Tlingit, for example, the Raven is trickster, transformer, and culture hero as well as world creator. As with the Africans, this supreme being is generally remote and not involved in current human activities. Even with his presence, Amerindian religious formula-tions are decidedly polytheistic. Several Western scholars have surmised that the notion of a supreme god among both Africans and Amerindians is an early imported influence from Christianity. In some cases, however, as with the Lakotas, the high god may result from the common tendency to personify everything, including the primary holy force animating all things and holding them together. Thus the Lakota/Dakota adjective *wakan*, which is akin to the Polynesian *mana*, becomes the "Great Mysterious" or "Holiest of Everything," Wakan Tanka.[165] Otherwise, the numinousness remains a largely nonpersonalized animistic force such as the Algonquin *manitu* or the totality of its potency, Kitchi Manitou. Among the Huichols of Mexico, "life energy force" is designated *kuperi*, of which both shamans and peyote are believed to have great amounts.

In the Amerindian acknowledgment of spiritual power is the attempt to influence and negotiate with it. But we never find an understanding of the supernatural as an authority *over* the terrestrial and human. In this con-text, Native American religiosity is incommensurate with the kind of structure found in the Roman Catholic Church, which seeks to affirm—and become the sole legitimate vehicle for—a supernatural omnipotence. As we have already seen, in Amerindianism, the high spirit, if there is one, is otiose and distant and does not constitute a ruling power. Any notion of obedience as such is therefore absent. Instead of obeying a higher author-ity, the emphasis is on cooperating with an other. "The basic goal in life . . . is to be in harmony with all natural and supernatural powers."[166]

This world and the spiritual world are regarded as mutual transforma-tions of each other. This suggests a dynamic of reciprocity and exchange between the two that is based on a fundamental notion of interdepen-dence. Ceremonial ritual, therefore, seeks to foster spiritual well-being in the otherworld. But at the same time, the otherworld is expected to aug-ment physical and emotional well-being in this one. Typically, for the Cherokees, Creeks, and Choctaws of the southeastern Indians, the sole purpose of ceremony is "to restore or maintain balance."[167] As with any re-ligion, an interpretive framework is established through which the super-natural is read. In the Amerindian context, nature is the all-encompassing canvas for transpersonal revelation in which the deity may occur, for ex-ample, in the outline of a flock of birds, through a natural phenomenon such as a waterfall or unusual rock formation, but most frequently in the vehicular form of an animal, occasionally as an anthropic vision.

The humanistic bias of Native American spirituality might be glimpsed through the worldview of the Navajo, which divides the cosmos into natural phenomena, the *diyin diné'e* (holy people) and humans (earth-surface-people).[168] All three, however, share the same life essence or kinds of souls. This life energy force is what the Lakotas designate as *wakan* and the Eskimo as *sila*, activating both the body and the soul essence itself.[169] But while an animistic vitality links what the Navajo consider the three realms of being, it also allows each to be vulnerable to the others. Despite their fundamental similarity, some natural phenomena and some *diyin diné'e* are understood as having dangerous attributes as well. Human illness or harm might result from the effects of these malevolent qualities. Navajo ritual, therefore, like most Native American rituals, tries to counteract such influences and render the patient immune, or *diyin* (holy).

If all established modes of communication constitute ritual, or all ritual is communication, religious ritual is distinguished from ritual or communication more broadly in making the primary relationship between the human and the divine or spiritual. The worldview framework establishes the individual paradigm through which a particular religious ritual communication occurs. In many Amerindian situations, this communication is directly between an individual and the spiritual. In many other cases, an intermediary becomes the channel between the person or group and the gods or spirits. The religious specialist may be a professional shaman (e.g., the Arctic Inuit *angakut*). In such cases, this becomes the adept's primary identity. In other circumstances, the specialist role may be only temporary, for a single rite or during its regular recurrences. The specialist may also act alone and independent of others, or he or she might be part of an organized society (e.g., the Sun Dance or Medicine Lodge societies).[170] We know too that the shaman or specialist may be called on to deal with a crisis, usually an illness, or he or she may be a functionary for certain calendrical occasions. In the broad diversity of Amerindian religiosity, the spiritual expert may serve as mediator or communicator with the spirits or gods, or he or she may be a representative of the spiritual, such as the masked Pueblo *kachina* or ancestral spirit dancers or the Navajo *ye'ii* impersonators. In other words, in American Indian richness and diversity in which hundreds if not thousands of tribal religious expressions existed, not all spiritual specialists were shamanic. There were and, to a lesser extent, still are a great variety of accomplished roles.

It is equally important not to ignore South America with its own significant and often spiritually vibrant native populations.[171] Apart from central Andean kingdoms (Chavin, Moche, Chimu, and so on) and the culminating Inca Empire, relatively complex chiefdoms formerly existed in the circum-Caribbean (e.g., the Taino Arawak of Hispanola) and sub-Andean (e.g., the Chibcha) areas as well. As in North America, many entire tribal cultures have ceased to exist, and their corresponding beliefs and practices have vanished (e.g., the Taino, Tupinambá, Abipón, Ona, Yahgan).[172] Others, such as the Guaraní (Paraguay), Tupian Chiriguano (Andean foothills), and Chocó (Panama) have managed to preserve much of their indigenous lifestyles by migrating to remoter regions of the tropical rain forests. The Cágaba of northern Columbia and the Warrau of the Orinoco delta have chosen relatively inhospitable areas in which to settle.[173] The Gê-speaking Apinayé, Canela, Sherente, Cayapó, Caingan, Carajá, and Bororo and the non-Gê Witoto have also been able to maintain beliefs in shamanism, animism, ancestor cults, celestial beings, and such deities as a rain god and/or an anaconda god in various regions of Amazonia.

In their heyday, the Incas had evolved a complex theocratic state centered on a supreme being (Viracocha), a subordinate pantheon of nature gods (Thunder, Weather, Sun, Moon, stars, Earth, and Sea) and *huacas* (regional or local supernatural powers, places or objects). Temple complexes housed images of the gods and provided residences for the priests. In the priestly Incan religion, an emphasis on ritual practice superseded direct spirituality or mysticism.[174]

Now dominating the highlands, the Incas survive today as the Quechua-speaking peoples, numbering more than five million. Though their religious practice is now nominally Roman Catholic—at best a form of folk Catholicism—they have retained a dichotomous understanding of the spiritual world that oscillates between gods and spirits, the terrestrial and celestial, good and bad, or Catholic saints and natural spirits/supernatural gods. A reliance on shamans has also been retained, and *curañderos* function as magical healers while public ceremonies still mark significant moments of collective life. Typically, the Peruvian shaman maintains an altar or *mesa* of power objects. In former Inca imperial times, the use of cocoa leaf was institutionalized. Today, Quechua shamans often use the entheogenic San Pedro cactus to induce trances. In recent times, Quechua has been decreed an official language of Peru along with Spanish. With language as a medium for maintaining religious ideas, traditional Quechua practices and outlooks fare a better chance of survival than do those among many other primal peoples.[175]

In contrast, the Mapuches of south-central Chile have resisted mission-izing influences better than have the Quechua and have preserved a purer form of their indigenous shamanism with its pantheon centered on Nenechen the celestial ruler, Old Woman his wife, Sun, Moon, Volcano, Southwind, and Abundance. Unlike the Incas, the Mapuches have no cen-tralization, no priesthood, and no large-scale ceremonies. Numbering only one-half million and without a highland bastion to protect them, they are more vulnerable and threatened with geographic dispersion by the hostile Euro-Americans who surround them. As have the Tepian-speaking Mundurucús of the Matto Grosso and the Yahgans of the western Tierra del Fuego, along with their Alacalúf and Chono neighbors, the Mapuches may succumb to acculturation, or *mestization*, in which traditional belief becomes obscured and lost in folk Catholicism.[176]

But even the Christo-paganism of *mestizo*, or "mixed blood" peoples, fre-quently retains shamanic practice on a folk level throughout South Amer-ica. The overall complex of South American Indian religiosity is oriented toward classic shamanism and shamanic healing, ancestor cults, pantheons of deities and animistic spirits, perhaps a supreme being/culture hero who is nevertheless a generally remote and currently inactive figure, and some-times a universal mother of all things (e.g., among the Cágabas). In some cases there is a tendency toward the development of temple idolatry (e.g., among the Warraus), as is found farther north in the Americas, with priests rather than shamans conducting public ceremonies. Often divination prac-tices form a regular part of religious behavior. Despite regional differences and contrasting emphases, in South America there is nevertheless a de-tectable similarity in understanding the supernatural in general and a basic reliance on shamanic techniques for interacting with it.

Another key element appearing in North and South American primal traditions alike and reminiscent of sub-Saharan African attitudes is the living presence of the name itself. The word is frequently seen as a spiri-tual potency in and of itself and not just as a representation.[177] Names and designations are regarded as sacred entities. Consequently, storytelling and ritual narrative assume great significance as creative acts and not simply as commemorations or symbolic reenactments of primordial events. But this indwelling of spirit extends from words and myths to the physical dimen-sion as well. Artistic objects have sacred potencies, therefore, in their crafted forms and also in the natural materials from which they are com-posed. It is this sacredness of the corporeal and the supernatural essence associated with it that is characteristic of the full range of pagan differentiation from the use of charms and rudimentary expressions of fetishism to more elaborate forms of ceremonial idolatry.

This complete interpenetration of the physical and spiritual, salient among all Native American worldviews in particular and integral to pagan religiosity, occurs in a fundamentally cyclical time-frame.[178] Linear temporality is at best a spiraling progress. While there may be advance, there is also return and perpetual renewal. Life, death, decay, and rebirth constitute the circular fundament for whatever limits may or may not exist in the conception of cosmic reach. In traditional American Indian religiosity, both interdependence and the encounter of time returning back on itself are supported by the accumulation of sacred tribal lore tied to nature as it is expressed through both the local environment and the transmitted pragmatic legends concerning the community's past.

As we have seen with African and other primal attitudes, Amerindians have "an instinctive reverence for supernatural powers, spirits, land, nature creatures, and human beings—both living and departed."[179] They stress the maintenance of equilibrium between themselves and nature. "Native Americans seek as their primary goal to live in balance in the present with the spirits everywhere present (rather than prepare for life in a world beyond death)."[180] Ideas of sin and salvation are absent, and instead, "the good of the tribe is always more important than the interests of the individual."[181] Nevertheless, seeking "a personal relationship with the sacred through vision is one of the most distinguishing features of many tribes."[182]

Intersecting with the wide diversity of tribal religiosities, Amerindian shamanic practices include various elements recognized more universally: departure and incubation, death and skeletalization, supernatural alliance and animal transformation, cosmological maps and routes to the underworld/otherworld, world tree and soul flight, thresholds of passage and return to the middle world, mastery of fire, and, among the Algonquins, Lakotas, Anasazis, Huichols, and others, solarization or activation of the internal sun.[183] Because of the ravages of Native American cultures by European missionaries, conquerors, and settlers, however, primal religions throughout the Americas are often precarious and in great flux. They have been subject as well to internal messianic frenzies such as the Senecas' Handsome Lake movement beginning in 1799, the early-nineteenth-century Prophet Dance, and the Ghost Dances of the 1870s and 1890s.[184] Indigenous elements have also merged with Christian ideas in the Native American Church's peyote cult.[185] Tribal institutions such as the Algonquin-Ojibwa-Chippewa Midéwiwin (literally, mystic doings) or Medicine Lodge society or the Lakota/Dakota Sun Dance have in the past been outlawed. These have nevertheless often continued secretly and have also been augmented through periodic revitalization efforts. The emerging powwow summer circuit that fosters intertribal exchange and other cross-Indian diffusions are generating new Pan-Indian movements to ensure that these particular indigenous American religiosities will be modified further but may still be sustained.

## Afro-American Spiritism

When African spiritist religious practices were brought to the Western Hemisphere, they were blended with not only Roman Catholic and other Christian elements but also Amerindian aspects.[186] While the purest form of Yoruba and West African religion in general is the Jeje-Nagô cult, which began in Salvador and the Brazilian state of Bahia, other Candomblés are less orthodox and incorporate other traditions and features: for example, Candomblé Angola and Candomblé Congo have fused with Bantu tradition, and Candomblé de Caboclo and Candomblé Angola have added native American features. Brazilian Umbanda, though, has synthesized African spirituality with more recent religious developments. Other forms have appeared throughout the Caribbean.

While sharing an American Indian intimacy with nature and the personification of natural fundamentals, black African spirituality is more urban and less rural. Despite their many similarities, they also exhibit some profound differences. One contrast with Native American religious expression that is found among the Afro-Latin cults is the prominence of the altar as a focus for devotion and a demonstration of the faiths' individuality.

On the African altar, we find that spiritist shrine objects of carved wood and ivory, cast metal, clay, fabric, and leather not only are utilitarian and decorative but also are charged with spiritual power through songs and incantations by the religious practitioner. This is part of a universal pagan need to communicate with spirit through tangible objects, one that the Afro-Brazilian and Afro-Caribbean religiosities have developed sensitively and organically and as striking features of their faiths. The altar items are augmented by prayers, songs, music, dance, and costumes as part of an aesthetic assemblage designed both to inspire the worshiper and please the god.[187]

These colorful and personally idiosyncratic shrines belonging to Afro-Latin spirituality constitute one of the faith's most salient and recognizable features. The mixture of the mundane and the religious characterizing the altar in Brazil, for instance, reveals Candomblé's intrinsic capacity to transform anything into a sacred object. In shrine development, trees or plants associated with a particular *orisha/orixá* (Yoruba god or goddess) are commonly found planted next to the deity's altar. These altars are also typically found adjacent to natural springs or artificial ponds.[188]

Whereas contemporary Western paganism largely represents an effort to reestablish a noncontinuous tradition—which in the New World comes from elsewhere—Afro-Latin spiritism not only is a direct and successful transplanting of an indigenous spirituality, it also, unlike Chinese developments in the Americas, more completely jumps the ethnic divide. Afro-Latin spiritism also has largely escaped the controversy of appropriation in Euro-Americans' interest in Amerindian religious institutions. As a fluid and highly adaptable black African complex, it has increasingly developed into a signature of large sections of chiefly urban Latin American populations of European descent. Afro-Latin spiritism is now becoming more and more popular among non-Hispanic peoples in the United States, especially in the gay community.[189]

As we have found with other pagan expressions, Afro-Atlantic spiritualities are local, with their form, arrangement, and practice dependent on the individual *babalawo* (diviner or high priest) or *santero* (priest or initiated practitioner) responsible for a particular ritual house (*ilé*) or ceremonial temple (*ileocha*; Portuguese *terreiro*).[190] The *casa de santero*, or priest's house, is the focus of worship and includes offering gifts of food (*amalá*), divination, drum and dance ceremonies, and trance possession. Shrine individuality, including which deity (or *orisha*) is selected as the primary focus of worship, is also determined in part by the local community and its particular needs. At the same time, whether in Cuba, the United States, or Brazil, these cults are ceasing to be strictly folk concerns of the poor and those from urban slums and are having increasing appeal among the more affluent middle classes.[191] As a New World spirituality, spiritism is spreading across a wide range of society.

The versatility of African spirituality is a direct continuation of the polytheistic depiction of the godhead. In the host continent of origin, the number of *orishas*, or ancestor spirits, range from 400 (401 in one system) to as high as 1,700.[192] There is a deity for every aspect of life: Changó rules thunder and passion; Ogun is the patron of iron and war; and Oshun is the goddess of love, marriage, and gold. Some *orishas* fall out of favor while others rise in popularity. The deities of the sun and moon are no longer worshiped much, and among the Edo to the east of the Yoruba in Nigeria, devotion to Obiemwen, the goddess of childbirth and fertility, and Ogiuwu, the god of thunder and death, has substantially declined. The Edo oceanic deity Olokun has taken over the functions of Obiemwen, including presiding over wealth, and has steadily risen in regard, as have the Yoruba-imported figures of Changó and Ogun.[193]

In the New World, the expected selective transformations have occurred. Sixteen *orishas* are recognized in Cuba, for instance. Even here, some are more popular than others. In the United States, a pantheon has emerged known as Las Seite Potencias Africanas (the Seven African Powers) as the religion has moved away from being grounded in mythological origins toward being formulated according to psychological and ethical archetypes.[194] These include the white god Obatala, chief of the seven; Changó; Ogun; the god of divination Orula; the phallic trickster figure of passageways Eshu; the goddess of maternity and saltwater Yemaya; and the goddess of life and freshwater Oshun. Sometimes these *orishas* are considered manifestations of a ubiquitous divine force or supreme god. But they are more often understood as ancestral human beings who, due to their extraordinary behavior as human beings, underwent a postmortem apotheosis. Spiritism's *orishas* are therefore ancestral spirits available for the welfare of descendants and human communities in general.[195]

Another key aspect of Yoruba plasticity and adaptability in which these deified spirits have coalesced derives from the association between the African *orisha* and the Roman Catholic saint. This was in large part a survival tactic, but it also represents a means of projecting empowerment and validation by an oppressed peoples onto an alien and hostile hegemonic superstructure. But the process is double-edged: The New World Afro-Latin cults also inherited the "European devil fetish" from their Euro-American overlords, something absent in native Africa where there is no radical polarization between the forces of moral good and evil.[196] Once the devil became known through the efforts of the Christian missionaries, the available apparatus of the Roman Catholic Church in the form of its panoply of saints came to be seen as an additional power source for nullifying the effects of Satan. Although this led to what is sometimes described as a syncretization between Catholicism and African spirituality, it appears that in the minds of most spiritists, the two religious systems are distinct and approached as separate.[197]

Another superficially similar feature between African religious under-standing and that of the Christian Church is belief in a supreme god as creator.[198] This figure in Afro-Latin spiritism, however, is essentially demi-urgic (subordinately formative). He—or he/she inasmuch as this supreme being is either androgynous or a composite consortium of male and fe-male deities—is a fashioner and not a creator *ex nihilo* through the power of word alone. Moreover, this entity remains remote, being what has been termed a *deus otiosus*, or "lazy god." He or she takes no interest in or in-volvement with human affairs, which are the province of the *orishas* or saints. As a result, there is no priesthood devoted to the supreme god and no formalized worship of him. Although this "lazy god" approaches hav-ing the status of a purely transcendental deity, this "religious fact" has little or no bearing on ordinary, everyday human affairs, which are the predom-inant and almost exclusive focus of Afro-Latin spirituality.[199]

Imported into the New World via the African slave trade, Yoruba, Ebo, Ido, Bantu-Congo, and other African influences have coalesced into the Afro-Latin cults of Santería or Ocha (Cuba); Santería or Lucumí (United States); Espiritismo (Puerto Rico); Shango (Trinidad and Granada); and Santuario, Candomblé, Umbanda, and Macumba (Brazil). These consti-tute highly distinctive, colorful, and passionate religious expressions. But beside their polytheisms and absent creator god, what makes these pagan religions?

First, these are primarily this-worldly concerns. While they have picked up or fused with other traditions, at base there is little interest in soteriol-ogy or afterlife affairs. Santería/Santuario seeks to help its adherents in everyday matters: prosperity, protection, curing, security, business advice, love, marriage, children, problem solving. Even in its interest in what we can understand as the "purely" spiritual, there is no degradation or rejec-tion of the physical. Afro-Latin spiritists employ the tangible in represent-ing and accessing the world of the *orishas*.[200] The interplay and exchange between this world and the otherworld are fully transactional. The gods are worshiped with prayer, song, music, dance, and material gifts, and they are expected to augment life in substantial fashion for their worshipers. These are faiths whose core is devotional reciprocity.[201]

Dialogue with the otherworld focuses on trance induction. The means involve the *bembe* ritual of drum-and-dance as the central practice of the sacred ceremony (*güemilere*).[202] But unlike the shamanisms of elsewhere, the preoccupation is to draw in a spirit rather than to send out a soul or spirit. The technique in these circumstances aims for the specialist or lay participant to be possessed by an *orisha*. In this state, the medium becomes the vehicle for communication from the spirit in the form of advice, warnings, or information. There is no entry into the spiritual realm as such but an incorporation of the spiritual into the here-and-now of tangible reality. In fact, it is claimed that during the trance possession, the human body is (especially) sacred. "Not only are the Orisha embodied, they use those human bodies to eat, drink, dance, speak, bless, and heal."[203]

Santería/Santuario is predicated on an understanding of *ashe*, or "divine energy." This is different from *emi*, or "spirit," the principle of life itself that the supreme god breathed into the original deities and human beings.[204] *Ashe* is the force that contradicts chaos: chaos as primordial confusion, and chaos as an abysmal nothingness. *Ashe* is exemplified and even concentrated in the *orishas*, but it also is inherent in all things. It amounts to a quasi-animistic, quasi-tangible presence akin to *orenda*, *manitou*, or *mana*. The perception of this numinous aura and the tapping into its beneficial influences may be said to be a chief preoccupation of paganism.[205]

But while the *ashe* is particularly present in the spirits of the *orisha* pantheon, each individual is believed to have a personal *orisha* of his or her own, a free soul functioning as a guardian spirit. The *ori inun*, or "inner head"[206] of spiritist belief, however, takes the form of a person's destiny and ultimate potential. This person's task is discovering the identity of his or her protecting *orisha*, predestined birthstone, sheltering plant, and guardian animal. Once known, if the last three can be kept on or near the person, at least in symbolic form, the individual, it is believed, will prosper. His or her capabilities will continuously expand, with great success.

Much of ordinary Afro-Latin practice beside the more formal renewal rites and the volatile trance induction ceremonies involves divination. This comes under the jurisdiction of Ifá or Orunmila/Orula, the former and present respective keepers of the Table of Ifá, the divinatory system of the Yoruba. The special priest, or *babalawo*, is the religious functionary in charge of the divining procedure. Palm nuts, kola nuts, coconuts, or cowrie shells or other seashells are thrown, and the patterns they form are then read in line with various myths, legends, religious verses, songs, prayers, and *orisha* praise names that the *babalawo* has devoted great amounts of time to learning. Another common divinatory device is the use of a special sixteen-part necklace that is interpreted in a heads-or-tales fashion according to how its disks or pieces fall.[207]

Initiation is another prominent institution.[208] In Africa, of course, there are the secret religious societies, adolescent rites of passage, as well as special initiations for particular religious functionaries: the *babalawo*, the *oloogun* or healing channel, and the *elegun* or special *orisha* medium. Before the full initiation, the Cuban *santero* and Brazilian *pai-de-santo* (father of a saint) or *mãe-de-santo* (mother of a saint; properly, Iyalorixá priestess) undergo a rigorous traditional training that often lasts up to three years. This is a procedure reserved for a select few alone. In current U.S. developments of Lucumí, all adherents are encouraged to experience the full initiation process, but the required training has often been abbreviated and, in some cases, may last for only three months.[209] While there is a growing interest in learning and performing ritual in the original Yoruba language and returning to traditional practice, there is also an increasing tendency toward acquiring Western ecclesiastical form. Due to the potential for problems with neighbors caused by drumming, there is also less emphasis on trance possession.

Another aspect in these cults is the rich association with magic. Magic is employed both positively and negatively. In paganism, ethics begins with the family, tribe, or community. Those perceived as enemies of the home group may become targets of hexes or debilitating spells. Whether the Brazilian Macumba/*quimbanda* or the Caribbean *brujería*, *palo monte*, or *palo mayombe*, the practice of harmful magic—often involving curses performed at midnight in a cemetery—derives principally from Bantu-Congo sources rather than Yoruba origins. The deity invoked in *despacho* cursing/hexing is often the trickster figure of Exu, Eshu, Elegguá.[210]

The Brazilian Exu Elegba is the "master of the directions of space and time." In his wooden statues, he is depicted with an enormous phallus, and when he became identified with the Catholic devil, the phallic spear extending from his head was transformed into a pair of horns. Exu, however, is the most human of the Brazilian *orixás*, beyond good and evil. He represents pure energy. In Brazilian Umbanda, he has many forms: Exu das Sete Encruzilhadas, do Lodo, do Cemitério, and das Almas, respectively, Exu of the seven crossroads, of the mire, of the cemetery, and of the souls. Exu Tranca Rua de Mar is the Exu who blocks the tidal street.

The practice of magic is not always negative. It also is used for rectifications and healings, in short, for all those this-worldly foci with which spiritism is generally concerned. Its harmful capacities are most traditionally associated with Dahomean rather than Yoruba sources. The spiritism of Haiti is less fused with Christian ideas than is that of Cuban Santería or Brazilian Umbanda or Candomblé.[211] There is also a divide between the spirits not found elsewhere. Vodun understands its *loas* or spirit deities and *orisha* equivalents as comprising two distinct families.[212] On the one hand are the benevolent Rada, headed by Damballah (identified with St. Patrick) and including *orisha* imports. The Rada stand for purity and harmony. On the other hand are the embodiments of wild energy and passion known as the Petró deities. They are more fearsome and certainly lean more toward sinister magic. Voodoo stresses the acceptance and worship of both Rada and Petró in the attainment of equilibrium and general well-being, as the neglect of one for the other is thought to create imbalance and a risk of danger.

Besides the influences of Christianity and Bantu-Congo magic on New World/Yoruba spiritism, a third development stems from Allan Kardec's opposition to the French Catholic Church in the nineteenth century. Born Hypolite Leon Denizard Rivail and living from 1804 to 1869, Kardec proposed what he termed a scientific form of spiritism. This system is composed of a spiritual hierarchy deriving ultimately from God, and while Kardecism includes belief in reincarnation, it also entertains the notion of spiritual advancement in which the human medium transmits light or enlightenment to a spirit to help reach a higher level. The Kardecian medium, therefore, conforms more closely to the role of the traditional shaman and less as the vehicle for spirit possession as found in the Afro-Latin cults in general. In the 1870s, Kardec's ideas became especially popular among the Brazilian middle classes, and despite the church's campaign against them in the 1950s, they have continued to gain acceptance.[213]

The growing inclusion of Kardecian understandings in Umbanda, Ocha, and Lucumí as well as other Afro-Atlantic religious practices reveals spiritism's potential for incorporating the transcendental despite its fundamental immanentist orientation. So while paganism may center its understanding of the spiritual or supernatural in the tangible world of physical reality, it does not preclude or even avoid the extension of the divine into a non-corporeal dimension. Afro-Latin spiritism reveals itself as a dynamic and adaptable religiosity exhibiting the full range of pagan spirituality.

## Contemporary Western Paganism

The question now before us concerns the relationship of contemporary Western paganism to classical Greco-Roman religiosity and the current indigenous primal paganisms with which the revived paganisms in the West claim affiliation and/or continuity. From the start, I wish to distinguish between what I am designating as contemporary Western paganism and what we can understand as contemporary paganisms in the West. These last include the essentially ethnic expressions of both Amerindian religiosity and Chinese practices. While Native American spirituality has moved beyond its tribal origins, albeit controversially, it is Santería and, to a lesser extent, voodoo that are moving more successfully into the Euro-American community at large from their ethnic, in these cases, Afro-Latin "home bases."

Both classical paganism and the indigenous forms still alive in the world today are characterized by polytheism, animism, humanism, magic, organic and numinous qualities, pantheism or at least a quasi-pantheistic immanence of deity, and, in part as a result of this last, idolatry. Consequently, we must ask how contemporary Western paganism measures up to or conforms to these features of paganism in its broad sense. In other words, where does contemporary Western paganism fit into the range of traditional pagan identity?

Contemporary Western paganism[214] is frequently referred to by scholars, academics, and often practitioners themselves as *neopaganism*. I wish to argue, however, that neopaganism is a particular—and predominant—form of Western paganism, an identifiable religion in itself, and so I shall henceforth capitalize it to stress this point. Along with Neopaganism, therefore, we have in the contemporary pagan scene of the West both reconstructed traditions (recopaganisms) and the more generic, natural, and spontaneous expressions that we can label *geopaganism*.

Folk religiosities survive even in the contemporary West. They are invariably local practices and in general more immediately concerned with, or connected to, the earth in one manner or another.[215] The venerational customs of the folk at large, the community of "ordinary" people, are often geopagan. Examples include tossing a coin into a fountain, spring, or well; offering ritualistic greetings like "good morning" or "good evening" to known or unknown passersby; or making a toast before beginning alcoholic consumption in gregarious situations. Although all culture is learned, much if not most geopagan behavior is subliminal and automatic. It comprises the unconscious but frequently repeated, that is, ritualistic, actions diffused throughout a culture. It may be found in our referring to the intoxicating ingredients in beverages as "spirits" or our calling film personalities "stars," "screen icons," or "movie idols," or our naming places of entertainment "music halls" or "theaters" and places of cultural treasure "museums"—here, whether consciously or not, in honor of the Muses.

Geopaganism is largely folk religion, or at least something close to it. It need not be purely unconscious and automatic behavior and, indeed, in the contemporary Western pagan milieu, often is not.[216] But almost invariably its rites are simple, organic, and spontaneously natural. As a conscious reaction or performance, geopaganism eschews great elaboration and complex ritual unless these have been sanctioned by long-standing, continuous, and local or regional tradition. When his or her devotional expression is deliberate, that is, intentionally performed, the geopagan is centered along with the immediate community on the earth with its springs, trees and groves, natural caves and grottoes, peculiar rocks and other unusual outcroppings, rivers, and hills and mountains. It is the simple practice of naturism, the veneration of the natural, that I am suggesting is the core expression of geopagan religiosity.[217]

Recopaganism differs from geopaganism in being more deliberate and consciously undertaken. Recopaganisms are the various attempts at reconstructing or reviving particular pagan traditions of the past.[218] These include the various druidical orders found especially in Britain and the United States. They also include the northern traditions of Odinism, Asatru, and Vanirism, Vanatru, or *seiðr*. We also find here contemporary attempts to revive the Egyptian and Hellenic mysteries. If geopaganism is at least incipiently polytheistic, recopaganism with its pantheons of Egyptian, Greek, Roman, Nordic, and Celtic deities is blatantly so. Recopagan practice can be recognized by its elaborate ritual and ceremonial dress. When and if it represents its gods and goddesses in concrete form, it can also be easily detected by its idols.

Neopaganism, while in part a Celtic revivalistic attempt, probably owes its inception primarily to the singular figure of Gerald Gardner. Just as the term Christianity subsumes or includes various subgroups or denominations like Catholicism or Methodism, Neopaganism also has individual expressions in Gardnerian, Alexandrian, and other forms of Wicca or the Crafte, in Goddess Spirituality, in the Covenant of Universalist Unitarian Pagans, and so forth.[219] Neopaganism may be broadly identified by its calendar of eight *sabbats*, or festivals; its ceremonial circle; its peculiar identity of the directions and elements; its ritual paraphernalia and invocations, chants, and songs; and, above all, its bigendered or bitheistic notion of deity.[220]

Often included in contemporary Western paganism are the various schools of ceremonial magic.[221] But even Wicca is in large part a magical practice.[222] If we understand magic as an attempt to violate the natural law

of exchange, that is, to obtain something of greater value in place of something less, we see the magical arts as a standard and recurring element
throughout classical paganism. Not all magical practice need be witchcraft, and indeed the transgression of the law of equal exchange is a fundamental endeavor of most religions. But paganism has always been at home
with magical practice and has been traditionally associated with it. In this
sense, Neopaganism is fully compatible with the sorceries and thauma-
turgies (miracle workings) that were presumably incorporated into pre-
Christian Greco-Roman religiosity.[223]

With regard to the humanism that underlies classical religion and philosophy and that we find more recently expressed through Confucianism
in particular, contemporary Western paganism—especially in its Neopagan forms—retains a diminished emphasis at best. With the increasing fa-
voring of the brain's right hemisphere over the left, today's emphasis on
feminine intuition over masculine rationality might be another reason
that humanistic centrality is no longer obvious in contemporary Western
paganism. Its antianthropomorphic tendency favors the mystical ubiquity
and interconnectedness of all life, which also appears to counter humanistic sentiment.[224]

Even contemporary Western paganism appears to recognize animism
and to incorporate a fundamental animistic understanding of the world.[225]
Contemporary animism may be different from indigenous and classical
animisms, but it is an animistic attitude or recognition all the same.
Whether present-day pagans in the West actually believe that inanimate
objects have spirits or that natural phenomena are caused by spirits, they
act and behave as if this were the case. But if an animistic attitude permeates Santería more than it does Neopaganism, it may have more to do with
the organicism of Afro-Latin spirituality: the organic quality of perception
and practice being threatened by the technological and rational societies
of the West. Conversely, the question of the numinousness of religion in
general and contemporary Western paganism in particular rests on a subjective evaluation and cannot be judged as something that has increased
or decreased, is present or absent, in Neopaganism as opposed to traditional, indigenous paganisms.

The most salient differences between Neopaganism and pre-Christian
and primal paganisms are found in the practice itself. Much of "original"
paganism involves temple and shrine worship. The basic format may be
described as "processional," whether formal ceremonial marching or the
informal proceeding from one shrine to the next as part of individual

worship. By contrast, the main Neopagan religious act is the casting and opening of the ceremonial circle,[226] with little if any devotion before an altar as such. Celebration is centered on the magic circle spatially and around it temporally. Neopagans have a set procedure for invoking the "elemental guardians" of each cardinal direction; dialogues and means of passing ideas, symbols, and talismans around the circle; a bread-and-wine communion; and sometimes the raising of a "cone of power" as a magical act and/or a culminating "spiral dance." Whether because of personal preference or geographic logistics, many contemporary Western pagans are solitary practitioners. In contrast, the predominant tenor in Neopaganism is congregational rather than individually devotional, as is the case in folk paganism. Nonetheless, all these differences in practice are more cosmetic or superficial than fundamental or essential, and Neopaganism's external form is just one more type of paganism alongside Shinto, Santería, Chinese folk religion, and Siberian shamanism.

On a more constitutive level, while contemporary Western paganism shares with paganism in general a spiritually materialistic or, perhaps more accurately, materialistically spiritual worldview, one centered on the immanence of the godhead, it has made some important shifts in both concept and practice. Pantheism has always had difficulty with the mundane, and modern Western paganism is no exception. The ordinary both is and is not sacred: the deciding point is attitudinal and depends on whether or not the perceiver is in an ecstatic state. Although in principle, everything may be holy, it does not always feel that way. Traditional devotional paganism resorts to time-honored aids and instruments to help achieve the required state of ecstasy. But mind-altering intoxications can be achieved only through tightly controlled permissible avenues in the West; the prevailing Judeo-Christian attitude does not believe in the individual's freedom to choose his or her own state of consciousness beyond certain well-established limits. Moreover, a kind of biblical hangover renders idolatrous expression both embarrassing and uncomfortable. This is particularly true for the Protestant influence, and although this same embarrassment and discomfort is less prevalent in Catholic and Orthodox circles, the cultic veneration of saints and icons is never considered idolatry.

The embodiment of an idea, or *idolon*, in tangible form, the incorporation of the holy in the corporeal, the worship of a physical object as a representation of the divine or the locus for an indwelling spirit or the sacred itself made manifest, is something generally absent from most neopagan and geopagan expressions of contemporary Western paganism.[227] This lack of idolatry as either an idea or a practice is one major distinguishing feature between contemporary and ethnic paganisms. What the contemporary Western pagan tends to do instead is reify the whole of nature into a divine object and/or process worthy of worship.[228] In our contemporary developments, nature itself becomes the idol.

But if the nonconspicuousness of idolatry is one contrasting element, the lack of an actual, as opposed to a nominal, polytheism is another. It is perhaps this single feature alone that places contemporary Neopaganism on the marginal fringes of paganism as a whole. The plethora of names for goddesses and gods often used by contemporary Western pagans of the neopagan school does not represent independent, substantially or cosmically distinct entities but, rather and simply, designations for either its Goddess or God.[229] Instead of espousing a polytheistic theology as is traditional of paganism, Neopaganism represents a bitheistic understanding of the cosmos. While this may be considered an "advance" over monotheism, the duality of the neopagan godhead can appear from a traditional perspective to be less pluralistic, multiple, or polytheistic than the Christian Trinity.

Consequently, we can assess the position of Neopaganism vis-à-vis paganism as a general category of a distinguishing theological perspective as commensurate with the range of diversity found in the other world religions. From a canonical viewpoint, it can be argued that neither Mormonism nor Jehovah's Witnesses are truly Christian. But in any religious affiliation are dissenters and critics of those who do not appear to toe an orthodox line. Paganism as a religion is not immune to these types of difficulties. In contemporary Western paganism itself, for instance, there is embarrassment and a distancing tendency between neopagans, on the one hand, and the more fascistic inclinations found in certain paths of the Northern tradition, on the other hand.[230] Without adhering to ecclesiastical fine points, however, I have attempted to look at the world's religious options from as broad an angle as possible. In this sense, few real alternatives are available, despite the vast and all-encompassing range of choice and variety within those few huge areas. Vis-à-vis paganism as a whole, Neopaganism may be comparable to the position of the Latter-day Saints or the Jehovah's Witnesses toward canonical Christianity, but we cannot consider that it is not pagan.[231] In addition, paganism as a religiosity has no centralized coordination or institutionalized organization. For those who claim the label of pagan, there is no recognized facility to deny it to them.

## Conclusion

In this chapter I have looked at Chinese folk religion, Japanese Shinto, primal tribal religion, shamanism, Amerindian spirituality, Afro-American Spiritism, and contemporary Western paganism in a quest for common features that constitute paganism as a world religion to rank along aside the other broad categories consisting of Christianity, Islam, Hinduism, Buddhism, agnosticism, and atheism. Among the features that emerge as noticeable are those of animism, pantheism, polytheism, immanentism, humanism, nature worship, numinousness, magic, organicism, fetishism, and idolatry. There is, however, no complete list of characteristics that can identify any specific practice as pagan. Most identities that we are permitted to recognize as pagan share in this pool, subscribing to some of its ingredients but not necessarily all of them. But if we could choose two features that constituted paganism, I would select a this-worldly attitude or preference and a recognition of divinity in, or as, matter, whatever else it may be.

Religion remains among the more contested of human institutions. The vast disagreements, even warfare, within any single religious identity often center on the question of who belongs and who does not. But in this undertaking, I am looking at religious expression and identity from a bird's-eye perspective. This is a search for the salient features of a neglected and unorganized theology.

Evaluating a religiosity is an intuitive venture. While we have looked for conspicuous elements by which to recognize and/or constitute a particular category, the final assessment of any individual practice rests on how it *feels* to the observer or participant. These last are not necessarily the same. Each is coming from a different angle, and each has different reasons for making his or her assessment. In this work I have tried to judge objectively as a spectator, but I recognize that paganism is something that one must sense. It is this particular sentiment that one encounters in a Chinese temple, a voodoo *honfort*, a classical shrine, a Shinto place of worship, a Hawaiian *heiau*, or whatever. There is in all these a numinous aura that spontaneously speaks to the soul. We can automatically recognize paganism along these lines as the Christian may likewise simply discern his or her own places of worship and practice. This venture into paganism has, accordingly, proceeded from this kind of general and intuitive recognition. I have subsequently attempted to delineate the salient features of these recognized identities and what they might share.

# 2

# Paganism as Behavior

The Hawaiian *heiau*, or indigenous pre-Christian temple, is usually a dry-stone rectangular structure. Its enclosing wall is low, and there is no roof. In essence, the surrounding wall is one of demarcation only. These are venerable enclosures, however, dating to precolonial times. Nevertheless, even today visitors find inside the *heiau*'s walls stones piled on top of one another, usually three high but perhaps as many as six, with each stone wrapped in the sacred *ti* leaf of Hawaii.

Because these offerings are found in the islands' *heiaus*, we can recognize them as evidences of pagan activity. There is, however, another significance here, one that transcends the immediate pagan context. In the previous chapter, we explored religiosities that could be considered pagan on the basis of their theologies, whether explicit or merely implicit. In this chapter, by contrast, we want to look more closely at pagan behavior. The small stone and *ti* leaf offerings in the Hawaiian *heiau* are illustrative of cultic behavior. I argue here that cultic behavior of the kind we have already seen in geopagan activity is in itself essentially pagan. Its most direct opposite, at least in the West, would probably be Protestant congregational worship, particularly Calvinist and perhaps Quaker and Unitarian as well.

Veneration in any religion is, or at least is akin to, cultic devotion. Apart from magical activity or the employment of techniques of magic to produce a desired effect, adoration or devotion is cultic. Usually when we speak about the cult of the Virgin Mary or the cult of any entity or activity, including reason, we imply intensity. But less passionate worship is noncultic only by degree and not by kind. In other words, the fundamental and atavistic human urge to express honor and homage is cultic or pagan.[1] It is something that is instinctually natural, even though its outward forms are learned through cultural transmission. Its cultic aspect becomes more obvious as the passion becomes more intense, and part of today's negative reaction to the very idea of cult stems from a resistance to anything more emotional than the norm and thereby potentially threatening to the status quo.

Our terms and their concepts for *cult, cultic, culture*, and *cultivation* derive from the Latin verb *colere*, "to till, to worship." Already we are permitted to see at root level the intimate interconnection between cultivation and worship. In both, there is a creation or making of worth, and as the agricultural origin and connotation suggest, value at this root level is understood as something tangible and real. If cultic behavior is learned, as is all behavior, it can nevertheless be argued that it is "naturally learned," that is, as something incipient and primordial in human development. Worship at this nonreflective and almost spontaneous stage of human growth, stripped of its theological overlay or baggage and expressive of the root level of religion, is what I am identifying as pagan.

Margot Adler's understanding of paganism is chiefly characterized by animism, polytheism, and pantheism.[2] Veneration at the earliest levels of human development almost invariably relates to apprehensions of personality in both the animate and inanimate realms. And even today, in its contemporary and indigenous forms, paganism is centered mainly on multiple personification. In other words, paganism is still largely animistic and polytheistic. But inasmuch as it is also pantheistic, it follows the naturalism of Robert Corrington, which holds that "there is nothing whatsoever outside of nature. The sacred is in and of nature and cannot outstrip nature."[3] The "mother" of nature as we know it—and have known it presumably since our origins—is the earth. But while we can still allow for the extraterrestrial as well as possibly the preternatural, Corrington's perspective on naturalism denies the extranatural or what Aquinas coined as the "supernatural."

Consequently, if worship is a natural impulse, as Peter Berger contends, cultic behavior that is directed inside nature is pagan. But religious or theological behavior that directs itself outside nature is transcendentalism of one form or another. Implicit in it—and distinguishing it from pagan behavior—is a devaluation of the natural. It is my contention that the cultic behaviors we detect throughout the world are primarily atavistic or spontaneous reactions that are natural and this-worldly. These are detectable as coherent actions in themselves despite their theological interpretations or reinterpretations.

In other words, from a behavioral point of view, paganism may be seen as part of religious activity itself, one that runs throughout not only the pagan religions themselves but the other world religions as well. In some cases, the pagan dimension of religious expression may be more clearly seen as pagan, as in Hinduism; in other cases, such as in Islam, this may appear to be less obvious. Veneration of the anima or animus or both is a natural human response. It may be deliberately performed, as in classical paganisms of the Greco-Roman world, or it may be more subliminal and unconsciously automatic, as we have seen in geopaganism.

Cultic behavior itself relates to, but can be distinguished from, the practice of magic per se. While magical practice is certainly a part of pagan expression, it can also be found in other, nonpagan, religions as well. Why, then, is magical behavior sometimes pagan while cultic activity is always pagan?

While contemporary Western paganism, classical paganism. and indigenous non-Western paganisms all relate in their incorporation of magic, most or at least much religion in general is suggestive of the magical: the countervening of the natural and empirical law of exchange. Quantum physics and nuclear physics are based on this principle of conservation, which, as a central tenet of science, maintains that any specific value or aspect of a system is always preserved. If there is a give, there must be a corresponding take. But the law of exchange extends to religion as well. Hindus refer to *karma*; Christians, to the rewards of heaven or hell. Religion is a composite of both magical and venerational rituals, but religious and pagan magic, as opposed to worship, seeks a violation of this equality of exchange. The magician may transgress the law by substituting something of lower value for the obtainment of something of greater worth. There is, however, no full cessation of the law of exchange. One does not transform nothingness into something. The principle is not destroyed but is simply unequalized.

In most religion, the employment of magic is understood as sacrifice. In religion as worship and not as magic per se, we attempt to secure the favor of the gods through offerings. In many cases, these gifts are symbolic. But any violation of the law of exchange is an expression not of worship but of the magical elements, which themselves constitute a religious norm. The magician, as distinct from the devotee or worshiper who offers gifts to the gods, who in turn may or may not then choose to act and return the favor, seeks to cause effect through the exercise of his or her will. This "purer" magic has become characteristic of contemporary Neopaganism in general. What is an offering or presentation in religion, like devotion or worship, becomes for the magician simply an expedient tool, something to be exchanged. In magic, the sacrifice represents a payment, as opposed to a gift.

It is important to mention that magic also is traditionally associated with deception or trickery. Usually this refers to the actions of the magician, but the magic also is inherently tricky. Consequently, an element of risk or danger is involved in the practice of magic. The law of equal exchange may be violated, but the inequality may go against the magician in certain circumstances. Freedom from the consequences of one's actions is not an automatic fait accompli in either religion or magic. Again, the law is violated but not suspended. Contemporary Western paganism has attempted to harness this violation with ethics. It speaks in terms of the law of the threefold return. What the magician or pagan practitioner of magic does, that is, sends out, returns three times, or three times as strong. This law of the threefold return is claimed to apply to good and bad actions alike.

Whether the consequence of unequal exchange is sought or used as an ethical check, it is a deliberate part of magic. Cultic behavior, however, has no aim in transgressing the law of equal exchange. And while it may be consciously performed, it need not be so to remain cultic. In fact, much of the learned behavior that can be termed cultic is unconscious, automatic, or reflexive. It is natural and becomes an organic part of the consequences that spring from any fundamental human need to worship or express veneration. Consequently, when magic is undertaken with a deliberate aim in mind, its rituals are consciously performed, always with an element of the artificial or the unordinary. Magic is the product of extreme will; it is often undertaken in times of stress and calamity as a response to events beyond the norm.

In contrast to the magical behavior of pagans and others, religious cultivation operates more within the natural norm. In its basic form, it seeks nothing beyond its desire to express some form of adoration to the divine or otherworldly. If the result is like the granting of a wish after throwing a coin into a well or the extension of the king's rule and reign after an equine/*ashvamedha* sacrifice, these are by-products, a goodwill exchange on the part of the gods, rather than a consciously obtained result secured through a rigorous exercise of the magician's will. Cultic behavior may be simple or complex, but its rituals are presentations rather than attempts to coerce. They spring from an atavistic and natural human propensity with the consequence that they are more spontaneous, more pagan, and more cultic. They may be predicated on an assumed, hidden, or latent contract with the supernatural, but this contract is not the commanding charter of the magician or priest. Rather, the cultic contract is based on such invisibles as trust, faith, and honor. It may expect little though hope for a lot, but it is generally premised on the creation of some kind of beauty that in some way resonates with the worshiper. Unlike the performance of magical rites, cultic ritual is more implicitly understood and recognized by the worshiper as an expression rather than a command, enticement, or self-centered creation, and any beauty that is its essence—whether rudimentary or elaborate—often carries no expectations but is simply offered. In other words, magical ritual is intentional and in some respects represents an attempt to tamper with nature. Cultic ritual may or may not be intentional; it may or may not be an automatic response developing from learned cultural behavior; but it is natural and works ultimately with the organic flow and not in violation of it.

The cultic is the very basis of worship. Its etymological origins in the Latin verb *colere* with its past participle of *cultus* refer to the tilling and cultivation of the earth and its soil. But at the same time, this word means "prayer" and "worship." In the pagan context, worship or the making of the valuable entails the physical and working with it. Cultivating the earth and making the crops grow are sacred acts. In both its tangible and spiritual senses, *colere* suggests nourishment. Cultivation and culture are themselves the cultic. In a figurative if not literal understanding, they are both physical and collective prayers.

In our anticult day and age, the term *cult* has received an enormous amount of one-sided, bad press. Its use connotes mind control, totalitarianism, brainwashing, deviance, deviousness, and sexual impropriety. But its more original and basic denotation suggests simply what is undertaken with intensity and passion. If the emotionally significant and enthusiastic have become suspect in our times, then our very times themselves must become suspect. But devotion to a person, idea, or activity undertaken with intensity is a natural human expression and fulfillment. It belongs to human life as much as do the foods that we harvest from the earth and its seas. The cultic is what refines and cultivates a particular preference or propensity. It primarily appeals individually, locally, and/or communally. It is not something that a priori has global or universal appeal, and for that very reason it is often suspect and condemned by others with different tastes and agendas. The cultic might be seen as the foundation of our search and growth as humans. It is where we at heart intersect with the mysterious, the as-of-yet unanswered perennial question, and the very wondrousness of the cosmos, a wondrousness through which the earth generates our sustenance and ultimately the very quality of our lives. But whereas the cultic may become deliberate and at times must be so, it is the spontaneous, unconsciously motivated, and automatically reflexive that is its foundation, the essence of paganism or worship or both: paganism as worship, and worship as pagan. Its rituals are rituals of cultivation rather than ceremonies aiming to influence preconceived events and achieve specific ends.

If freedom and health are recognized as universal humanitarian goals, no less an end of human endeavor is the pursuit of comfort. Idealists often tend to reject this last as an unworthy and illegitimate direction. Comfort is equated with the mundane and hence considered of inferior value. But when balanced by the other goals, comfort need in no way be detrimental, and in any event, it is certainly the motivating factor behind a greater deal, if not the majority of both individual and collective enterprise. A fourth aspiration, and again one frequently spurned as incompatible with "modern," progressive life, is that of worship. What we often have here too is not the rejection of worship per se but of either what is perceived as ignorant superstition or the unacceptable tenets of one or another organized religion.

When I toured the world for two years in 1981 and 1982, I found myself repeatedly struck by the almost universal phenomenon of veneration by people everywhere, regardless of culture or faith. In fact, even where the venerative act runs counter to the official dogma or accepted theology, the elements of adoration are still to be found. Granted, such forms are more obvious in the so-called Third World if not in Asia or the Far East as a whole, but their constancy is such that I was led to seek their equivalent in such Protestant bastions as North America and northern Europe. Wishing to know both how people venerate as well as what they do, I accumulated notes and observations to this end. What follows is my understanding of this behavioral aspect and its validity if not necessity in today's fast-paced world and the advent of a free, healthy, and comfortable life in the twenty-first century.

The venerative act appears to be either theistic or nontheistic and, in the former, directed toward either animistic or nonanimistic projections. In other words, worship is focused or not, and if it is focused, it is expressed toward what we may term the *anima-animus* or a more purely

abstract or sectarian conception such as the Brahman, the Buddha, Yahweh, the Christian God or Trinity, or Allah.

In reality, however, there is no clear-cut line between any of these three
forms of veneration. They overlap and in their pure sense exist only as
academic classifications. More vernacularly, worship is frequently to be
seen as an automatic and accustomed act. It is often performed with only
minimal conscious awareness. In fact, it appears to be so instinctive a part
of human nature that if it is not an integrally universal form of behavior,
its causes must be sought in the nuclear archetypal configurations on
which each of the various world cultures is rooted.

The major religious cultures whose venerative, cultic, or pagan behavior
we explore are the Christian, the Islamic, the Hindu, and the Buddhist. In
this venture, I am restricted to my own firsthand contacts plus the supplemental knowledge I have been able to gain through my research. Nevertheless, it is principally in the religious domains of these specific, official, and
"universal" theologies that I examine here the venerative modes of their adherents' behavior. In other words, the major religious competitors of paganism are Buddhism, Hinduism, Islam, and Christianity and, conceivably,
along with its less committed form of agnosticism, atheism. None of these
five religious options is a pagan *religion*, though each is variously infused
with identifiable pagan *practices*. In the remainder of this chapter, I look at
these practices as they appear in these nonpagan religious identities.

Before proceeding further, however, let me reiterate what I mean by
"veneration." From the outset, I intend as broad an interpretation as possible, though keeping in mind that veneration has two sides, one internal
and one external. Regarding the former, the concepts of respect, reverence,
awe, and love come to mind. Generally, these are directed toward a deity,
person, or object, but this need not always be the case. Because the internal aspect of veneration is subjective, for purposes of observation we must
restrict ourselves to the detectable instances of the act of venerating. Idolatry is one of its most obvious manifestations, but other expressions of
honor, reverence, and adoration may or may not appear as a ceremonial
tribute or a set form.

In general, the object of worship is distinguished by attributes of sacredness or some other characteristics of worth, esteem, or respect. Veneration, then, deals with something considered special and is the outward or
tangible acknowledgment of this attribute of specialness by one or more
individuals. In the context of understanding "pagan" behavior, our interest
is not in the forms of worship directed toward the official formulations of

the godhead, except possibly to the degree these forms are also to be seen as expressions of people's love for the animating principle of all life and nature. The fundamental dichotomy between worship and the "higher theological concepts" is more obvious in Brahmanism and Buddhism. In the face of the impersonal absolute or the fundamental nothingness, worship is superfluous, and yet the fact that devotees of these religions continue devotional practices betrays a deeper need embedded in humankind, one that I am identifying as pagan.

The case is less obvious in the focus on the personal god of the Levantine religions (Judaism, Zoroastrianism, Christianity, and Islam) but nonetheless may be argued. The flaunting of the prohibition in some of these beliefs against the worship of both other gods beside God and graven images is again an indication of the ubiquitous tendency toward a perception of spiritual multiplicity. Most of us recognize that reverence of Yahweh, Allah, or the Trinity is no less an instance of veneration, even if we contend that it is a reflex of an earlier, more primordial acknowledgment of animating forces.

However, in the cultic-pagan context, veneration takes its root in more automatic and tangible expressions like the spontaneous tossing of a wishing coin into a well, and so we concentrate on these forms and their associated beliefs such as animism, shamanism, phallicism, and idolatry. Concurrent with the act of worship is where the act takes place. Demonstrable veneration almost invariably occurs in (or in front of) what may be termed a shrine or temple, be it private or public, domestic or communal. In its origin, the word *shrine* refers to a receptacle (e.g., a box or chest) that contains some sacred relic, but this meaning has been extended to include not only the tomb (i.e., casket) of some venerated person but also any place hallowed or honored through the presence or association of a venerated object.

In a strict sense, there is little difference between a shrine and a temple. Although the latter usually refers to the edifice itself and may be merely an enclosed area, it also usually indicates a place for the worship or presence of a deity. In Japan, the generic "temple" is used for buildings of Buddhist worship, whereas the "shrine" is reserved for Shinto and worship of the *kami*, but this is a special case. In general, the temple represents the focus by humanity on divinity. In popular usage, however, the concept of divinity may be envisioned as anything special, valued, or prized. This includes particular activities as well, and we shall return to this attitude when we discuss the developments of secularized veneration. For the moment, let us be aware that the repetition of veneration in any form in any specific location allows us to consider that location as either a shrine or a temple, and conversely, the detection of a sanctuary constitutes our primary source for witnessing of the objective reality of veneration, that is, the subjective process by which for a moment beyond time and beyond the woes and concerns of the world individuals can surrender themselves to the grace of a postulated influence.

Consequently, our basic question is why we know, for instance, when encountering a Candomblé altar that despite its prolific Christian iconography, it is pagan. The "how we know" may have several answers, but the "why we know" rests on the fact that it *is* pagan. Paganism may use a wealth of different symbols and external paraphernalia, but its essence rests on an underlying subliminal, organic, and natural apprehension that may be either blatant or subtle in differing degrees but that is detectable. Anyone already of pagan sympathies will recognize the pagan essence whenever it appears in whatever the setting. While this sounds like an "it takes one to know one approach," we should keep in mind that this recognition is at best something cultivated; it may have a natural and spontaneous origin, but it is a sensitivity that is developed as well. Much of my own development along these lines occurred in India and with my encounters with Hinduism. Hinduism is a religion that is officially world denying but in practice is about as flawlessly pagan as they come. During my nine-month sojourn in India in 1981, I deliberately set out to explore both the Indo-European origins and the pagan legacy of contemporary Hinduism through its temples, shrines, pilgrimage sites, festivals, and accompanying cultic behaviors.

## Hinduism

As the birthplace of perhaps the oldest major world religion, India affords us a rich arena in which to study cultic veneration, how it is expressed and how it intersects with nonpagan religious frameworks. In its overall mix of peoples and differing traditions, India must certainly be unlike any other area in the world. Often compared with China, India is said to excel in individual liberty, whereas the People's Republic of China scores instead in equality. If, however, the Indian political achievement guarantees freedom, the social pressure to conform and keep to one's station as dictated by the rigors of caste greatly moderate the range of individual mobility. Nevertheless, it remains a land that embraces perhaps the widest diversity of behavior to be found anywhere. India is a world of uncanny contradiction as well as almost laboratory magnification. In India, everything is exaggerated to such an extent that as a result, it becomes more salient and readily detectable. Because of its ancient but still vibrant pagan inheritance, it is the perfect place to begin any investigation into the "countercultic" expressions inconsistent with an hegemonic theology.[4]

My first sight of Bharata came during the taxi ride from Dum Dum Airport to a hotel in central Calcutta. I was stunned by the sheer number of people, the riot of color, and the overwhelming interaction of movement of all kinds: speeding trucks, the slow shifting to the roadside by human-drawn rickshaws, women on foot carrying huge bundles on their heads. People lived everywhere and in all conditions of affluence and poverty, permanence, and transience. Occasionally I glimpsed a roadside shrine, sometimes with gaudily painted figures of deities, but in the chaotic presentation of pure sensation and through my own lack of familiarity, most chapels flashed by unrecognized.

Several days later, accompanied by the Armenian patroness of my hotel, another taxi took us to Dakshineshwar, the complex where Ramakrishna served as temple priest. Ramakrishna's bedroom, now a shrine in which only silence is enjoined, possesses the aura that accrues from the presence of a highly venerated person. Within the complex itself, twelve large black *lingams*, each in a separate chapel, face the central sanctuary dedicated to Kali, wife of the god Shiva, the *lingam* (literally, phallus) being the iconic representation of Shiva. But my ignorance was such that I had little idea of what is considered the proper way to approach these shrines.

Even worse was the next day when, alone, I walked to the Kalighat, Calcutta's main temple, reputedly constructed on the site where a finger fell from the corpse of Shiva's original wife Sati as it was being dismembered while the lamenting god carried it across the heavens. I circled the compound and bought candies and a couple of strands of red flowers as offerings. Reluctantly leaving my expensive Western sandals with a boy as required, I entered the central structure, but inside the doors of the sanctum sanctorum were shut tight, and I found myself caught amid the almost unbearably hot press of people. Some devotees merely tossed coins and took their leave, but I waited with the rest for what seemed an interminable length of time.

Eventually the doors were flung open and in the great melee that ensued, I held my offerings above my head to protect them against the pushing and lunging of the crowd's frenzy. Being recognized as a foreigner, the guards pulled me to the threshold of the goddess's shrine where one after the other, the attendant priests plied me for monetary contributions. Having hidden most of my funds, I would have had to undress to reach them and thus declined further payments once the limits of my pocket cash had been reached. Vermilion paste was placed on my forehead, and to my surprise, after contact with the idol—Kali's red tongue being all that I recognized in the rush and confusion—my offerings were returned to me. Also to my surprise, my sandals had not disappeared, though the couple of coins I gave to the boy were hardly to his satisfaction. I gave the sanctified candies to the throng of screaming children that had gathered around me, but a beggar to whom I had also given a sweet held it up to his forehead in moving gratitude. This was my first understanding of *prasad* (divine gift) in which flowers, fruit, water, confections, or even one's own offerings are given to a devotee as a gift from the deity. Exhausted, I then returned to my hotel. The next day I took a night train to Banaras.

This most ancient—perhaps the oldest in the world—and holiest city has always enticed me as if it were some kind of numinous magnet. Although I had been told by earlier visitors to the Far East that there were many more appealing and pleasant places throughout India, there had never been any doubt in my mind that this was where I would go first and would establish as a home base. To my frustration, the train sat within what I was told was a view of the city for two hours owing to the engine failure of another train farther ahead on the same track, but eventually I arrived and, after a cold shower in my hotel, hired a rickshaw to reach the center of town. In the Roman festival calendar, the day was the *feriae* of the Terminalia, not only marking the end of the year but also commemorating the *terminus* or property-demarcating boundary stone, and I thought it appropriate for the occasion to see the great stone *jyotir-lingam* (lingam/phallus of light) housed in what is popularly known as the Golden Temple. My ride from the hotel near the bank of the Varana River across the city to the holy area fronting the Ganges was reminiscent of the taxi ride to Calcutta except that the openness of the cycle rickshaw allowed for more direct exposure to the hodgepodge of activity and traffic that is Indian life. Shops little more than open-fronted cubbyholes lined the roads the entire route. In front of them were juice stands, fruit wagons, and prepared-food carts with all sorts of unrecognizable items. Ramshackle buses with horns blaring pushed their way through the crowds of pedestrians, bicycles, cycle rickshaws, and occasionally motorized rickshaws and autos. Cacophony and chaos are the only way to describe it all to the unaccustomed eye, but everywhere punctuated by the dark beauty and dazzling smile of the Indian face and, of course, by the ubiquitous, always in the way, holy cow.

My rickshaw wallah deposited me into the care of Kailash, whom I would describe as a *yatrawal* (religious guide for pilgrims) except that he is not a brahmin but a member of the *vaisya* caste and hunts for Western tourists rather than Indian pilgrims. Telling him of my desire to visit Vishwanatha, Kailash asked with surprise, "Dressed like that?" in apparent reference to and rejection of my Western clothes. "Besides," he continued, "you must first take a bath in the Ganga, and it is now too late for that."

Eventually I purchased a *khurta* (shirt) and *dhoti* (long wraparound cloth), and once back at the hotel, two bearers showed me how to wear the latter. At 5:30 A.M. the next day, I set off for the Ganges and there bathed shortly after sunrise. I was escorted by Kailash's henchman Lalu, and after leaving the chilly river, we were met by Kailash himself. The two arranged for a priest to escort me through the main temple and several nearby shrines. My "tour" was at such a breakneck speed that I was scarcely aware of what I saw. Instead I glimpsed merely a psychedelic kaleidoscope of what seemed numinous archetypal flashes. Perhaps in the rush, I touched the Vishweshwara stone, but I shall never know for sure. And all the time I encountered the brahmin nemesis, the handing out of an odd-numbered amount of rupees as *dan*, or baksheesh. I at least had known enough not to take with me more than a limited supply of money. As it was, I had to borrow sixty rupees from Kailash for various expenses, including payment of my guide.

Hinduism may be described as a constantly growing amalgamation of the pre-Aryan neolithic practices with the Vedism of the subcontinent's Indo-European populations.[5] The Vedic belief itself centers on the god Indra, a projection of man, and his alter ego Agni, the god of fire. It is a nature-oriented composite that is both positivistic and this-worldly, finding the essence of deity in energy and brightness. The central celebrated act is the slaying of the cosmic, antihumanistic, rain-withholding, darkness-spewing serpent Vritra by the thunderbolt-wielding hero god Indra, a reflex of which is the legend of St. George and the dragon. As the champion god of India's Indo-Aryan conquerors, Indra naturally became an aristocratic deity. At the same time as the Indo-Aryan conquest of India, the country's indigenous priests, who were brahmins, were reduced to an inferior position. But the native priests were also literate, which distinguished them from the remainder of the dark-skinned original inhabitants. As a result, the brahmins first recorded the sacred hymns of the Aryan rulers and then continued a two-millennia writing career through which they gradually superseded the nobles and reasserted their position of authority and dominance. The brahmins literally wrote themselves into first place. Eventually, the antidivine dragon Vritra was declared to have been himself a brahmin, thereby transforming Indra's once glorious and order-establishing act into what became the worst and most unforgivable sin of all, brahminicide.[6]

The brahminic takeover of India and the Indian mind has been one of the most astonishing con jobs in human history.[7] Its totality alone is staggering, all the more so due to its blatant obviousness. Already by the later portions of the Rig-Veda, the most ancient collection of Hindu sacred verses, the Brahmanic speculations and intrusions appear. These continue especially with the Atharvaveda, the last collection of the oldest sacred writings, and even more so with the Brahmanas, ritualistic and liturgical prose writings, and their development of what became known as Vedanta. The Brahmanic philosophy in essence is completely opposed to the joyous, life-loving, and worldly notions embraced by Vedism and teaches instead that all is illusion and that to escape from the endless round of wearying rebirth, one must extinguish all desire and seek oneness with the absolute, the Brahman or Atman.

At first, the path to this end of nonidentity was through the elaborate ceremonies developed by the brahmins from the earlier, simpler Vedic prototypes. But no ritual could be performed without the presence if not the direct mediumship of the brahmin himself.[8] The highest virtue was declared to be the giving of alms—especially cows—to the priest, and through the premium placed on light-skinned brides, the brahmin caste eventually emerged as the lightest skinned of all India's social divisions, preempting that of the golden nobles themselves. It was not considered ironic that the darkness of the groom mattered not at all.

This then is Hinduism, a widely embracing complex of beliefs that at its core is the Vedantic philosophy that all is one, all is Brahman, and that each individual identity and separation is a grand illusion from which it is best, if not obligatory, to escape. The bible of Hinduism, however, is not the Vedas or Brahmanas but the epics of the *Mahabharata* and *Ramayana* and a collection of works entitled the Puranas that arose first in counterreaction to the Buddhistic reaction against Brahmanism and later through the more deadly threat of the invasive, iconoclastic Islam. The Puranas fully accept the tenets of Vedanta, but they merge with it popular beliefs and legends and, at the same time, organize India into one grand pilgrimage circuit under the auspices of the brahmins.

Consequently, the official religion of India may be termed Brahmanism, that is, the religion of the Vedanta philosophy. However, if the effort of all activity is the extinguishing of desire and the attainment of *samadhi*, or release, then ritual and worship, *arati* and *puja*, are lesser and, in a sense, discountable goals. Ideally, the life of the ascetic is the one course of choice, and accordingly, the *sannyasi* or *sadhu* (renunciate) is always acclaimed in Indian circles as the most noble of all people.

In apparent contradiction, veneration by the Indian is among the most fervent to be found anywhere. Although nearly every Hindu repeats the Brahmanic injunction that "God is One," his or her devotion to a diverse range of deities remains unabated. And although the Hindu gods and goddesses may be worshiped with the idea of attaining *moksha*, or salvation, all are honored as well in hopes of fulfillment of various desires, usually mundane ones such as the granting of wealth, offspring, advancement, or success or as the curing of an ailment or the removal of an obstacle.

In short, the earthly orientation of Hindu worship, though perhaps encouraged in part by the officiating brahmin's desire for wealth accruing through his self-declared indispensable role in the performance of ritual, directly opposes the essence of Vedantic philosophy. For in its true sense, veneration rather than renunciation is the pursuit of worldly pleasures through the favor of the gods.

Kailash was surprised by my interest in the worship of the Hindu deities and in turn took a greater interest in me. He allowed me to accompany him during his evening round of *puja* (worship) and introduced me to many shrines as well as the proper forms of Hindu reverence. I accepted him as my guru all the more so because he was not a brahmin.

In the caste system as it eventually crystallized, the *vaisya* rank third, beneath the *kshatriya* (warriors) and princes in second place and the brahmins on top. The name itself derives from the root *vis*, meaning "all" in reference to, among the original Aryans, the *vaisya* being the people at large. In India of today, the aboriginal inhabitants, the Danavas and Daityas, became the lowest caste, making up the largest proportion of the population, but the *vaisya* occupy a position that seemed to me at least to possess only a modest degree of elitism and yet represent the broader spectrum. In other words, they are closer to the ordinary level of society, less academic and specialized, and this was the area on which I wished to concentrate.

Among his confreres, Kailash had the reputation of being "very religious." He was scrupulously consistent and never missed his evening devotions, but the rapid pace at which we visited one shrine after the next was hardly what I would call contemplative. Making matters worse, I arrived in India with a comfortable but inconvenient pair of Western sandals, which had straps to be tied and untied when taking them on and off. The citizens of Varanasi and the visiting pilgrims usually had simple *chapals* that could be merely slipped on and off. It was impossible to find my larger size at any of the shoe shops, and eventually I had a pair custom made, only to have them stolen when I was again visiting the Golden Temple. Later, I succeeded in finding an unattractive pair in a bazaar during a visit to Delhi which, thanks to the ability of Indian cobblers to repair just about anything, lasted not only the rest of my nine months in India but also throughout the other Asian lands I visited afterward.

Through Kailash and general observation, I learned that the prerequisite for all Hindu worship is the sacred bath. This is usually taken in the morning, and in Banaras, the bathing ritual is almost invariably connected with the river Ganges. As Kailash explained, a token washing is acceptable if the full bath is not taken, which entailed wetting the hands and feet and perhaps the face. We often took this symbolic bathing from the riverbank just before the evening devotions.

The morning Gangasnan (Ganges bath) in Banaras is a dramatic sight. The river in this holy city is considered especially sacred, since it flows, in contradistinction from its normal course, from south to north (*uttar-avahini*). Moreover, because Varanasi is considered the permanent residence of Lord Shiva, the river is believed to be always washing the god's feet. As a result, thousands of pilgrims and local residents flock to the riverbank at the break of each day.

Although most Indians use the rivers for normal bathing purposes, during the *snan*, or sacred bath, the use of soap is not encouraged. Nor are specific rites performed beyond the utterance of "*pranam*" or "*Maa Ganga ki jai*" in salutation to the river or the recitation of Vedic mantras such as the Gayatri. Beside the mother Ganges, the bather may address other gods as well as the *pitris*, or ancestors. Flowers, rice, fruits, coconuts, betel leaves, and coins also may be tossed into the river, but oblation may be as simple as pouring water back into the river through the fingers of one's cupped hands. In general, however, Gangapujan (Ganges worship) is to be distinguished from Gangasnan, although it often is only the time devoted to personal worship or the ritual performed after the bath that distinguishes the sacred lustration from ordinary ablution.

All over India, the morning bath in the holy rivers and *kunds*, or sacred tanks, is performed. In Banaras, however, it is particularly teeming and colorful. On the various *ghats*, or flights of steps down the banks of the river, special priests called *ghatias* sit on wooden platforms (*takhata*) and look after the clothes and personal effects of the bathers.[9] They usually keep mirrors and combs for their clients' use as well. After receiving a *dan*, or ritual gift, they apply the *tilak* mark to the foreheads of the bathers. These *ghatias* may keep small *lingams* or idols of Ganesha and Vishnu on their *takhatas*, but in general they perform little ritual except occasionally to assist the devotee in Gangapujan.

After the *snan*, or bath, most worshipers visit one or more temples such as that of Shitala, the smallpox goddess, or Sankatamai, another manifestation of Shiva's wife. Almost everyone, however, also venerates Shiva's *lingam* in the Vishwanath, or Golden Temple. I found that the best time for this last was shortly after the temple doors opened at 4 A.M. The only problem with this was that the Ganges bath at such an early hour was usually colder than one might have wished. But before the throngs arrived later, the sanctum sanctorum was exceptionally peaceful and the approach to the black phallus was easy. Garlands were on sale from the flower stands that lined the narrow alleys leading to the shrine, and here one could also leave his or her footgear in the custody of the peddler. For *darshan* (seeing, witnessing) of the Shiva idol, the visual sighting is considered sufficient, but in Vishwanath the tactile approach is especially in vogue, and after placing one's flowers around the stone, presenting a coin as well or giving it directly to the attendant priest, and pouring Ganges water brought from the river over the *lingam*, one usually places one's hands on the emblem. Often, however, this was nearly impossible, as the shrine room is surprisingly small and can be choked with devotees generally in an incredibly frenzied state with much pushing and shoving that frequently required great athletic strength to keep from being pushed into the small tank in which the *lingam* stands.

During the morning, the Vishwanath stone almost completely disappeared from view beneath the amount of flowers, water, and milk that accumulated in the tank. When possible, the priest would remove a garland from the idol and toss it around the neck of a worshiper. On other occasions, he was forced to clean out the tank, and a pile of soggy, crushed flowers could often be seen just behind the sanctum sanctorum, usually to the great delight of a cow or two that had wandered into the temple enclosure.

After *darshan* of the *jyotirlingam*, one generally visits the subsidiary shrines within Vishwanath itself, or the nearby sanctuaries of Gyanvapi, Annapurna, Rama, and Kashikarvat. Because the elephant-headed son of Shiva is the god of beginnings, one usually called on the shrine of Dhund-hiraj Ganesh before that of the Golden Temple. I learned from Kailash that the proper way to dispose of a garland that one had received as a *prasad*, or divine gift, was to hang it on a tree, throw it into the Ganges, or give it to a cow.

The other usual *prasad* dispensed at most temples was a thumbnail-size ladle of water often sweetened, flavored with *tulsi* leaves, or mixed with milk. This was poured into one's right palm: always the right hand as this is the one from which all offerings are both given to the gods and received from them.[10] My favorite *prasad* was either a banana of which the Indian versions are beyond compare with anything I have known in the West, or the delicious juice of a freshly broken coconut that someone occasionally would have just offered to the deity.

The basic form of worship is *abhisheka* (from *abhi*, "maximum," and *sheka*, "respect").[11] The act of *abhisheka* itself occurs with the continual dripping or streaming of water on the idol through a small hole in the base of a pot suspended overhead. This is preceded by various mantric recitations once the *raksha*, or protection lamp, has been placed before the deity. In the Rudrabhisheka (formal worship of Rudra/Shiva) at least, though I witnessed much the same with other deities as well, the *lingam* is bathed with *panchamrita*—milk, honey, *ghee*, curd, and sugar—and then washed with Ganges water before the *abhisheka* proper occurs, during which Vedic verses are chanted. Finally, the deity is washed again with holy water and then "dressed," with clothing for Vaishnava deities and a sacred thread for male gods.

There are two modes of official *puja*, or veneration, as well as more elaborate forms of the Rudrabhisheka.[12] Nevertheless, these various kinds of Hindu worship are essentially pagan in motivation, incommensurate with the official Vedantic theology of renunciation and escape from *maya* (cosmic illusion). An in-depth investigation of Hindu *puja* and its many variations—both priestly and vernacular—becomes an intricate insight into a particular variety of living paganism: in this case, a paganism that is behavioral but denied both theologically and officially. On the vernacular level, Hindu worship concerns itself with earthly well-being, but even the more complex ceremonies suggest something other than theological transcendence and worldly release.

Aside from individual *puja*, devotees gain *darshan*, or the witnessing of the divine, also by attending any of the various priestly ceremonies. The rite of *arati*, or waving of an earthen or brazen lamp before an idol, may be performed by any worshiper and at almost any time, but the official occasions of *arati* by the priests are four and relate to waking, feeding, washing, decorating, and retiring the idol of the god or goddess.[13] In a broad sense, Hindu *bhakti*, or devotion, especially as it developed over time into the emotional expression of experiential adoration for deity, is the idolatry associated with and biblically condemned as paganism.

Hindu veneration also includes the *pinda dan* rites performed to one's ancestors in which balls made from rice, various flours, beans, and the like are offered. In addition, the *antyesthi kriya*, or last rites, include death preparatory acts, cremation, and postcremation purification. But perhaps the largest venerational category is the votive worship relating to an individual's rites of passage.[14]

Veneration would not be complete if it did not include collective celebrations for specific festivals. Whatever else they may be, festivals appeal to our inner yet hidden source of inspiration. They are one of "the most complex and colorful forms of ritual."[15] At the same time, festivals offer an intimate look at the people who celebrate them. The colorful calendrical celebrations of Hindu India once again offer a unique kaleidoscopic understanding of a central behavioral, cultic, and pagan aspect of humanity.

My first Indian holiday was the all-India annual commemoration of the festival dedicated to the god Shiva, the Mahashivaratri. Technically, a Shivaratri or "Shiva's night" occurs on the fourteenth of every waning moon, but the one that falls in Phalguna (February–March) is the Maha-Shivaratri, the Great Night of Shiva. In the coordination of the Hindu year with the lunar prototype of the Roman festival calendar, the Mahashivaratri coincides essentially with the original beginning of the Roman year, or the first of March, and has some interesting parallels. The Roman festival is called the Matronalia, but the *feriae* are sacred also to the god Mars, who in many respects approximates aspects of the god Shiva. Although in the West, the year's commencement has shifted to the first of January, the New Year's Eve celebrations continue with the raucousness that is frequently found in connection with the Mahashivaratri.

Shiva's festival has two parts: *upas* and *darshan*.[16] In Banaras, the activity intensifies as Shivaite shrines everywhere are being decorated and the last touches of paint are applied. At midnight, Shiva's marriage with Parvati is celebrated. The Shiva *upas* tends to be solemn for the most part and consists of the singing of *bhajans*, or devotional songs. The true rejoicing is that part of the ritual entitled Shiva *darshan*. Devotees call on not only the shrines of the major Vishwanath temples but often many of the *lingam*s throughout the city—even those normally ignored or forgotten during the rest of the year—heaping them with flowers and inundating them with Ganges water.

As I approached the Golden Temple for Shiva *darshan* on the Mahashivaratri, I found the main entry of the complex on Vishwanath Lane barred by guards prohibiting entry and the alley to the right of the temple closed. I circled the entire block and entered the court of Gyanvapi (the "well of wisdom") at the rear of the temple which today also contains the mosque built by the Muslim emperor Aurangzeb (1658–1707). The courtyard was thronged with worshipers waiting to enter Vishwanath. The gates leading to the narrow passageway running along the rear of the temple before turning toward the small auxiliary entrance on the compound's left (west) side were closed.

I waited in the crush of people for an hour, managing also to lose to a pickpocket a small change purse containing about fifty rupees as well as the key to my room. The gates were opened for only brief periods to allow a limited number of devotees through at a time (women waited and entered separately), yet the lunging of the crowd was positively dangerous, and once past the portals when I was swept along in the rush and over the slippery pavement, there were times that I thought death might be near. I used all my strength to keep from being crushed against the walls. Finally, disheveled and filthy, I entered the temple which, because of the limited access being allowed, was relatively peaceful. I managed to touch the *lingam*.

That night, the shrines of Shiva everywhere were lit with colored lights, sometimes accompanied by blasting music, candles, earthenware oil lamps, and flowers and fruits heaped over the *lingam*s. This is the night of vigil and for many consists of singing *bhajans*, or devotional songs, throughout the night. In continuing the parallel with the Roman Matronalia, New Year's Eve festivities are also a form of vigil, although in our calendar they have shifted to December 31/January 1.

Fortified with a hashish mixture known as *bhang*, one makes the rounds of as many shrines during the night as one can. Following his *puja* before a particular Shiva shrine on the Man Mandir Ghat, Kailash gave me some *bhang* sweetened with milk. This, I learned, was what everyone—the men at least—consumed on Mahashivaratri. I was also beginning to learn about the Hindu fast. Later in the night, we stopped at Kailash's house and were served special Shivaratri "fasting" foods. Beside some tasty unknown fruits, I enjoyed an exquisitely delicious kind of pancake of which I could eat only three because they were so heavy and felt like cement in my stomach. Still later, I returned to Vishwanath, which was now marvelously quiet and without the crowds. Inside the inner sanctum, the priests occasionally threw a powder of colored, sparkling dust at the worshipers but mostly at one another. It was both amusing and mysteriously beautiful.

Two weeks later, at the time of a full moon, is another New Year's type of festival and again one of all-India importance. This is Holi.[17] It is preceded by several days in which one wears only old clothes, since the likelihood of being sprayed with dyed water remains high. I realized now that the inner sanctum colored dust–throwing activities of the Vishwanath priests were only a prelude to the more serious business of Holi. The general revelry and the possibility of being drenched with a bucketful of colored—usually red—water culminate with the Holi day on which the moon is full. The evening before Holi itself, the Holika fires in just about every locality are lit to burn through the night. One circles one's neighborhood fire three times, mutually rubs ash on the foreheads of friends, neighbors, or acquaintances, and then embraces them. The overall Holi interval is a time of conviviality, and Kailash, who normally never touches liquor, made an exception and became quite inebriated several nights running.

On the morning of Holi day, following the Ganga bath, I was once again given some *bhang* with milk, this time by my landlord's uncle, a *ghatia* or river priest. Attempting to reach the Golden Temple through the melee of flinging dye was an unforgettable experience, and I wondered what, if any, connection there was between the Holi paint and the custom of Easter egg dyeing in the West. To my surprise, Vishwanath attracted few people. Most shops also were closed. By noon the whole atmosphere of the city had greatly mellowed, with men and boys strolling the streets proudly exhibiting their trophies, that is, their stained clothing. This became the moment of the quietest and emptiest Kashi I ever saw, but already there were signs of an overall resumption of normal, if not supernormal, life.

At noon, the custom of spraying one another with liquid colors ends, and everyone bathes and changes into new clothing acquired especially for

Holi. A warm and exuberant amiability sweeps over the celebrants. At a juice shop I occasionally patronized, though I usually thought markedly unfriendly, I was greeted most effusively by the staff and owners and even handed a free nutmeg-flavored *lassi*. By evening, the Ganges was inundated with a myriad of small, twinkling earthenware lamps drifting downstream. Riverside temples were decorated with colored lights. Later, when encountering Kailash and others, I was doused with red powder. So much for the new clothes. It was then that I learned that after the noon hour, the new vestments, and the ceasing of colored water, one was to rub dry vermilion, green, or silver powder onto one another's foreheads, though it usually was over the entire face and head. Then one embraces three times. I noticed many of the young men placing their hand briefly on the another's crotch as well. Inebriation was high by this point, and so was the deeply emotional expression of affection.

Holi, like the lunar Roman Ides of March to which it corresponds, is a New Year's festival, although in the Hindu calendar, the year properly begins with the new moon following Holi, the first of the lunar month of Shukla Chaitra. Another New Year's celebration begins with the sun's entry into the astronomical sign of Aries. Indians use a sidereal determination of the zodiac rather than the tropical system of the West in which, relative to the fixed position of the stars, the first point of Aries moves backward (the precession of the equinoxes). In the Indian Nirayana system, the vernal equinox or sun's entry into the sign of Aries (Mesha) relates to the relatively fixed position of the star Spica and corresponds roughly to April 13. It was this date on which the Ganges is first believed to have descended to earth, and it is in the city of Hardwar, where the river leaves the hills and enters the great Gangetic Plains, that the most meritorious occasion for Gangasnan takes place. The attendance of this ritual was my third Hindu festival.

I had read somewhere that the moment of greatest sanctity in the bathing section of the Ganges in Hardwar (called the Har-ki-pairi) is considered to occur with the moment of sunrise on what is called the first of the month Vaisakhi (though it is really the first of the zodiacal sign Mesha) on April 13. Most bathers, however, seemed oblivious to the sun. Although the river was extraordinarily crowded, there was much less bedlam than I had expected, and I enjoyed the mixed reactions of people shivering with cold, babies and children tearfully screaming in fear of the water as parents plunged them beneath its surface, and the overall exhilaration and laughter. It was a time of fun and joy.

On the evening of the same day, I returned to the Har-ki-pairi. Both sides of this dammed section of the river were pressed with worshipers, and with the lack of a breeze it was almost intolerably muggy and uncomfortable. But just before the dark of night when the flies had finally abated, several paths were cleared on the west side opposite from where I was, and priests descended the steps to the water's edge carrying aloft huge torches. I counted ten in all, and to the accompaniment of countless bells—both handheld and in the various nearby shrines—and drums, the torches were waved about and repeatedly lowered to the water's surface. I assume there were also chants or repetition of various mantras, but with the broadcasting through loudspeakers on our side of what I came to refer to as Hindi movie music, I could not tell. All the same, the *arati* was impressively moving and dramatic as the sky darkened to black.

During my stay in India, I attended several popular festivals. Although the Juggernaut festival is held in Puri during June and July,[18] it is celebrated throughout India as well, and in Banaras small processional altars with depictions of Krishna, Balarama, and their sister Subhadra appeared throughout the various neighborhoods. Most of these seemed to be the concern of children, but *rathayatra*, or chariot processionals, were also set up in Vaishnava temples, and *arati* was performed before them. In Kashi, in addition, a *mela*, or fair, containing an enormous chariot was held. Of the three figures or avatars represented, the white Balarama was larger than the black Krishna because, as was explained, he was the elder brother. Since the essence of the Juggernaut is a visual affair, devotees made a special point to touch their eyes during *puja* in honor of the *ratha* (chariot), but Kailash also went to the length of touching each of the vehicle's many wheels. During the serpent festival of Naga Panchami near the beginning of Shukla (waxing moon) Shravan (July/August), snake charmers suddenly appeared throughout the city, and people presented coins, bowls of milk, and other items to their *nagas*—usually large hooded cobras—as part of the occasion's *puja*. Paper *naga* images are attached to household doorways, and a large fair and special adoration is held at the Nag Kuan in the northern section of the city.

For the Janmashtami of Krishna Shravan, the birthday of Krishna, I was in Maharashtra and had only the chance to observe a swing placed before an altar of Lakshmi-Narayan which was profusely and enchantingly decorated with plants and fresh green sprigs. In Banaras, because of the large Bengali population that especially reveres the wife of Shiva, the nine-day

Dasara or Durga Puja celebrations of Shukla Ashvina (September/October) are particularly fervent. The Navaratra, or Nine Nights, were probably originally the festival of Indra commemorating the defeat of Vritra and the conclusion of the consequent monsoon season, but today they honor Durga, wife of Shiva, and her victory over the buffalo demon Mahishasura.[19]

For Durga Puja, throughout the city, huge painted clay images of the goddess as an extremely beautiful eight-armed woman appeared.[20] Below her was her vehicle, the lion, astride the carcass of the water buffalo, as well as a wounded but muscular Mahisha all flanked by the deities Sarasvati with a goose and Skanda with a peacock on the right and Lakshmi with an owl and Ganesh with a rat on the left. These *murtis* (images) were explained as a Bengali innovation, whereas the indigenous residents of Kashi traditionally celebrated Navaratri as a more private domestic affair focusing on the *kalasha* or *ghata*, a round water pot symbolizing the goddess.[21]

All the Devi temples of the city were cleaned and decorated with flowers, fresh leaves and branches, and colored lights and, of course, were much more crowded than usual. The first night a transvestite danced in the Shitala temple to the awed delight of a large assemblage. Each day, moreover, was dedicated to a particular manifestation of the goddess, each with her own shrine.[22] Most of these shrines were small and as a consequence constituted a great press of people, thereby denying all but the most perfunctory expression of devotion and nothing at all like contemplation or reflection.

In the worship of Durga's manifestation Mahagauri at the Annapurna temple, a temporary bridge was constructed to allow worshipers to enter without obstructing the circling of the central sanctum in special constructed passageways presumably separating men and women. Some were to circle the goddess 108 times; Kailash made twenty-one circumambulations, but I and my escort settled for eleven rounds. As red is the favorite color of the goddess, she is worshiped on this occasion with special crimson flowers. In the evening, the visiting of the various Durga images set up by numerous organizations was reminiscent of the viewing of Christmas lights in the West.

On the tenth day, called Vijaya Dasami, the *murtis* or images are carried from their *puja pandals* (ad hoc shrines) well into the night amid great hoopla and past a carnival-like atmosphere replete with sword-wielding dancing demons to the Dashashvamedh Ghat where they are then boated out onto the river to be discarded in a final immersion (*visarjana*). As this day also commemorates the victory of Rama over the *asura* demon Ravana, the occasion has also been the time to enact a cycle of plays known as the Ram Lila. These dramas relate the story of Rama, his wife Sita, and his brother Laksmana as found in the *Ramayana*. For the residents of Banaras, they are sponsored by the city's Maharaja and held across the river from Kashi in the former king's residence of Ramnagar. As a result of Rama's culminating victory, the following day the city witnesses the enormously popular reunion of the champion with his brother after fourteen years of exile, the Bharat Milap. Then, three days later, back across the Ganges at Ramnagar, there follows the predawn enthronement of the returned Rama, the *arati* thereof, and a tearful and calming climax to the shove-and-pull energies of the assembled crowd as well as the epic story (lasting a month or more) of this greatly loved Vishnu incarnation.

If the excitement of Dasara and Ram Lila were not enough, hardly two weeks later at the end of Ashwina and beginning of Kartika, there follows the most popular Hindu festival of all, the five-day Divali.[23] In Kashi, the first two days, Dhanteras and Hanuman Jayanti, are not especially observed, although because we were attending the Sanskrit Conference being held at Benaras Hindu University, several of us went to an ayurvedic exhibition of traditional holistic remedies at the house of Shiva Kumar Shastri in honor of the god of medicine, Dhanvantari. There we received *darshan* of the deity in the household shrine on his *jayanti* (birthday, from the Sanskrit word for victory).

Also on Dhanteras, all metal goods shops put on a glistening display of newly polished pots and pans and the like until late into the night, as this is also the time of Dhanapati, that is, Kubera, the lord of wealth—his riches being symbolized by metal—and every housewife makes a purchase. Evidence is everywhere of houses and temples being repainted, and the following day all the domestic cleanings are completed in readiness for a possible visit from the goddess Lakshmi.

In the correspondence between the Hindu and Roman lunar calendars, the new moon day of Divali itself coincides with Halloween. As with the Celtic calendar and the festival of Samain, the following day has new year's connotations. For Divali, the temples are decorated and covered with strands of colored electric lights which, if the city's supply of electricity does not fail, remain illuminated, but often at this time of year when the monsoon rains have been less than usual, the city is plunged into darkness, which becomes all the more enchanting as then one can see the tiny *deepak* lights burning in almost every window and on the rooftops while fireworks light up the sky overhead, firecrackers crash in the streets below,

and the Ganges too is covered with tiny floating lamps. The day is also celebrated as Kali Puja, and hence the shrines of Kali remain open deep into
the night. Every shrine and altar is crowded with *deepak*, the small earthenware oil lamps.

The following morning, the first of the waxing fortnight of Kartika, is
known in Banaras as Annakut. This is the festival of *bhogas*, that is, edibles
such as milk sweets, fruits, cooked vegetables, boiled rice, and legumes
(chickpeas, lentils, *mung*, and *ahar*), which are piled into small mountains
in front of the deities. Beside baskets and dishes of offerings, every available temple space is garlanded. At the Shitala Mandir, the smallpox goddess is represented on this occasion with a full sitting idol rather than the
more usual silver mask set onto her carved stone block. Even the *lingams*
wear glistening masks.

The Vishvanath *lingam* is completely covered with a metal encasement
bearing a facial likeness and a canopy of flowers and leaves stretches overhead. At this last, I unknowingly entered through the main portals, which
were being used as an exit for the throngs coming from the Gyan Vapi
courtyard, but by this time, because I knew the son of the chief *mahant*
(priest), I got away with it. An entire model temple composed of candy
had been constructed in the central area over the *lingam* of Vaikunthesh-
vara, while the back section of the complex was filled with an array of
foods with only a small corridor leading to it to allow worshipers to pass
and approach the sanctum sanctorum.

The temple of Annapurna is the main focus of the day. Here, as in the
other sanctuaries, *bhoga* are piled high and elaborately shaped into architectural configurations. Upstairs, a special room with highly decorated
ceiling, magnificent lamps and mirrors, and so forth is open for only three
days out of the year and contains a highly revered golden idol of Annapurna for which crowds pour forth for *darshan*. Downstairs, in the main
shrine, a standing silver image of the goddess now appears holding a ladle
in which a *laddu* (a kind of sweetmeat) is being offered to a standing
Shiva. On the following day, Yama Dvitiya, a festival in which brothers and
sisters reaffirm their bond, many Hindus observe a fast that is broken the
ensuing morning when the priests distribute the *bhoga* as *prasad*.

The last festival I observed in India on this trip was Rasa Purnima,[24] the
full moon of Kartika, and on this occasion I was on the shores of the Bay
of Bengal at Puri. Because Kartika is considered perhaps the holiest month
of the year, the time when all the Hindu deities are thought to descend to
earth, special rites and *vratas* (vows) take place, but the full moon day is

considered especially sacred. In Kashi, bathers enter the Ganges as early as 2:30 A.M.; in Puri, there were crowds on the beach already by four. Mostly youths were in the ocean water, but I saw elderly women taking *snan* as well. Firecrackers and sparklers were everywhere evident, but it was the placing of cane or palm husk floating lamps (*ahals*) that occupied everyone's attention. That these lasted scarcely two seconds before being inundated and extinguished by the onslaught of the sea did not seem to deter anyone.

The Hindu festival occurs against a temporal backdrop in which every day is sacred to one or more of the gods.[25] In Banaras, the tiny shrine of Shani fronting Vishvanath Lane was particularly thronged each Saturday as devotees waved small lamps before the idol in hopes of averting Saturn's malevolent influence.

In Hinduism, the festival is a temporal equivalent of the geographical *tirtha*, or pilgrimage center.[26] Consequently, both the festival time and the sacred place are considered occasions for heightened, extraordinary numinous presence. Shivaratri, Holi, Dasara, and Divali have become celebrations of all-India importance; Vaisakhi and Rathayatra have more local associations but again are of Pan-Indian significance. Varanasi and Hardwar are *tirthas* and also two of the seven sacred cities, the others being Ayodhya (birthplace and capital of Rama), Mathura (birthplace of Krishna), Kanchi, Ujjain, and Dvaraka (capital of Krishna).[27] This last, in the west, is also one of the four *dhams*, or "divine abodes," which include the Himalayan Badrinath in the north sacred to Vishnu, the Orissan Puri in the east containing the famous Jagannath (Krishna) temple, and Rameshvaram on an island in the south leading to Sri Lanka where Rama dedicated a *lingam* to Shiva.[28] Consequently, India as a whole has been apportioned and partitioned into a complex, multilevel grid of holy places that become expressive of cultic veneration as a myriad of different but interrelated forms.

Beside Banaras, eleven additional centers contain a *jyotirlingam*, or self-resplendent phallus, and Banaras is also one of the 108 *pithas*, or "seats" of the goddess.[29] India also contains seven sacred rivers as well as sixty-eight *svayambhu*, or naturally formed *lingas* meriting special devotion. An examination of both the Hindu year and Hindu geography reveals a calendar and continent full of special occasions and places. The *tirtha* is a spiritual "crossing place," a geographic point where heaven and earth are closest together. The festival is merely the time when the ability to "cross" is the most intense.

In Brahmanized Hinduism, the *tirtha* is explained as being of greater "purity" (*suchi, pavitra*) and the spot where one is more likely to achieve *moksha*, or liberation. But in the underlying folk religion descending more directly from the earlier Vedism and the pre-Aryan neolithic religious sentiment of the subcontinent, the earth is not rejected as impure or of less sacred value than heaven. Instead, the *tirtha* is a specially charged point in which aid and grace from the unseen is considered to reach and benefit the worshiper in tangible terms. Consequently, despite the official Vedantic theology, the more earth-centered, this-worldly practice of the lay Hindu constitutes a virtual counterveneration that in all its essentials is pagan.[30] It is for this reason that along with the sacred places, I am emphasizing the annual round of festivals in India. These holidays reveal the organic contours of vernacular expression that relate a people to here-and-now celebration and interest rather than to a transcendental theology. This kind of concern and the emotional, festive behavior associated with it convey paganism as a natural and popular response that persists despite any overlay of world-denying dogma and creed.

Moreover, in connection with the Indian *tirtha* we can gain an understanding of the significance of the worldwide mantic center. The sacred node is sacred not in any generic distinction from the ordinary world in general but in the sense that it functions as a portal through which divine access to humankind and men's and women's access to the gods flow most freely. For the pilgrim, on the one hand, the *tirtha* is the place for the expiation of sin, and on the other, it is where one's worship is most effective in bringing about the merit and blessing derived from the gods. The *tirtha* is a "ford" between the otherworld and this one.

There is no doubt that in Hinduism, each holy power center possesses mythological connections with one or more deities. The Hindu pantheon is vast to the point that it transcends any truly comprehensive approach. Yet only a limited number of deities, avatars, and heroes are popularly worshiped: Shiva, including his fierce manifestation as Bhairava; Shiva's consort Devi in both her mild form as Uma or Parvati and her terrifying form as Durga or Kali; their elephant-headed son Ganesha; and, to a lesser extent, their second son Skanda (Karttikeya); the god Vishnu, his wife Lakshmi, and their incarnations as Rama and Sita and as Krishna and Radha or Rukmini; the monkey god Hanuman; and the sun god Surya.[31]

Occasionally such Vedic figures as the fire god Agni, the craftsman architect Vishwakarman (Tvashtar), and the god Varuna, now ruler of the oceans though formerly of the heavens, are worshiped. Indra, the king of the Vedic gods, has all but disappeared. I could find no living shrine to the deity throughout my travels in India and only some evidences of cult to him in such Hindu border areas as Nepal and Thailand. In the idol shops of Banaras, where almost everything was available, I could find no statues of Indra, and the shopkeepers always seemed surprised that I would ask for one. The cult of Indra appears instead to have been transformed into the worship of Skanda-Karttikeya (and particularly his Dravidian veneration as Kumara or Subrahmanya) and, even though he descends equally from the Vedic Rudra/Agni, of Shiva.

Consequently, the six orthodox sects of Hinduism are the Vaishnavas, Shaivas, Surapats, Ganapatyas, Saktas, and Smarthas worshiping, respectively, Vishnu, Shiva, Surya, Ganesha, Devi (Shakti), and all five of these, the most popular deities of Hindu India.[32] There are, however, few Surapats. And although several of these figures have various antecedents in the Vedas, they are chiefly Brahmanic and Puranic creations incorporating many aspects of the pre-Puranic and still to be found indigenous *numina*, namely, the *yakshas* (tree and vegetation spirits); *nagas* (aquatic divinities); *devis*, *matas*, or *satis* (goddesses); and *birs* or *viras* (male folk deities).

This autochthonic or indigenous animism includes not only India's ubiquitous tree worship but also many cults deriving from the perception of negative spirits (*rakshasas*) from which the various adorations of *ganas*, *bhairavas*, and *barahmas* (different sorts of local spirits) have crystallized.[33] A number of specific cults in Kashi have emerged from the non-Brahmanic or Laukik folk culture.[34] Many of these folk cults are found on the outskirts or along the Panchakosi route of the city, but such law-and-order figures as the club-bearing Dandapani and Kala Bhairava have their shrines instead in the very heart of Banaras. These cults tend to fuse with those of the more official, Puranic deities, but their veneration is often specifically distinguished by the use of vermilion and nonvegetarian offerings, including wine, *hukka* (meat), and *ganja* (*Cannabis sativa*).[35]

The animating spirits of nature, both positive and negative, and the souls of the deceased are linked at the folk level of religion.[36] Although the folk deities have obviously, but not always, been assimilated to the official gods as attendants or manifestations, chiefly to Shiva and Shakti, we can also see in the very persistence of these *laukik* spirits the Indians' original animistic perception.[37] This last continues its vitality beneath the later accretions of Vedantic philosophy and Brahmanic *shastras* (the rule books of orthodox worship). This animating factor behind most acts of veneration is not confined to Hinduism but extends to virtually every mythological religious system. In essence, it comprises the attribution of conscious life to all material existence and suggests an invariable, natural human proclivity.

The worship of gods and goddesses, the cults of folk deities, and the belief in animating forces is a universal and root-level phenomenon in which, from the beholder's viewpoint, the world becomes personified and thus somehow manageable in a sense that it might not otherwise be. Theologians recognize this as an earlier developmental stage than animism as the consideration that all objects and natural phenomena possess an individual spirit. This earlier perception is referred to officially as *preanimism* or *animatism*,[38] but regardless of classification, it appears that most venerative expressions reveal a mutual affinity through an implicit or explicit recognition of what I term the *anima* and/or *animus*. These are the animating female and male poles by and through which every material form of reality acquires a personality and thereby becomes a potential subject for propitiation.

In their Latin meanings, *anima* and *animus*, respectively, refer to "breath" and "mind." Both terms are used in the sense of "soul," and therefore we have expressions for both the breath or life soul and the intelligent or conscious soul, the ego. In actual Latin usage, the meanings can be exchanged, but generally, the *anima* denotes the vital principle, the breath of life, the animal principle of life, or even life itself. *Animus* indicates the rational soul, reason, intellect, mind, consciousness (as a physical entity, or the vital power on which consciousness depends), or will power. To understand these terms in the sense I am using them here and throughout this book, it is important to distinguish them from the psychological constructs created by Carl Jung and to recognize them instead in their original quasi-terrestrial, animistic senses.

Together, the *anima* and *animus* constitute the range of vital possibility through which forms possess sentient life, and the veneration of any object, tree, idol, or symbol is the means by which the general perception of animation becomes personalized. A *tirtha* in essence, then, is any place in which such a transformation takes place. In actual usage, however, the *tirtha* refers to a particular spot that through custom, history, or the collective power of veneration is recognized in general as an area especially charged with the force of numinous animation. Whether place or object, the comprehension of such tangible expression of the sacred is pagan in that there is no rejection of the earth or material as unclean, inferior, or in any way unsuitable as a vehicle, locus, or manifestation of the holy.

*

In Indian worship, the *birs* and *devis* are more or less transparent reflections of the perception of *animus* and *anima*, and their distinction from the Puranic figures of Shiva and Shakti as well as the other mythological deities is one only of degree.[39] The designation of both beings, *bir* (or *vira*, male) and *devi* (goddess), is Sanskrit and suggests an animistic understanding as much among the incoming Aryans as it does for the indigenous residents of the subcontinent. The *bhairon*, *barahm*, or *bir* is usually symbolized by a vermilion-covered stone that, though not always perceptibly phallic, seems obviously the prototype from which the more stylized *lingam* of Shiva emerged.[40]

The *bir* stones are often difficult to distinguish from the *amma* or "mother" stones used frequently as emblems for the female *grama devata*, "guardian deity."[41] These latter are usually rounder and less elongated and may even, like that of Shitaladevi in Kashi, be found as crudely carved blocks. Although it cannot be proved, the evidence recurs so regularly that the link between funerary markers or stones and the localization of worship directed toward *pitris*, *virulu* (heroes), *pishachas*, *bhutas*, village deities, *ganas* (or demigods), and even the more orthodox figures remains highly likely. Another cult stone, the *koil*, is used to mark the graves of the holy men who are not cremated. They may also indicate where a saint has been buried alive. These tend to approach the less elongated shape of the *amma* stone rather than the more phallic implication of the quasi *lingam* of the *viras* but may nevertheless be regarded as links between the protective power symbolized by the goddess and the commemoration of the honored hero.

I first encountered a *koil* in a charming temple to Kali at the foot of the hill holding the Chandi Devi temple at Hardwar and mistook it first for a *lingam*. I was informed at the time that the *sadhu* who was buried underneath it had lived at this shrine and subsisted solely on goat meat and wine. The fondness of flesh, blood, and spirits is a characteristic of both the Shakti goddesses and the folk deities and, understandably, could influence the diet of anyone who served them.

At the Gumbiripir, or "peace," temple we visited regularly each Sunday evening in Banaras to honor its living *baba*, we brought only flowers, sweets, and *ganja*. The *koil* was the center of the shrine but was never visible, as it was permanently covered with colored cloths and the daily offerings of flowers. It would be uncovered, Vijay explained, once the *sadhu* died and was buried underneath it. Subsequently, however, Kailash offered a different and, as is often the case in India, conflicting story concerning the veneration of this stone. As there was also a Hanuman shrine here, I assume the vegetarian worship was determined by Vaishnava dictates. The Gumbiripir temple is situated amid a great expanse of railroad tracks which, the local story claims, the British were forced to construct around the shrine, as they were unable to dislodge the small complex owing to the great sanctity attached to it. Kailash explained it in this way: Once a highly revered ascetic lived at this site. He entered *samadhi*, or "absorption," and had himself buried alive underneath the spot where the *koil* now stands. Many, many years later, when the shrine was neglected and all but forgotten, the British authorities wished to clear it for the installation of railroad lines. The local people supported the project because they wanted to discover whether the *sadhu* was still alive as claimed. Every morning, however, the workers found that what they had completed the day previously had to be done all over again. Finally, the decision was reached to construct the tracks around this spot rather than through it, and the shrine became popular once again.

Every Sunday evening that I was in Banaras, at least Kailash, Vijay, and I would hire a scooter rickshaw for the bumpy ride to the edge of the tracks. Sometimes more of us—eight including the driver—would pile into the vehicle for the visit. We had, of course, already completed our baths—actual or token—as well as the usual round of evening *puja*. Normally, one does not take food until after completing one's worship, which often meant that we would not depart for the temple until late. Because my Indian companions had their evening meal afterward at home at midnight when all the restaurants were closed, I would renege on this particular ceremonial approach and dine beforehand.

The peace *baba*'s temple is an open, flat-roofed structure in which the *koil* sanctum occupies the back center of the left-hand side. At the front to the right of the main area is the small shrine of Hanuman. Behind this and to its right is what I took to be a living quarter. Bells of all kinds are suspended from the low ceiling in front of the sanctum. Coins are often tossed from passing trains. From the farthermost point that the rickshaw could reach, it is about a fifteen-minute walk to the temple, crossing numerous railway lines, passing the length of a large warehouse, and crossing more tracks before reaching the path leading to the small complex. On arrival, Kailash and Vijay would loudly announce themselves to the *baba*. Being an extremely old man, the *baba* often was asleep, although others were always there as well. Uniformed police, too, occasionally came to worship.

After removing our sandals, we would wash our hands and feet and rinse our mouths from an exterior water tap at the far corner of the building. Then we would enter the temple and place our candies, flowers, perfumed cotton sticks, *kapoor* (camphor), and incense on the *koil* and kneel in front of it while touching our foreheads to the ground. The *baba*, who by this time was always crouched next to the shrine, would open our offerings. We removed the flowers, each of us placing a garland over the already covered sacred stone, tossing the loose petals, and taking a second garland to the small shrine of the monkey god. Our incense was also now lit and divided between the two sancta.

We would then sit back while Kailash prepared the *chillum*, a kind of conical pipe used for smoking. Although Kashi *ganja* is excellent, after I had been to Kerala, I became the usual supplier of what we smoked. Kailash sometimes added a bit of hashish. While waiting, I was always amazed at the number of insects, especially the gigantic ants, that moved over the altar area. Once, a rat brushed along my leg as we were sitting on the floor. I was never able to follow the conversation among the *baba*, my friends, and the others, but it usually took the course of gentle banter.

Once the *chillum* was prepared, a smoldering coil of cord was placed on top, and it was then set before the *koil*. Everyone rose now and took a place next to one of the many bells that adorned the ceiling. Vijay would then light the *kapoor*, and as he waved it in performance of *arati*, a youth would play the tabla while the rest of us clanged the bells and chanted, creating that marvelous din so characteristic of Hindu worship.

This interlude would last anywhere up to ten or fifteen minutes. When it concluded, we would each in turn move forward and kneel before the shrine and wave the blessings of the flame toward us with our hands. Then we circumambulated the altar area, sometimes entering through the back right side and touching the *koil* as well. Re-reaching the front, we again knelt, placed a rupee on the altar, and touched the feet of the *baba* while he placed a *tilak* (sign or mark) of ash on our foreheads.

Finally we would sit again in front of the sanctum or outside on the edge of the raised dais in front of the temple and light and smoke the *chillum*. Vijay would distribute the candies that had sat in their open boxes throughout the service and now constituted *prasad*. We often did not stay much longer after this. One of us might reenter the temple and kneel in front of the shrine briefly, ring a bell for a last time, take some more water, and then depart for our waiting rickshaw. The irony of these Sunday visits for me (and others as well) was that often I felt somewhat ill beforehand (as one most frequently can in India) but totally exhilarated and recovered by the time we left.

In many respects, the format of worship at the Gumbiripirbaba temple was much like that in the more Puranic main shrines of the city, but in hindsight it seems more akin to the veneration of the *ganas* and regional deities. A *sadhu* is a kind of local hero. More directly connected with adoration of the localized *yakshas*, however, was the tree worship every Saturday during the evening *puja*. Many of the larger, older, and more venerable trees of Kashi have at their foot a small shrine containing an image of Hanuman. Since monkeys live in trees, this always struck me as appropriate, but I also have wondered whether the monkey is considered a living embodiment of the *yaksha* thought to dwell in the tree. In southern India, instead of Hanuman representations, one usually finds *naga* stones or altars by trees dedicated to the local serpent deity.

Kailash and Bhaiya Lal venerated a *pipal* tree near the former's house and at the top of the Man Mandir ghat where they were accustomed to take their evening bath. Ghee lamps were lit and waved along with incense sticks (the flame of which I learned from Bhaiya Lal one never extinguishes by blowing from the mouth) both at the main tree and in front of a Hanuman shrine set into a nearby second tree. We circumambulated both, but the first tree we circled eleven times. Hindu veneration has countless variations, but a general form unites the various individual performances of *puja*. Worship is in fact the main element, for although it is directed to almost everything, it is the act itself that is important and not necessarily the specific deity. Once I asked Kailash and Bhaiya Lal who a particular goddess was in the Shitala temple to whom we paid homage during the evening *puja*, and they had to ask the attendant priest. (We were told that it was Lakshmi, although I learned a few years later that even this information was incorrect.) It is this very fluid form of veneration that led me to believe that beneath the plastic images, trees, and stones lies the implicit recognition of the ubiquitous *anima-animus*, the very heart of pagan veneration. The Romans likewise prayed to the *deus loci* "whether male or female" (*si mas si femina*), without knowing for sure which it was.

The great Hindu temple sites that tourists usually visit in India include Elephanta, Ellora, Mahabalipuram, Bhubaneshwar, Puri, Konarak, and Khajuraho.[42] Several of these, besides containing historic monuments open to all, also contain living shrines. Basically, for a Western devotee in

India, it is a hit-or-miss affair, as some bar foreigners from entering. Some people I knew entered temples that I could not, and vice versa. In general, however, most temples are not only open to foreigners but welcoming as well, provided they approach as a pilgrim and not strictly as a gawking tourist.

Aside from those in the state of Orissa, the great temple complexes of Hindu north India were destroyed by the Muslim invaders, but in the south I was delighted by several fabulous preserves.[43] Often these are like miniature mythical cities of another world. Symbolically, they are said to represent the cosmic Mount Meru described in the Puranas, Hindu scriptures dating from the fourth century c.e., as the center point of the universe.[44] The northern style of temple architecture is characterized by curvilinear towers, whereas the southern or Dravidian form is in the shape of truncated pyramids. The *vesara* style combines elements of both the northern and southern schools. It is, however, the Dravidian architecture that remains the most impressive in the sense of the full temple complex. The *devalaya* (house of god) is surrounded by a high wall, and its gateways at the four cardinal points are the distinguishing feature of the southern temple, towering and profusely sculptured structures called *gopuram* (cow gate).

Here again, the Hindu temple offers an explanation of what may be accepted as a living pagan practice. The great pagan temples of Egypt, Mesopotamia, Greece, Rome, and the Americas as active residences of a deity and loci for his or her worship survive at best today as only fossilized vestiges. Even in mainland China, virtually all the former temples to Confucius have been destroyed, and although offerings are made spontaneously, the Altars of Earth, Sun, Moon, and Heaven (containing the Temple of Heaven) are at best only museums and not functioning edifices of worship. Apart from the Temple of Heaven and the Shinto shrines, most temples in China, Japan, and Korea are constructed according to the "palace style." These range in size from grand edifices to small shrines barely large enough to house an altar. But for living temple precincts, the temples of Buddhism and Hinduism and the shrines of Shinto afford the greatest insight into the grand creations of the classical and Mesoamerican worlds. Among these, those of Hinduism and Shinto retain the greatest pagan affinities. However, in Shinto, such centers tend to function more as devotional shrines than as generic organized temples, so the strongest parallels with pagan temple worship are apt to be found in Hinduism.

Inside the enclosing wall of the Hindu temple complex are a series of subsidiary shrines beside the sanctum sanctorum. There is a kitchen for preparing the cooked food, a cooking shed, storehouses, a sacrificial shed, a well (often providing the best supply of fresh water in the village), a flower garden, shops selling devotional goods, administrative offices, and sometimes a bathing *kund* or even a larger pleasure tank for an annual floating processional. In front of the congregational pavilion is found the flagpole carrying the emblem of the chief deity: a lion for Devi, the Nandi bull for Shiva, and the mythical bird Garuda for Vishnu. Beyond this is the pedestal containing a lotus or the deity's footprints, used for the offering of flowers and ceremonially cooked food such as rice sprinkled with vermilion powder to the *parivara devatas* (minor powers) necessitating appeasement. Next to the sacrificial pedestal is often the lamppost and, in Shiva temples, a Nandi (Shiva's mount), and in those of Vishnu, a Garuda (Vishnu's vehicle). Apart from its regularly recurring format and countless individual variations, the Hindu temple is a living house for its deity, one equipped to receive and handle a great number of daily visitors. It remains the chief locus on which Hindu veneration is focused.[45]

In southern temples, the *arati* may be performed as much as six times per day, including worship sometime after sunrise and also between 8 and 9 A.M., and the *panchamrita* ingredients are oil, ghee, milk, water, and scented water. The idol is, of course, undressed for the bathing, and once it is reclothed, it is also smeared with sandal paste and decorated with flowers and ornaments. Cooked food is offered, including betel leaf and nut, but not until the doors of the *garbhagriha* are reopened does the *arati* proper occur, accompanied by hymns of praise and music. The basic ritual involving Shiva and Vishnu is described as the paying of royal honors.

Apart from the daily worship, there are three important temple ceremonies. The first is the temple consecration ritual in which both the unwanted demonic spirits are induced to depart the premises permanently and the deity is invoked into the image after its eyes have been opened. The consecration ceremony of a temple is understandably a more elaborate celebration, culminating with the concluding bath by the officiating priests. This is a most popular moment and is often heavily attended by numerous devotees. The *naimittika-pûjâ* is the worship on special occasions such as Shivaratri and Dashahara (Dasara). These festivals are celebrated variously in different temples and may extend over several days. They might include the *rathotsava*, or car festival, in which a special processional idol is paraded through the streets—often in highly decorated *rathas*, huge replicas of temples on wheels—or it may be a special annual event of its own, a *brahmotsava* representing the marriage of the deity, or some other special happening connected with the god's legend. The Jagan-natha (Juggernaut) procession of Puri is the most celebrated of these. In the Hindu commemorative year the *rathotsava* is among the most popular events.[46]

The ritual life of the temples for *ganas* and *yakshas* is practically the same as that in those of the Puranic deities, though often the priest is not a brahmin. Animal sacrifice is also a distinguishing feature, as is the absence of Vedic incantation. The more original Vedic sacrifice also occasionally takes place in India, but it is not a part of Puranic temple worship. It may, however, be performed on a temple grounds or in some other connected capacity with a popular place of worship. These are the elaborate rites recorded in the Veda appendages known as the Brahmanas.[47]

Today, the Vedic *soma* (ritual drink) sacrifice seldom is performed, and the construction of a fire altar even more rarely.[48] Several years are required for preparation before the rite can be begun, and because of the great cost, the sacrifice is traditionally performed only by kings, nobles, the very rich, or those able to collect large subscriptions. Expenses include not only the feeding of the required priests but also those who, like myself on one occa-sion in Bangalore, are in regular attendance. But as thrilling as it was to witness a sacrifice and the worship of the original Vedic deities, it became all the easier to understand the consequence of how, at the hands of the brahmins, the earlier religion had become an overburdened ritual. The larger and more elaborate and prestige-gaining ceremonies were obviously the prerogatives of only the most wealthy. The common argument is that ritual became more important than the gods themselves by the time the Brahmanas were written, and this, along with the solidification of the caste system, paved the way for what became the Buddhist reaction and rejection of the Vedic religion.[49]

Kailash had a story concerning Baba Sharma who, returning from the Ganges one morning, entered into conversation with a Pundit Krishna. After a while, Baba Sharma remembered that he had forgotten to say a "*Namaste*" greeting to the river goddess, Ma Ganga, but Pundit Krishna al-layed his consternation by informing that he was on his way to the river and would greet it on the *baba*'s behalf. When Pundit Krishna arrived at the water's edge, he folded his hands, bowed his head, and proclaimed, "*Namaste*." To his great surprise, a voice came from the river and repeated back to him the *Namaste* greeting. But that was not all. A female arm next raised itself out from beneath the water's surface holding aloft a dazzling diamond-and-emerald necklace and handed this to the pundit with the instructions that he was to take it to a certain Mahendra Moti. At this point in the story, Kailash stopped, and I was forced to ask, "What happened? Did he give the man the necklace?" "Of course not," Kailash replied with a great smile. "He was a brahmin." The greed of the brahmins, I learned, is proverbial.

To recover the pagan substratum of Hindu India, it is necessary to have some understanding of the role of brahminism and, in particular, the brahmins themselves in the historical transformations of Vedism. At the same time as the brahmins were establishing the *srauta* rituals for which they were proclaimed the indispensable agents, the later Vedas and the Brahmanas revealed a speculative trend that led to the ultimate reinterpretation of the earliest hymns as Vedantic philosophy. Some of this speculation is undoubtedly legitimate and the germinal notions of world-weariness may also have been felt by those who reflected on the deeper mysteries of life, but because the world-rejecting Vedantic philosophy strikes directly at the world-loving joie de vivre of the Aryan faith, the Vedanta clearly became a tool by which the brahmins asserted their preeminence and position of authority over the rulers and nobles of the Aryan invaders. In gaining the dominant role concerning spiritual matters, the brahmins superimposed a radically different theology onto the indigenous and Indo-Aryan forms of paganism that preceded their ascendancy.

In time, the Buddhist religion succeeded in dominating Brahmanism throughout India, and it is significant that the Buddha was himself a noble. In essence, however, the Buddhist philosophy has the same import as does the Vedanta, especially regarding the doctrine of transmigration, the endless round of rebirth from which one tries to escape. Nevertheless, history proves that the brahmins were not permanently defeated, and curtailing the earlier emphasis on *srauta* ritual and attending instead to the devotional needs of the general public, Puranic Hinduism resulted. This newer religious fusion managed to combine a speculative transcendental philosophy with vernacular practice in a way that is similar to the establishment of Christian hermeneutics with popular devotional customs in Europe.

The reconstituted Brahmanism that reigns in India today has unified the subcontinent in a manner that no mere political effort could. The entire country is united through its division into a complex of sacred *tirthas* with which the basic Puranic legends are interwoven and repeated. The brahmins have in fact succeeded in creating India as one enormous pilgrimage circuit, and this has been perhaps their most successful ploy, for the act of journeying to a sacred place, belonging to no single religious creed, is a universal and vital aspect of veneration.[50] By incorporating this natural propensity into a unified theological system, the brahmins have established Brahmanism, that is, Brahmanical Hinduism, as the unifying and entrenched influence behind Pan-Indian culture.

Along with the shift from aniconic Vedism to that of Hindu idolatry, the visiting of holy places has become the mainstay of popular Hinduism. I have already mentioned the seven sacred cities, including Kashi, and the four *dhams*. During my sojourn in India, I also was privileged to receive *darshan* of five of the twelve *jyotirlingas*, namely, Vishweshwara at Banaras, Rameshwara on the island of Rameswaram, Mahakaleshwara at Ujjain, Amareshwara on the island of Omkara in the Narmada River, and Grishneshwar at Ellora. Each of these has a contrasting aura. Their settings and the approach to them are different and allow one to grasp the great diversity of Hindu veneration despite the encompassing unity of the Brahmanic credo. From the simple propitiation of the multitude of manifestations of the *anima-animus*, Hinduism has succeeded in developing the practice of *bhakti*, "love, devotion." This venerational fervor is directed foremost to Shiva, Vishnu, Krishna, and Devi, and it becomes the expression contained in the popular rites of *puja* and *tirthayatra* (pilgrimage).

As a pilgrim, a devotee becomes temporarily a *sadhu* or *sannyasin*. His or her visit to sacred locations, his or her ritual declaration of intention, either directly or through the mediumship of a priest and whether *sakama* (in fulfillment of a vow, seeking a cure, or desiring a specific blessing) or *nishkama* (without desires, i.e., as sheer adoration of the deity), his or her bathing in holy waters, honoring divine images, and receiving *darshan* of both place and deity are in essence a duplication of *nitya yatra* (the daily pilgrimage), the focus sought behind ordinary *puja*. It is from his or her ancestors', the Indo-Europeans', love of travel that the Hindu's pilgrimage derives its origins. In fact, from this same impulse Indo-Europeans have come to dominate, numerically at least, the world's population. The basic attitude is perhaps best summed up in the Vedic Indra's injunction to seek happiness by wandering (Aitareya Brahmana 7.15).

For modern Hindus, this desire to travel has been shaped and directed chiefly through the *mahatmyas*, Puranic hymns of praise glorifying a particular holy place and its presiding deity. But the *tirtha* and *nitya yatras* of contemporary Hinduism, being conceived as they are under the dictates of Brahmanic Vedanta, are often undertaken or performed as rites of atonement. It is thought that the more difficult and greater the hardship that is endured, the more merit will be earned. In this spirit the observances of fasts—and of course the more extreme forms of asceticism such as lying on a bed of nails or suspending one's body by hooks piercing the skin—have become a part of Hindu religious expression. An orphan I unofficially adopted during my stay in Banaras, who was a devotee of Hanuman, scrupulously observed a "fast" of sorts each Tuesday, the day sacred to the monkey god, although this amounted just to the avoidance of salt and most man-made foods such as breads and rice. Fruit was allowed, and in the evening, the consumption of a sweet seemed nothing short of mandatory, presumably due to Hanuman's great love for candy.

Notions of penance and the desire for atonement from sin and impurity are a large part of Hindu *snana* (bathing), but in *puja* and other forms of veneration underlying the encroachments of Brahmanism and Vedanta, one perceives a deeper, more popular, and organic level in the worship of India: the sheer *bhakti* or adoration of the gods or, ultimately, the *anima-animus*, and the desire for health, wealth, progeny, position, and happiness. Why Hindu worship appears to be pagan is because at heart it *is* pagan. Despite the Vedantic overlay of "official dogmas and doctrines" that deny ontological reality to the world and its concerns, the Indian religious response is largely subliminal and strongly reflective of an older and more persistent cultic urge that centers on life rather than escaping from it. This natural, this-worldly, and animistic response found in vernacular Hinduism is not the Brahmanism of denial, bodily mortification, quenching of desire, and elaborate theological speculation but a fundamental spiritual zest that is more correctly recognized as unadulterated pagan behavior. It expresses paganism as a natural proclivity and the root of further religious developments.

## Theravada Buddhism

After India and its vibrant Hinduism, our study could become tame and anticlimactic. But the veneration of the *anima-animus* becomes all the more subtle, which is my chief contention: that despite the official, usually theistic or transcendental, religion of a state, culture, or peoples, what may be termed a perennial countercult remains detectable, whether focused or not. India provides the insights, tools, and patterns with which to recognize the same persistence of countercult veneration in the other major world religions. The experience of Hinduism in the land of its birth is like viewing religion through a kind of privileging and exaggerating magnifying glass. Certain trends and activities stand out even more clearly. And while these same remain less obvious elsewhere, the ability to perceive cultic or pagan behavior in Hinduism prepares the observer to find similarities beneath the more official accretions of Buddhism, Christianity, and other religions.

Buddhism itself is like a Protestant form of Hinduism.[51] It has several varieties, but the essential differences present fewer obstacles or difficulties among its different forms than we might find, for instance, among the varieties of Christianity. While Theravada Buddhism is perhaps a purer, less adulterated form than Mahayana and/or Vajrayana, countercult becomes something mainly existing *in addition* to its Buddhist practices. In Mahayana and Vajrayana or Tibetan Buddhism, by contrast, the pagan elements have been more completely incorporated *into* the Buddhist expression itself.

Of the countries embracing Theravada Buddhism, that form of Buddhism remaining closest to the original teachings of Gautama Buddha, I have visited only Thailand. Sri Lanka is the only one of these countries containing a sizable Indo-European Buddhist population, the Sinhalese. Theravada Buddhism—also known as Hinayana, "the lesser vehicle"—flourishes in Sri Lanka and Southeast Asia.

Buddha did not deny the existence of matter, but since he stressed the complete quenching of desire in order to be free of all material ties and hence the cycle of rebirth, his philosophic teachings differ little from the ideal of Vedanta.[52] The Buddha's *nirvana* of the void is essentially the same as the brahmin's *moksa* or *samadhi* with the absolute Brahman, although technically Brahmanism is labeled theistic idealism, whereas Buddhism is a form of atheistic materialism. One of Buddha's major innovations is his total rejection of social distinction and any a priori superiority of the brahmin. The pride of birth and lineage that is part and parcel of the caste system is intolerable to any Buddhist. In such "Indian" countries as Muslim Pakistan and Bangladesh, despite the complete lack of Hindu color, one is struck by the atmosphere emancipated from the absence of the suffocating restrictions and pressures of *varna*, that is, the position into which one is born and the notions of social impurity. This same ability "to breathe" one also finds in Thailand.

When I first arrived in Bangkok, the capital of "the Land of the Free," the city was in the full swing of preparations for its 1982 Rattanakhosin bicentennial celebrations. Temples and *stupas* (reliquary shrines) everywhere were in process of restoration and regilding. Amid the buzz of activity and excitement, I was fascinated by the graceful, relaxed, and exquisitely beautiful people who had never known the yoke of colonialism and therefore did not harbor deep-seated or residual resentment of foreigners. Although Thailand was then a poor country, after India I could readily perceive here a greater level of affluence and economic manageability. In both the social and technological areas is a degree of hope that is absent in India. Also during my brief visit here, I enjoyed a marvelous cuisine as well as delicious and exotic fruits. The best-tasting chicken I have ever consumed was from a street stand in front of Bangkok's central train station.

As a Protestant form of Hinduism, Buddhism inherited from the older faith its cosmology, mythology, and many of its Hindu deities. Iconographically, the Buddha is frequently flanked by Brahma and Indra in attitudes of adoration. One feature in the history of religions is that colonial outposts tend to preserve earlier characteristics that subsequently were lost or replaced in the motherland. Because Buddha came to be regarded as the ninth avatar of Vishnu, the general inference is that Indra represents the iconographic antecedent of Shiva and became established outside India before the final rise of the Hindu triad (*trimurti*) in the homeland. In Thai temples, Indra is portrayed with a green body, is worshiped as one who aids those in distress, and is believed to rule Daovaduengsa on Mount Meru, the closest of the various heavens to earth.

The priests of Hinayana Buddhism are properly monks. As with the Hindu brahmins, the priests, or *bhikkhus*, constitute a special social class and receive a mandatory deference from the laity, above even that due the king.[53] Apart from their priestly functions, the *bhikkhus* also function as surrogates by which one offers sustenance to one's departed relatives, for in offering food to monks, one's dead are considered to have automatically received the same. During the sermon or blessing recital, people may pour water from a cup into a receptacle that is later emptied at the root of a tree as a meritorious gift to the dead. But if a bowl of water is placed in front of the altar during a temple service, the priests will let drops of wax fall into the bowl from a lighted candle as a means of sanctification. When drunk, this water is considered protection against illness, misfortune, or harmful spirits. When a monk comes to a house to pray, a spun cotton thread is placed around the edifice as a means of averting calamity. In these ritual customs, we are able to witness an underlying vernacular perception of multiple personification that has little if anything to do with the attainment of the Buddhist goal of nirvana.

More officially, for any temple ceremony that takes place in the *bot*, or assembly hall, the presence of all members of the monastery—with a quorum of five priests—is required, for morning and evening prayers as well as sermons. The *bot* always contains a large image of the Buddha, although other smaller Buddha images may be grouped in front of it. There is also an altar for both monks and laypersons to burn incense (joss sticks) and beeswax candles. In addition, laypersons may offer flowers—usually lotuses—or wreaths and bouquets as well as small pieces of gold leaf that are stuck onto the images. The walls of the *bot* are frequently covered with frescoes portraying the life of the Buddha or scenes from his previous lives, infernal torments, and heavenly pleasures. Statues of deities, fearsome giants, or lions may guard the entrances, and stylized depictions of *nagas* (snakes) line the edges of the temple roof. Boundary stones mark the temple precincts.

As with Hindu temples, one always removes one's shoes before entering a *bot*, and, once inside, takes care not to point one's feet at another by tucking them underneath and behind oneself while kneeling. Besides the *bot*, the *wat*, or monastic complex, may also contain a separate preaching or worship hall; open resting pavilions; living quarters in which each monk has a cell with perhaps a basement for his boy attendants; the *mondop* for storing the Tripitaka, or sacred scriptures of Buddha's teachings; a crematorium; *prangs* (elevated, fingerlike cylinders with a rounded top); pagodas often used for burial; and *chedis* (bell-like domes either containing holy relics or used as emblems of them).[54] Despite the basic austerity of the Buddhist monk's life, I continually found the *bhikkhus* to be buoyant, curious, open, and friendly. I felt no sense of oppressiveness, and coupled with the Thai people's naturally gentle manner, I was regularly struck by their captivating charm which so often could be totally absent from a greedy or holier-than-thou Indian brahmin. In fact, nowhere in Thailand did I find a temple, Buddhist or Hindu, that, if not already closed and locked, was not readily accessible and in any way forbidding.

Theravadins believe that on reaching nirvana, the Buddha ceased to exist once and for all.[55] Nevertheless, this does not prevent veneration of his image, though in essence what is being worshiped is his memory and his teachings. In fact, the Three Jewels of the religion are the Buddha, the Dharma (Law, now contained in the Tripitaka, or Three Baskets) and the Sangha (monastic community), and each of these receives separate homage during prostration.[56] Moreover, Buddhists always burn three incense sticks, one for each of the jewels. Besides worshiping images, Hinayanists also revere various relics of the Buddha or Buddhist saints, such as bones or ashes, imprints of the master's foot, or even the outline of his shadow.[57]

In Bangkok, the Golden Mount atop an artificial hill contains relics of the Buddha presented by Lord Curzon, as viceroy of India, to King Rama V. A footprint of the Buddha is worshiped at Phra Buddhabaht on a hillside beyond Saraburi, often amid large annual celebrations, whereas Phra Buddha Chaya is a cliff on which the configuration of the Buddha's shadow has been preserved. Homage also is paid to *bodhi* trees grown from seedlings or grafts of the original under which Gautama's enlightenment occurred. What this ubiquitous veneration in the Theravada context suggests—especially in light of the nonpersonification interpretation of its official theology—is the persistence of a natural vernacular impulse to worship.

Adoration of relics, images, and ideas is a part of the Theravadin's religious expression, even if the perception of personality or life usually so closely associated with the focus of veneration is absent. Just how depersonalized the focal point of such worship is by the laity is, of course, debatable. Without permanently joining a monastic community, the layperson forgoes the possibility of becoming a celibate and relatively ascetic *arahat* and achieving final extinction of the self and is left to hope instead for the rewards of heaven and the avoidance of punishments in hell. But already we have entered the realm of the *anima-animus*. As we shall see, beneath the official overlay of Theravadism in which more than 90 percent of the Thai population are counted is a popular level of worship that is essentially a direct refutation of the tenets of Buddhism.[58]

One aspect of folk worship relates to the poetic title of Thailand as Suvarnabhumi, the Land of Gold. This is undoubtedly due to the use of gold leaf in popular devotion which, to me at least, was perhaps the most striking feature of the people's veneration. These tiny squares are sold by the religious paraphernalia stands where one also buys candles and incense. They are thin, small gold paper quadrangles held between wax paper. When I bought candles at the Indra Wiharn, about five gold leaves were given to me along with them. Devotees place them over virtually every available idol so that Thai shrines literally glitter with gold. Although each sheet is hardly a scrape, the accumulated expression throughout the country must total to a fabulous sum of wealth.

The Hindu deities that came with the importation of Buddhism are generally depicted as worshipers of the Buddha as a supreme being and, like men and women, seekers of ultimate release from the wheel of re-birth.[59] Because of past good deeds, the gods are acclaimed as souls reborn in heaven. But Hinduism—or the worship of Hindu divinities—operates independently from Theravadism.

In the past, through conquest and expansion, Indian princes estab-lished various kingdoms and empires stretching across Southeast Asia and into Indonesia.[60] The island of Bali remains today an outpost of Hin-duism. Hinduism itself, however, flourishes in Thailand as a popular countercult underneath the Buddhist rejection of existence as sorrow. The Javanese Hindu kingdom of Majapahit (late thirteenth century) and the Khmer Empire of Cambodia (sixth to fifteenth century) established the cult of the *devaraja*, or "god king." As an incarnate god on earth, the monarch ruled by virtue of establishing a pyramidal temple complex as a symbolic re-creation of the cosmological mountain Meru. Angkor Wat, with its central tower of diminishing tiers, is the foremost example.[61] Similar models can be seen in the Khmer outposts of Pimai, Panon Rung, Lopburi, and Sukhothai, the last conquered in the Thai migrations southward from China and becoming their first capital in the thirteenth century.

Vestiges of the *devaraja*, or "god king," cult can still be seen in the selec-tion of the name Rama for all Thai kings and in the use of brahmin priests to perform the country's royal functions. But whereas the *devaraja* cult was a political expression seeking religious legitimization, the royal wor-ship of Shiva and/or Vishnu developed its counterpart among the people. Part of this Hindu side of Thai heritage is seen in the temple frescoes de-picting the elephant-headed Ganesha as god of learning, the supreme Shiva as the god of gods, and the fabulous Garuda bird, the mount of Vishnu. There are also the *lokapala*, or guardians of the four corners of the world: usually Indra on his elephant Eravan in the east, Yama or Skanda on a peacock in the south, Varuna astride a goose in the west, and Agni or Vishnu on his mythic vehicle in the north. On the walls of the royal tem-ple of the Emerald Buddha in the complex of the Grand Palace, the epic story of the Indian *Ramayana* is depicted.

Other mythic figures, though less obviously Hindu, are Ramasoon, the god of thunder; Mekkhala, the goddess of lightning; and Nang Toranee, the goddess of the earth. This last, also known as Grandmother Sangasi, an archetypal parent of humankind, has an outdoor idol shrine—more properly, a fountain—in front of the hotel where I lodged in Bangkok, the Royal Hotel at the far corner of the Pramane Ground from the Grand Palace. The earth goddess sits high and beyond reach, so I could not tell whether her golden face was the result of popular attention or the manner in which her image had been constructed. She was dressed in a deep rose cloth wrapped around her torso. With her right hand, the goddess is grabbing her hair near the scalp and guiding it with her other hand toward a large gold leaf–adorned cauldron in front of her pedestal, into which water flows from her long single lock of hair. Nang Toranee is considered the deity who gives water to the earth. Also considered a goddess of prosperity, there is ample evidence of cult at this shrine, which includes food offerings and garlands galore. Colored cloths are tied to the railing surrounding the statue, and candles and joss sticks are burned in front of her image.

A popular Hindu cult in Bangkok is that of Brahma at the Erawan shrine. Properly, Erawan is the (often three-headed) elephant mount of Indra. However, during the construction of the Erawan Hotel, on whose grounds the shrine is constructed, several mishaps occurred, and after consultation with local soothsayers, it was determined that the planned chapel must be dedicated to Brahma rather than Indra. Eventually many miracles were attributed to this god, and today the four-face golden idol is venerated night and day with incense sticks and offerings of flowers and garlands sold by a crowd of insistent peddlers surrounding the area. Farther along the same street is the Indra Hotel with, also, an Indra shrine, the only evidence of a living cult to the deity that I discovered.

At Lop Buri, the Thai capital in the seventeenth century and about a three-and-a- half-hour train ride north of Bangkok, there are numerous tenth- to thirteenth-century Khmer ruins. One of these, the Kala temple dating back to the tenth century, contains a lintel depicting Vishnu asleep on the cosmic serpent Ananta. In front of this is a new San Phra Khan chapel built in 1953 which contains a broken-armed Vishnu with a Hanuman idol to the side. Both of these are completely covered with gold leaf and draped with colored cloths. A series of gold-papered buddhas are also to be found, but the temple is definitely Hindu, and to the delight of the local monkeys, devotees leave ample supplies of edible offerings. At the time I visited, four temple dancers, privately hired as an expression of gratitude, gracefully performed within the precinct.

In Chiang Mai, the northern capital, there is less Hindu influence. In the city's oldest temple, the Wat Chiang Man dating back to the thirteenth century, there is a dark crystal Buddha, the Phra Sae Tang Tamani, which is revered for its rain-bringing and evil spirit–averting powers. In fact, several Buddha idols throughout Thailand are renowned for their supernatural abilities to protect or bring blessing, for example, the fourteenth-century polished bronze Buddha of Wat Mahathat in Phitsanubk. There is also some evidence of popular worship of Avalokiteshvara, the bodhisattva of mercy, and Maitreya, the Buddha of the future.

Along with both Buddhism and Hinduism, many elements of a more aboriginal form of animism are readily detectable throughout Thailand.[62] For instance, in front of the western facade of Bangkok's oldest monastery, Wat Phra Jetubon (Wat Pho), is a highly decorated and venerated *lingam*. When I visited this, I performed a Hindu *puja* and noticed afterward that the various Thais present seemed noticeably pleased.

At the opposite end of the Grand Palace from the Wat Pho is a small temple containing another deeply worshiped pillar, the *lakmuang*, or foundation stone of the city. It is surrounded with flowers, candles, and incense in honor of its resident spirit, and it is also a place where sacred dances as expressions of thanksgiving are regularly performed. The detectable stone-cult of Thailand includes the healing stone *vajra* in front of the eastern entry to the temple of the Emerald Buddha. Apart from this locus of cultic activity, another is directed to the veneration of large or special trees. I saw one of these trees at the Underground Temple of Chiang Mai. It grew in a small enclosure, and tied to it was a bunch of colorful feathered arrows. In general, worshipers tie strips of red cloth around the venerated tree and make various offerings as well.

By far, however, the most definite recognition of the *anima-animus* is the omnipresence of spirit houses throughout Thailand.[63] Virtually every property has constructed on it a small templelike residence for the spirit of the land on which one has constructed. This miniature house, usually raised on a pedestal, is placed preferably on a corner of the property where the shadow of the main building will not cross it. The idea behind the venerative attitude toward these "doll houses" is to protect against or prevent harm from the guardian spirits of one's building and of the land on which the building has been erected. Banks, hotels, and other commercial establishments also have set up these small but often elaborate sanctuaries to placate the forces of the land. At road bends where traffic accidents have occurred, similar shrines are constructed to appease the obviously offended genii of the thoroughfare area. Segments of colored gossamer cloth are frequently tied around the pedestal or to the railing surrounding the platform on which the spirit house itself sits. Besides the usual candles and joss sticks, food and drink are offered, and one may find models of various figures or animals such as the elephant, symbol of fertility, placed in or around these tiny but highly decorated shrines.

The spirit cult expressed by these "houses" as well as that involving trees, stones, or the elements such as wind, rain, and water is the direct heritage of the indigenous animism of the land. This traditional perception is still the essential religion of the tribal peoples of the far north. It extends to belief in *nagas* (divine snakes), *kontans* (like the Indian Gandarvas, i.e., celestial singers and musicians), *kinorus* and *kinnarees* (male and female half-bird, half–human beings). There is also recognition of *prets* (agonized spirits who have escaped from hell), *phee kasues* (spirits that feed on human entrails after entering through the anus), and *phee pobs* (possessing spirits).[64] Especially feared, however, are the ghosts of women who have died in childbirth.

It is important to realize that in Thailand this animistic belief is not confined solely to the poorest levels of society and uneducated folk. Even governmental and administrative officials with a Western education subscribe to these ideas. Consequently, the construction of large skyscrapers also can be determined by recognition of the spirit world. An instance of this can be seen in Bangkok along Ploenchit Road where the entrance of a modern bank has been modified. This followed consultation with a geomancer who determined that the troubles occurring with the establishment were due to the shadow cast by a flagpole across the street toward the banking structure. As a result, the entry of the building was redesigned to suggest the mouth of an angry dragon whose menacing look keeps the negative influences at bay. All has gone well since this otherwise modern-looking architectural feature was added, in harmonious keeping with the contemporary building as a whole.

Thai animism and popular Hinduism—or at least the veneration of Hindu deities—encompass the people's needs for aid and protection from the intangible dimension of the *anima-animus* and function as this-worldly emphases in contrast to the world rejection of Theravada Buddhism. Even Buddhist festivals are modifications of Indian observances whose calendrical system was imported along with the missionary thrust of Buddhism.

The important rite of paying homage to teachers of *khon-lakon* dancers and *piphat* musicians takes place on the first Thursday of June. Both the gods (Shiva, Vishnu, and other *devas*) and the spirits of departed teachers are formally invited to attend the performance. They reputedly witness the homage paid to living teachers along with the initiation of pupils, and they are encouraged to accept the offerings wrapped in banana leaves of rice, liquor, *baisi*, hog's head, duck, and chicken. The *bhikkhus* are, of course, present and begin the ceremony by chanting and then accepting the food before administering their blessings. The ritual itself consists of various dances, circumambulation of the altar with a lighted candle in the right hand, the sprinkling of holy water, the administration of *tilak* to the brow of each pupil, and the encircling of the head of each with sanctified strands of cotton. The conclusion of the homage and initiation ceremony of dancers and musicians is the scattering of puffed rice to induce the divine and spiritual teachers (gods and ghosts) to return to their proper abodes. In this single rite of paying homage to teachers, one can see how the various Buddhist, Hindu, and animistic elements of Thai belief are blended into a harmonious whole.

In regard to Buddhism, four main commemorations are held during the year, each corresponding to the Indian *pûrnimâ*, or day of the full moon.[65] Apart from these more strictly Buddhist festivals, the Thai also celebrate such Hindu holidays as Naga Panchami, Dasara, Divali, Vasanta Panchami (the beginning of spring), and Holi, or at least vestiges of them. Among the more obvious is the highly popular Loy Kratong celebration in honor of the goddess of water that occurs in conjunction with the full moon of the month of Kartika. For this festival, small "floating" (i.e., *kratong*) banana-leaf baskets are "sent adrift" (*loy*) on rivers and canals everywhere. These are filled with scented flowers, token foods (rice, betel leaves and nuts, papayas, etc.), a coin, joss sticks, and small candles as offerings to the water spirits or to Mae Khongkha, "the Mother of Water." One's wish is believed to be obtainable if the *kratong* flame continues to burn. Striking is the similarity with the floating lamps of Rasa Purnima at Puri or the hanging of lamps for this time in wicker baskets atop long bamboo poles at the Panchaganga Ghat of Kashi. In Banaras, these "sky lamps" are said to light the way to the otherworld for the spirits of the dead. In Thailand, similar to the Indian funerary *shraddha* rites are the *sarta* offerings of rice cakes mixed with honey. These correspond to the Hindu *pindas* except in more practical Buddhist fashion, they are offered directly to the priests on behalf of departed relatives. During the monks' ensuing chant, a water libation is poured onto the ground to quench the thirst of the dead.

Another remnant of a "brahmin festival" in Bangkok can be seen in the giant swing near Wat Suthat, a bright red teak wood structure standing nearly twenty-five meters high from which acrobats used to swing as part of the celebrations of the annual harvest. Brahmins also are connected with the beginning of the planting season, for it is they who determine the date of the celebrated Plowing Ceremony presided over by the king and held at the Pramane Ground. On this occasion, barefooted but colorfully red-dressed priests lead garlanded bulls that pull the sacred plow through the soil. To the chants of the brahmins, rice seeds are blessed and sown, and predictions are made concerning the outcome of the year's crops.

The still-practiced new year's holidays of Thailand reveal one of Hindu folk religion's strongest manifestations. Because the Thais follow the Indian sidereal reckoning, which adjusts for the precession of the equinoxes, the vernal equinox today falls on April 13 rather than March 20 or 21 in the West's tropical determination. The sun's entry into Aries is celebrated as the Songkran, or water festival, stressing the very element that dominates the same day at Hardwar and other places in India. In Thailand, the holiday lasts for three days, and as a new year's commemoration, it becomes a time for cleaning houses, honoring elders, as well as the general horseplay in which water is splashed everywhere and everyone gets wet.

The goddess Songkran is depicted riding the vehicle symbolizing the current year: rat, ox, tiger, rabbit, dragon, snake, horse, goat, monkey, rooster, dog, or boar. In this we see the Chinese influence in the names and sequence of the animals used for the year's designation. With its parades, fairs, pageants, dancing, and music, Songkran is found in both villages and cities. It survives in Bangkok mostly only in the suburbs, for at one time the capital celebrated new year's day instead as April 1, the nominal equivalent of the beginning of Chaitra (March/April), the first of the year in many Hindu calendars. Once again, this holiday takes the form of squirting and splashing people with water, often perfumed or even dyed, so reminiscent of the Holi revelry two weeks earlier in India. This idea of water as a lustrating, blessing, and fecundating vernal agent unites all these celebrations, which probably derive from a single antecedent. Processions with masked figures as well as depictions of male genitalia also suggest prototypical fertility rites. There are boat races and fish carried by beautifully attired maidens to the Mekhong River where they are released, as well as birds freed from cages on this day, and the nighttime illumination of the rivers with thousands of lights.

The new year is also the occasion for honoring the relics of one's dead, which are kept in urns in front of the household idol of Buddha. People in general and especially aging relatives are also honored at this time and their blessings sought. The Buddha images are lustrated in a ceremony attended chiefly by the elderly. In particular, a famous statue, the Buddha Sihing, is now placed outside on the Sanan Luang next to the Grand Palace so that people can pour lustral perfumes on it. But because the Thai government has declared the Western calendar to be the official one for the nation, many of these rites and celebrations in the capital itself have shifted from April 1 to January 1.

There are of course several other national holidays in Thailand as well as various ones of more regional or local significance. At this point in our discussion, however, it is enough for us to recognize the Hindu influence that permeates the Buddhist if not other religious sentiments both here and throughout Southeast Asia. For instance, in neighboring Malaysia, among the more important celebrations of the year on the sixth of Magha Sukhra (January/February) is Thaipusam, the birth of Kumar-Subramanian (Skanda, the son of Shiva), a Hindu festival popular throughout the Dravidian south of India. This is observed especially on Penang and at the Batu caves near Kuala Lumpur and is primarily a penitential occasion with those undergoing austerities carrying in procession decorated frames with skewers that pierce the bearer's flesh.

But if Thaipusam suggests the more self-abnegating propensity of Vedantic theology, the general tenor of Hindu practice as a whole along with the indigenous survivals of animism itself reveal in Southeast Asia, and in Theravadism in particular, something quite different. Instead, we find a vibrant form of veneration that comprises celebration and the expression of gratitude as well as the making of "merit" and the seeking of fulfillment of one's wishes. This is not the life-denying declaration of Buddhism but the happier affirmation inherent in the spontaneous, this-worldly pagan recognition of the *anima-animus*. We find this same countercultic behavior beyond Theravada in the other form of Buddhism as well, that of the Mahayana.

## Mahayana Buddhism

Mahayana has incorporated more indigenous folk or pagan elements into its overall corpus than has Theravada but coexists with a countercult religiosity that flourishes independently in the various countries where Mahayana is found. Japanese Buddhism coexists with Shinto, and Chinese

Buddhism functions contiguously with Confucianism, Taoism, and the country's folk religion. Beside China and Japan, a third Mahayana country is Nepal. Here, Mahayana functions alongside Hinduism. Despite the exodus from India in the face of the Muslim onslaught and the resultant growth of Hinduism, Nepal belongs to the central Asian complex that includes Tibet and Mongolia. The form of Buddhism that was established in Nepal, Tibet, Mongolia, China, Korea, Japan, and Vietnam thus differs radically from Theravada or Hinayana.[66] We might argue that this development is understandable, as it offers something more substantial and personal than the abstract and otherworldly (or antiworldly) theology of original Buddhism.

In India itself, the birthplace of Buddhism, the religion has long since disappeared. For instance, the once great monastic and pilgrimage center of Sarnath outside Banaras is now just a place to view archaeological excavations, a museum, and token temples established by various Buddhist countries amid an overall emptiness, which can nevertheless be refreshing after the noise and crush of Kashi. All the same, Buddhism died in India not only because of the cleverness of the brahmins but also because Hinduism was able to offer the people something they wanted and to which they could respond. If in Thailand a countercult operates in defiance of strict Buddhist tenets, in Mahayana that countercult has been incorporated to the extent that it has become a fundamentally all-embracing faith. Although it dovetails with the void of nirvana, it includes a full range of emotional appeals for virtually every type of person.

On a comparatively superficial level, one distinction between the two branches of Buddhism is that the sacred scriptures of the Southern school of Theravada are written in Pali, the language of the Buddha, but that in Mahayana Buddhism (the greater vehicle), they have been translated into Sanskrit. But the real difference from the Southern branch, or Hinayana Buddhism (the lesser vehicle), is Mahayana's emphasis on a belief in a paradisiacal afterlife in place of the nirvana of the void.[67] Consequently, Mahayana offers greater metaphysical speculation, recognition of an extensive pantheon, and the nonascetic consideration that the goal of the *arahant* (or *arhat*) is selfish and less evolved.[68] In Mahayana, adherents attempt to reach salvation—or, more properly, bodhisattvahood—with the purpose of helping others attain salvation as well. In other words, stopping short of becoming a buddha and achieving final extinction of self, the bodhisattva remains in this world and, because of his or her accumulation of merit and compassion, seeks the emancipation of everyone.

As a result, the Mahayana pantheon has three or more tiers in which the multitude of buddhas who have taught the faith on earth and achieved final nirvana upon death are secondary if not useless for popular worship.[69] Instead, the bodhisattva, or potential buddha, is the real focus of veneration. Of these, Avalokiteshvara (lord of the world) and Maitreya (the future Buddha) are the most revered.

Beyond these popular figures, is the concept of the *jinas* or *tathagathas*, also known as the *dhyani*, or meditating buddhas, which rule the cardinal directions as well as the cosmic center.[70] Consequently, the notion of a supreme buddha, an *adi* or primordial buddha often named Vajradhara (holder of the Vajra) or Vajrasattva (whose essence is the Vajra), has developed out of these five heavenly buddhas traditionally arranged in a *mandala* configuration, or circular symbol of the universe. Among these, the historical Buddha, Siddhartha Gautama, is merely an earthly form.

Along with the various buddhas and bodhisattvas of the Mahayana pantheon are also countless deities as well as demons, often borrowed from earlier levels of folk belief and frequently converted into tutelaries or spiritual family members of the various *tathagathas*.[71] With its greater emphasis on metaphysical speculation, Mahayana Buddhism generated numerous schools and subsects, each with its own theology and rituals.[72] Although none of these developments may be described as explicitly pagan, they nevertheless contain pagan emotional and venerational elements representing the same kind of theological compromise we find as a vernacular response to an official transcendental doctrine.

Another school in Mahayana Buddhism is Tantrism (in China, Chen-yen; in Japan, Shingon). The essence of this approach is the achievement of illumination and salvation through magical rituals and, in particular, the use of *mantras* (Japanese *shingon*), *mandalas*, and *mudras* (symbolic ritual gestures) as well as meditation and sexual acts. Tantric Buddhism has an extensive pantheon and often focuses on elaborate temple worship. In Tibet, Nepal, and Mongolia, this Mantrayana form of Buddhism, fusing with the shamanic folk cults, emerged as virtually a third vehicle called the Vajrayana.[73]

The Vehicle of the Thunderbolt, Vajrayana, takes its name from the emblem and weapon of Indra. Behind much of the Tibetan-Nepalese pantheon is found the Indra hypostasis. The thunderbolt (or diamond) was appropriated by Tantrayana as the symbol of enlightenment or the essence (if not the void) of buddhahood. Strictly speaking, the counterpart of the Vedic chief god Indra is the figure of Vajrapani who holds the *vajra*, now stylized as a multipronged wand. Vajrapani is included as the bodhisattva associated with the Tathagatha Buddha of the east, Akhsobhya (the Imperturbable Buddha). Nevertheless, the central Buddha, sometimes identified as the Adi Buddha, is also associated with the *vajra* under the name of Vajradhara or Vajrasattva. Known also as Vairocana (the Great Sun), this is the Mahayanists' highest deity.[74] As with Puranic Hinduism, however, much of the Vajrayana iconography and symbolism may be viewed as a reidentification of those originally belonging to the Rig-Vedic chief of the gods, the deity Indra.

To escape the prolonged enervation caused by the perpetual humidity and heat of the monsoon season, I left Banaras and flew to Kathmandu, the capital of Nepal, and ensconced myself in the air-conditioned luxury of the Soaltee Oberoi. By the time I had settled, however, it was already midevening when I set off without map, language, or other aids to see what I could see. Somehow, through the dark I managed to reach Darbar Square in which Nepal's tall pagoda temples formed black silhouettes against the even blacker sky. The exotica might just as well been straight out of Ravel's *Shéhérzade*. Its exquisite beauty was then marred for me when I was nicely but firmly refused entry into the double-tiered temple of Krishna near Asan Tol. I was allowed to approach, though, the ground-level shrines, one to Ganesha (Asok Vinayaka) and another to Anna Purna. I noticed that worshipers often did not remove their shoes at these shrines.

The most evident devotional form in the Kathmandu Valley is Hinduism or, rather, elements of Hinduism. Consequently, Hinduism proper cannot be considered a countercult of Buddhism, as it is in Thailand. The Nepalese faith, however, is a fluid composite of Brahmanic, Buddhist, Tantric, and indigenous concepts and practices. This syncretization is also the very essence of the Vajrayana form of Buddhism with its elaborate pantheon whose home is Tibet.

The Nepalese temple is generally a square wood, stone, and brick structure, often freestanding and sometimes surrounded by a courtyard. Frequently around the temple is a colonnaded circumambulatory passage, and oil-lamp railings encircle the structure as a whole. One or more bronze bells hang near the main entrance, which usually are rung by devotees at the commencement and conclusion of *puja*.

The temples in Nepal may have more than one door, and sometimes all four sides are open. Examples of this last are the Mahendreshvar pagoda at the Makhan Tol and the Shiva temple near the Vishnumati River at the end of the Maru Hiti, both in Kathmandu. The latter, however, has lattice coverings over the three auxiliary sides, and between these and the sanctuary proper the family taking care of the temple have installed themselves, chickens and all.

The downward sloping angle of the overhanging roof (or roofs) which meets the supporting wooden struts, often is highly decorated, sometimes with erotic scenes or *mithuna* couples, which is the central characteristic of the pagoda style. Small bells are underneath the overhang, and at the structure's top is either a simple spire or a multiple bell-and-umbrella shape. The tapering pagoda may be as high as three stories, with each level possessing its own roof under which might be found open balconies. The inner sanctum is never large and is often lit only dimly while exuding the aroma of old wood impregnated by the smoke accumulated from years of burning butter lamps and incense. Horns of sacrificed animals are embedded in the walls of some temples.

Kathmandu's Darbar Square is filled with a complex arrangement of pagoda temples. These range from the old and huge wooden Kasthamandapa (after which the city may have taken its name), which is more an open pavilion for temporary lodgers, though it also contains shrines, to the enormous elevated Taleju temple that dominates the entire area. A walk through this maze of shrines and pagodas and the profusion of carved wood is pure otherworld enchantment.

Between the Kala Bhairab shrine with its seventeenth-century black stone, six-armed, angry-looking idol and a three-story *sikhara* temple to Krishna is a two-storied pagoda dedicated to Indra, albeit empty save for a *lingam*. Not far from this is the Seto Macchendranath (Lord Indra of the Fish) sanctum. At first I was hesitant to enter his complex for fear of the brahmanic rejection of *mlecchas* (untouchables or foreigners), but what I took to be a large temple was in fact a paved public courtyard with a pagoda in the center.

Macchendra, the patron deity of the Kathmandu Valley, bringer of rain and abundant harvests, is not a Hindu divinity but an incarnation of the bodhisattva Avalokiteshvara who belongs to the lotus family of Amitabha, the celestial buddha of the west. Macchendra is, however, an excellent example of the interchange between Hinduism and Buddhism in Nepal, for his other main title is Lokeshvara (lord of the world), another name for Shiva. Although he is also sometimes confused with Vishnu, Macchendra is also known by such Shaivite appellations as Nartesvara and Nilakantha. He is Karunamaya (the compassionate one) and Bunga Deo (named after the village where his image is kept for six months of the year). This wide range of names and the widespread veneration confirm that he is one of Nepal's most popular figures.

The temple of Seto Macchendranath is a copper gilt–roofed pagoda with a ground-floor shrine in which is found a white-faced, buddhalike image. Various stupas as well as different statues, usually of Avalokiteshvara, surround the small central building. Rows of prayer wheels stretch along three sides of the sanctum proper, whose pillars, railings, and supporting struts reveal a mélange of Hindu and Buddhist iconography. Because this was a Buddhist temple, my fears were unwarranted, since the complex was open and not restricted by the Nepalese concepts that birth and caste alone determine one's inclusion in the Hindu faith. This is a general attitude I encountered throughout the Kathmandu Valley.

By contrast, in Patan (Lalitapur), the ornate Hiranayana Mahavihara Buddhist temple and monastery were readily accessible. The Mahayana influence is everywhere detectable, including a copper-gilt mandala of the five *tathagatha*, or celestial buddhas (known as a *vajra dhatu-mandala*), and icons of Avalokiteshvara, Padmapani, and Lokeshwara. Not far from this last, however, is the fifteenth-century Kumbeshvara temple of Shiva containing a ground-floor shrine where, to my surprise, I received *prasad*. At the south end of this temple's court is a lattice-covered area containing a highly venerated life-size idol of the fierce form of Shiva (here designated Unmateshvar Bhairab). This includes an even larger-than-life-size erect *membrum virile* particularly popular among barren women.

One of the most heavily attended temples was that of Mahendreshvar at the Makhan Tol in Kathmandu near Darbar Square. It was built in the sixteenth century by Mahendra Malla and dedicated to Pashupati (Mahendreshvar), Shiva as "lord of the animals" and patron deity of Nepal. The temple was reconstructed in 1963 and now consists of a sanctum with four portals with closed grill gates up to which throngs of worshipers press both day and night for *darshan* of the *mukha lingam* inside, that is, the emblem of Shiva carved with four faces. The two-storied pagoda itself sits on a stepped podium.

On a festival night during my stay in Kathmandu, music celebrations took place in the pavilion adjacent to Mahendreshvar. Behind the temple a platform had been set up and piled with a mountain of nuts, fruits, and foods. In front of it was an altar whose central object was so covered with flowers that I could not recognize it. Perhaps it was either the symbolic image of Gujeshwari Devi (two *kalashas*, or pitchers, joined together) or the four-armed stone sculpture of Kamadeva (god of love) with erect *lingam*. As usual, worshipers clanged the two bells found before the temple.

The devotional focus of Lamaism or Tibetan and Himalayan Buddhism that replaced the central image of the preaching, meditating, ascetic Sakyamuni of Theravada is the cosmic schema of the *vajra dhatu-mandala*.[75] Developed from the concepts of buddhahood as light, sovereignty, and power embodied respectively in the celestial buddhas, or *tathagathas*, of Amitabha, Vairocana, and Akhsobhya, the cosmic diagram of the Vajrayana with its magicoreligious significance most likely emerged from an earlier world-representational schema employed by the shaman. The transcendent Buddha of Vairocana has now become the central figure of the *vajra dhatu-mandala*. He is partially suggestive of the Adi Buddha. Amitabha is assigned to the west; Akhsobhya, to the east. All together, there are now five celestial buddhas, and each *tathagatha* or cardinal direction is associated with a color, symbol, vehicle, virtue, and vice as well as a consort, bodhisattva, and *yi-dam* or tutelary deity symbolizing the particular vice or failing.[76]

In Nepal only the white and green forms of Tara are generally significant in regard to the *tathagatha* consorts. Originally a Hindu deity and wife of Brihaspati (the planet Jupiter), Tara (star) was abducted by Soma (the moon) with whom she bore Budha (the planet Mercury). Important to the development of Tantra and occasionally identified with Devi, Tara has become the most popular goddess in Vajrayana Buddhism. She is called Savioress and is worshiped as one who can quickly mitigate the effects of illness and misfortune. Tara is frequently linked with Avalokiteshvara as his consort. Tara may also, however, manifest a fierce form, although in this context only as the Blue Tara (Khadayi Yogini)—also known as Ugra (ferocious) Tara and Vajra Tara—does she have any cult in the Kathmandu Valley. In this form, she is often identified with the blood-thirsty Kali.[77]

A characteristic aspect of Tantrayana is the *yab-yum* (father-mother) position assumed by various deities, chiefly the *yi-dam*, with their consorts.[78] The idols portray the male and female in sexual embrace symbolizing a mystical union. The god may have an animal face (such as Yamantaka's bull head), a demon's visage (such as Vajrabhairava), or several faces (such as the four-headed Sambara). The god may also have many arms, each holding various attributes like a chopper, drum, skull cup, severed head, impaled body, wand, and elephant skin. The goddess (in Sambara's

case, Vajravarahi, the adamantine she-boar) sits astride the lap of her partner, whom she faces.

With Sambara-Vajravarahi, the union is described as the expression of
the female as transcendental wisdom joined with the male as compassion,
the means to salvation. It is almost certain, however, that the esoteric rites
of original Tantrism included acts of physical union between devotees. On
the autochthonous folk level of worship, the oneness of the male and female, the *animus* and *anima*, is the epitome of the force of animation and
participation in the dynamics of the godhead. Generally coupled with this
aspect of animism and shamanism is phallicism, an association that may
explain why many figures in both Hinduism and Vajrayana are shown
with erect *lingam*.

It is through the class of bodhisattvas and their associated *yi-dam* that
Hindu and other deities have gained a position in the Vajrayana pantheon.
This process is further augmented by the inclusion of the Taras as well as
*yoginis* (Tantric sorceresses) and *dakinis* (initiatory mystic fairies designated mothers and called *khadhoma* in Tibetan).[79] A general perusal of
these figures and their alignments readily shows the historic, artificial, and
eclectic growth of the iconography of the *vajra dhatu-mandala*.

In the example of Manjusri is the personification of learning and wisdom who is also considered a form of Yamantaka (conqueror of death,
one of Shiva's titles) associated originally with Gautama Buddha, later
with the lotus figures of Amitabha, and finally a member of the family of
Vairocana. Manjusri's consort is Sarasvati, who is the Hindu goddess of
learning and the wife of Brahma.[80]

Avalokiteshvara (the lord who gazes downward) is perhaps the most
venerated figure besides Tara in Vajrayana and Mahayana Buddhism, despite the relative popularity of both Manjusri and Vajrapani. In Nepal,
Avalokiteshvara, especially through his identification as Lokeshvara (lord
of the world), has become an embodiment of both Shiva and Vishnu. In
particular, Chintamani Lokeshvara (Lokeshvara of the wishing gem) is
worshiped in order to acquire wealth. As with any bodhisattva, in iconography when Avalokiteshvara is present with his "spiritual father," the
Tathagatha, here Amitabha, he is depicted as standing. But when he is
alone in his own sanctuary, he takes a sitting position.

Devotees light a lamp or incense in front of images of Avalokiteshvara,
the other bodhisattvas, and the Buddhist deities. They prostrate themselves three times and may make a request or simply express gratitude for
a favor granted. Even in front of the statues of Gautama or other *manusi*

(human) buddhas, they may raise a lamp, although technically speaking, these figures have passed beyond being. Even so, worshipers may express religious vows and objectives, and so strong is the animistic projection of personality, they also may make ordinary requests and desires to the Buddha's idol.[81]

A key endeavor in Buddhist and Hindu reverence is the acquisition of merit. One popular mode in Buddhism of gaining this is by repeating various mantras, or mystic formulas, of which the most renowned is the *Om mani padme hum* invocation of Avalokiteshvara. The syllables, however, are regarded as having power even apart from the sound of their utterance, and consequently, in Mahayana, prayer wheels have been devised, ranging from huge barrels to handheld varieties as well as those lining a temple's walls. A single turn of the prayer wheel is the equivalent of repeating the mantra it contains, multiplied by the number of times (e.g., 400) that the mantra is printed on a single page and the number of pages (e.g., 100).[82]

Avalokiteshvara is said to have sprung into existence from a white beam of light that emerged from Amitabha's right eye. A tear from the right eye of the compassionate Avalokiteshvara in turn gave birth to the White Tara; another tear, from the left eye, became the Green Tara. Hardly distinguished from Tara is the popular embodiment of Avalokiteshvara's compassion known as the goddess of mercy in both China (Kuan-yin) and Japan (Kannon). The Newari Karanda-Vyuka presents the bodhisattva's most important non-Tantric form, Padmapani (lotus in hand), as the emanator of the Hindu pantheon.[83]

An unusual aspect of Tibetan Lamaism is its belief that various human beings are emanations of bodhisattvas (particularly of Avalokiteshvara and Manjusri), the *tathagathas*, gods, demons, or *khadhomas*. These incarnations are called *tulkus*, and they are thought to coexist with their emanators.[84] The most famous of these were the fifth Dalai Lama of the Yellow Hat sect, who was considered an incarnation of Avalokiteshvara (Tibetan: Chenrezigs), and his religious teacher, the Panchen or Tashi Lama, who was declared a *tulku* of Amitabha. Each of these spiritual leaders inaugurated lines of successors who are recognized as *tulkus* of their predecessors rather than as direct reincarnations of Avalokiteshvara or Amitabha, respectively. Moreover, the Dalai Lama is a double incarnation, as he is also a *tulku* in the spiritual line of Gedundub, the disciple of the founder of the Yellow Hats, Tsong-kha-pa, himself an incarnation of Manjusri.

Lines of *tulkus* are also believed to come from various gods (e.g., the indigenous Pekar), goddesses (e.g., Vajravarahi), *tathagathas*, bodhisattvas, and *ku kongmas*, that is, humans as *ngagspas* (sorcerers) or even parents of famous people. Here we move closer to the pagan idea also found in the ancient world of Greece, Rome, Egypt, and Mesopotamia of heroes parented by gods, the god king, the demigod, and even the apotheosized human. With the *tulku* as well as the doctrine of the three bodies of the Buddha[85] is a reflection of the central pagan notion stressing interaction and interconnection between the divine and the human. *Tulkus* are distinguished from such other Tibetan concepts as the *trong jug* and the *tulpa*. The former is the disembodied wandering of one's self or even the translation of one's self into another body during which time the original body remains inanimate. The *tulpa* is an apparition created by a lama or magician that coexists with its originator (sometimes even independently) or may even continue after the death of its creator.[86] Although the *tulpa* may appear as corporeally real as a human, deity, animal, or object, the *tulku* is an actual physical incarnation whose birth is predicted by his or her predecessor.

The belief in *tulkus* began with Dus-gsum-mkhyen-pa (1110–1193), the first head of the important Red Hat sect of the Karma-pa who supported the rulers of Tibet from the fifteenth to the seventeenth century. He foretold his rebirth as his own successor, giving such information as where he would be born and other details for purposes of recognition. In one unreformed Red Hat tradition, the *tulkus* of Padmasambhava or his disciples are recognized as coming into being only when special instructions or corrections are required.

Related to the idea of the *tulku* is the Nepalese tradition of the "living goddess," Kumari. Considered an incarnation of Kali Devi or of Tara, a young girl of five years or less is selected from the Buddhist Banra caste. If she is passes certain tests and esoteric rites, she is recognized as the virgin goddess and installed in her palace, the Kumari Bahal, on Darbar Square in Kathmandu. Here she lives in seclusion, performing various ritual duties, attending the Indra and Bhoto Jatras, and presiding over the chariot festival of the autumnal Kumari Jatra. Her incarnation ceases, however, once she exhibits any loss of blood, through menstruation or allegedly even an ordinary cut.[87]

The Vajrayana of Tibet is distinguished by the development of Lamaism, both the reformed and unreformed varieties.[88] In the Kathmandu Valley, Buddhism has all but merged with Hindu veneration, and indeed, on a popular level, the two are scarcely separated. Beneath the panoply of these forms, an autochthonous folk belief is also apparent, and the same has applied—at least until recent times—in Tibet. In fact, throughout Nepalese Vajrayana and Tibetan Lamaism with their assimilative pantheons, the earlier, indigenous deities can be found, betraying the perennial animistic countercult to the tenets of the more official Buddhistic religion.

The Tibetan folk religion, which undoubtedly parallels the ecstatic shamanism of Mongolia, produced its own monastic system replete with rituals and scripture as a pagan reflection of Buddhist organization in an attempt through camouflage to survive in the face of Lamaist opposition and ascendancy. This specialized form of the "religion of men" is known as Bon (or Bon-po) and has survived in some regions of Nepal as well as in its influence on the unreformed sect of rNying-ma-pa (ancient sect of the Red Hats). Bon recognizes a founder in (the probably legendary) gShen-rab-mi-bo, a world-ruling god Sangs-po 'bum-khri, and a god of wisdom gShen-lha 'od-dkar. The Tibetan state oracle of the *chos skyong* has been absorbed by syncretic Lamaism from the pre-Buddhist Bon rites involving the shaman's trance and possession by an evoked spirit.[89]

Compared with Theravada, Mahayana Buddhism with its wish-granting deities and saviors already represents an intrusive incorporation of folk belief. The *vajra dhatu-mandala* is itself most likely a transformation of the cosmic diagram ritualistically employed to represent the world concept of the shaman. Each deity or demon is accorded a direction and localized in a particular region. Tibetan legend holds that the country's hostile local spirits were magically pacified by the Tantric master Padmasambhava and thereby took their place in the divine hierarchy as *dharmapalas*, the sworn guardians of the faith and its adherents. This ability to absorb indigenous figures and native cult entities in Mahayana has produced in Tibet a Lamaist pantheon more complex than that of any other faith. Nevertheless, the folk religion that in large part gave rise to both Bon Po and Lamaism can still be found within and behind the Lamaist development of Tantrayana.

Before the Chinese takeover, Tibet was home to various colleges of ritual magic (two in Lhasa acting in behalf of the state) whose adepts, the *gyud pas*, used the prescribed techniques to propitiate or subjugate the untamed and negative forces. These were then either magically enchained and kept as prisoners or were granted perpetual worship in gratitude for their assistance or at least desistance from harm. These forces were thought to dwell in trees, rocks, mountains, rivers, lakes, and a variety of local places, and both shamans and Lamaist magicians sought to subdue and transform them into useful servants. The Lamaists also tried to convert these forces to the Buddhist religion.[90]

While the orthodox doctrine of Buddhism is opposed to religious rites, the worship of protective genii of the house, the hearth, the tent, the field, the earth, and the mountain, as well as the *yi-dam*, *chos skyong*, and bodhisattvas modeled on them, speaks for the popular retention of the animistic prototype of veneration. Through ritualistic efforts, this folk belief seeks to secure welfare, cure disease, exorcise hostile influence, and elicit guidance in the other world or *bar-do* (the intermediate realm after death).

The preparation and use of charms stem from this same religious impulse. Consequently, from the official monastery to the local shaman's individual orb of influence, sanctified water, holy pills, prayer wheels, formulaic flags, paper charms, images, traveling altars, and ritual *phur-ba* daggers descended for the general population and its protection. Particularly desirable was the portable amulet case that might contain an image (frequently of Tara), wood-block printed or handwritten mantric formulas, relics, fragments of an article belonging to a holy man or sorcerer, or objects blessed by a lama. The amulet cases were frequently worn, especially when traveling, but otherwise kept on the household altar or in an outdoor shrine erected especially for this purpose. Or along with relics, sacred scriptures, and other objects associated with holy men, the amulet was placed in a relic shrine or stupa.[91]

Worship of such charms always consists of three prostrations (akin to the Chinese *kowtow* or the Indian practice of lying flat on the ground), clockwise circumambulation, and the making of offerings.[92] As with the adoration of idols in the gods' houses (Mongolian: *lha khangs*), devotional gifts include flowers, incense, perfume, and various foods, although the most common offerings are water, grain, and butter lamps often placed in copper bowls.

I believe that pagan veneration is rooted on the domestic altar. Human beings have from time immemorial worshiped the sun, various astral and atmospheric phenomena, the elements, and special objects or places. But it is the household shrine—often linked to the hearth—that is the fundamental expression of human perception of the numinous or divine and the protective influences separating humans from the wild while safeguarding their families and, by extension, their communities, tribes, and states. The domestic altar serves as a prototype in the nomad's tent as well as in the communal shrine, temple, or monastery.

In Tibet, although the altar has traditionally always held at least one image, many idols, venerated objects, and ceremonial instruments may also be found there.[93] All these artifacts, along with the rich symbolism embodied in scroll paintings, have spread throughout the world the fame of Tibetan artwork with its fine sense of detail and ornamentation. Much of this tradition is indebted to the accomplished Newari craftsmen of Nepal commissioned by merit-seeking Tibetans.

Various charms, talismans, grains, or semiprecious stones sometimes are placed inside the images used for worship, either the double *yab-yum* figures or the single icon.[94] On the altar, these might be clothed with small garments or draped with cloth. Usually a butter lamp is always kept lit, though others may be added, the lighting or refilling of which with fresh fuel still constitutes a general expression of veneration in Nepal and other areas of the Tibetan diaspora.

Food offerings consist of the usual Tibetan diet of barley flour and butter made into cakes, although ceramic models are sometimes substituted. Beside amulet cases, incense burners, dishes for foods or rice, and vases for flowers, a Buddhist altar carries a *vajra* and a *ghanta*, or bell. A mirror may also be included as well as various musical instruments like the conch, bone trumpet, wood oboe, cymbals, and skull drum. Offerings are thus made to a musical accompaniment and/or the recitation of hymns.[95]

In true keeping with the survival of this-worldly cult interests, not all rituals are dedicated to seeking salvation and nirvana but may also be directed toward more material objectives. These may be procurement of rain, happiness in love, success in a venture or over an opponent, recovery of lost articles, exorcism, general propitiation for favor, submission of spiritual foes, or even the death of a human enemy. Hail-averting ceremonies are also deemed necessary for a good harvest. The Red Hat sects permit barley beer despite the Buddhist prohibition of all alcoholic beverages, and it is used primarily as an offering to the more violent deities like Vajrabhairava.[96]

Popular worship in Tibet and Mongolia includes placing votive offerings (usually carved stones or plaques) at auspicious places.[97] These range from crossroads and bridges to heights and mountain passes. Stone offerings, that is, stones stood on end or piled into cairns, are established in honor of local genii or mountain gods.[98] Rivers and lakes also are venerated, while springs, as occurs universally, receive oblation in exchange for their use in making wishes. Worship extends likewise to particular trees that are generally demarcated by a surrounding railing. Rocks and stones, too, are honored. In Nepal, round stones are appeased as representations akin to the autochthonous *devi*.[99]

The Buddhist practices of Nepal, if not Lamaism itself, are included in the orb of Vajrayana with its integrated and yet not always so integrated forms of folk cult. Many of the practices so far discussed, such as those connected to sacred place, are purely pagan and have little to do with the transcendental and nihilistic orientation of Buddhism per se. But even when these popular, earthy, and emotional customs are fully incorporated into Buddhism, they reveal the pagan nature of much Buddhist practice if not of cultic behavior itself. They are invariably indicative of natural vernacular concern and organic expression rather than the theologically motivated behavior of rejection and asceticism.

Corresponding to the notion of sacred places is, of course, the idea of sacred times. Along with holy pilgrimage centers are special festival occasions. The earlier, commemorative cycle belonging to shamans and nomads may be glimpsed in the solstitial and seasonal festivals of the Mongolian peoples that include sun and fire worship, honoring the culture hero Genghis Khan and the blessing rites of the herds.[100]

In Nepal, the year is divided into festal and *vrata*, or votive observances, but the calendar of events and Buddhist celebrations is structurally Hindu.[101] The Nepalese of the Kathmandu Valley commemorate the usual Indian holidays.[102] Kartika Purnamasi appears to have diffused into several, chiefly local, harvest goddess festivals: Mahalaxmi Village Puja, Gujeswari Jatra, and Indrani Puja, culminating near the successive new moon with Bala Chaturdasi on which grain seeds are scattered for dead relations.[103]

In addition, the Nepalese calendar includes spring and winter chariot processional and bathing ceremonies in honor, respectively, of Rato (Red) and Seto (White) Macchendranath, which are highly popular local celebrations, perhaps the chief foci of the religious year. Around September is the Indra Jatra, an obvious descendant of the Vedic Indramaha. This festival is a recognition of the rains believed sent by Indra when he first hears the frogs croaking in June. The many-headed and many-armed image of Biswarupa (all forms) is now displayed, representing the pantheistic world god slain by Indra according to the Rig-Veda. A part of the Indra Jatra is the Jatra of Kumari in which the "living goddess," accompanied by two boy attendants representing Ganesha and Bhairava, proceeds by chariot into the public, granting to the multitude her *darshan*.

The only Nepalese festival I attended during my stay in Kathmandu was that of the scapegoat monster Ghantakarna on the fourteenth of Shrawan krishna (July/August). On that day I rented a bicycle to visit Deopan and other sites on the outskirts of the community. Not knowing the day's customs, I repeatedly had to run through cord set up by young boys at various neighborhood crossings, and by not paying the required toll I learned later that I had become a relative of Ghantakarna, or at least a hardworking man.

The fees were being collected for the funeral of the scapegoat that occurs at the end of the day. Reed-and-leaf effigies are burned (these being more abstract than anthropoid in appearance) while an untouchable whose body is completely painted seeks alms. Afterward, a funeral procession goes to the Vishnumati where Ghantakarna is cast into the river.

Later that night I set out again from the hotel toward Darbar Square. The evening was warm and semihumid but unusually still as most people keep to their houses, being afraid to venture out into the dark lest Ghantakarna come back and seize them. This is the night during which witches are believed to call on their deities. Accordingly, lamps and "spirit bowls" are placed outside in the streets and especially at crossroads to appease the local powers for another year. These offerings consist of rotting boiled rice, onions, garlic, husks, and strips of colored cloth tied to small wooden stakes. It appeared to me that the neighborhood dogs were simply waiting for the wicks to burn out.

The Ghantakarna practices stem directly from the folk veneration of animistic spirits—both friendly and harmful—that underlies the devotional system and "high religions" of Nepal as well as Tibet and Mongolia.[104] The folk pantheon on which it is centered is a tiered system. At the top is a figure who might variously be the Erketü Tngri (Mighty Heaven) or (Köke) Möngke Tngri ([Blue] Eternal Heaven) of the Mongols, the Bon Po high god of white light, or the Vedic Dyaus (Jupiter). Associated with this high being at the center is a more active entity: the Mongolian Qormusta, king of the heavenly beings, or the Vedic Indra, personification of "Heaven's" thunderbolt.[105]

If this celestial hierarchy is translated into a concrete configuration, it results in something like the *vajra dhatu-mandala* with the various auxiliary figures corresponding to the *dhyana* buddhas of the cardinal directions surrounding a central or even primordial entity. Among the Mongolian heavenly beings (*tngri*), various Buddhist-Hindu adoptions such as the Buddha, Vishnu, Kubera, Devi, Indra, and Vajrapani came to be included. As the active personification of the high god, Qormusta/Indra also holds an affinity with the middle region, the atmosphere, whose wild spirits are often conceived of as red warriors or hunters, albeit protectors nonetheless. These are the armed equestrian heroes of the Tibetan dGra lha (enemy god), the Vedic Maruts, or the Mongolian Sülde (*genius*) Tngri, Dayitsin Tngri (enemy god), and Geser Khan. Mountain gods are also included as divinities of the middle realm.[106]

Various heavenly and atmospheric beings have been singled out for a special cult. These include the fire god or goddess (Vedic Agni; Mongolian: Odqan Ghalaqan) and the "white old man" (the Mongolian Tsaghan Ebügen who has been compared with the European St. Nicholas). Other prototypes are the "seven old men," that is, the constellation of Ursa Major. Such culture heroes or ancestors as the Mongol's Genghis Khan and the Nepalese Chankandeo (an apotheosized merchant) also are worshiped.[107]

In addition, mountain gods belong to the spirits of the lower or terrestrial sphere. The cult of the heights extends to the cult of the earth, and more diversified than those directed to the beings of the upper and middle regions, the lower gods include deities of the land, the waters (the *nagas*), rocks, trees, as well as house and hearth. Here is the earth mother herself.[108] In pure animism, however, as local manifestations the earth *genii* have no set gender and range from the Indian *devi* or *amma* and *bhairon*, the Nepalese *mai*, to the Tibetan *sa bdag* (lords of the earth).

The important point of the high and folk religions of Central Asia is that despite the tripartite cosmological division perceived within the godhead, the categories are linked with one another. Moreover, because of the variety of nomenclature, gender, and function of any particular configuration, these cult are dealing with the basic animating principle in which the *anima* and *animus* are merely shifting polar and functional manifestations rather than specific retentive identities. It is the veneration of them that is significant, not their role in a theology or their position in a pantheon. What recurs unfailingly is that they are regarded as protective and favorably bestowing and may therefore be propitiated for such.

If the Central Asian complex is one of the main expressions of Mahayana Buddhism, another is found in Japan. Here, Shinto is the foremost form of indigenous pagan sentiment, but unlike most paganisms, Shinto is largely aniconic. Instead, it is in the Buddhist temple that Japanese idolatry finds its chief expression.[109] In many respects, despite its orientation toward transcendent values and world negation, Japanese Buddhism conforms to venerative expressions of the *anima-animus*, as much, if not more than do the Mahayana forms found in Nepal, Tibet, and China.

Kyoto is one of Japan's more impressive cities. Though for tourists, a much more manageable city than Tokyo, Kyoto is nevertheless formidably large. As the former imperial capital from 794 until the Meiji Restoration in 1868, the city is still used for the coronation of a new emperor. As a whole, it is a wonderland of magnificent architecture, royal gardens, broad and stately avenues, and panoramic scenery. But despite its overwhelming artistic and cultural heritage, Kyoto is a modern complex the equal of any urban conglomeration in Japan.

Although it was the Shinto shrines that were of foremost interest to me, I could not help but be impressed by the hundreds of lovely Buddhist structures.[110] At the time I was visiting Japan, many of these sanctuaries were enhanced all the more by the beauty of the flowering plum trees or the incipient stages of the cherry blossoms for which the country is renowned.

The Japanese Buddhist hierarchy also includes many Hindu figures: Indra as Taishakuten, Brahma as Bonten, Vaisravana or Kubera as Bisha-monten, Sarasvati as Benzaiten, and so forth. Buddhism in Japan has also furnished such popularly worshiped personalities as Kannon (queen of mercy), the bodhisattva Fudō (destroyer of evil), and Jizō (guardian of the spirits of dead children).[111] Along with this pagan tendency toward poly-theism, much of Japanese Buddhism—particularly Shingon and some of the Tendai sects—takes a magical stance toward the procurement of bless-ings or prosperity and the deflection of adversity, including recovery from illness.[112] The usual procedure in Buddhist worship is making petitions to the deities, reciting mantras, performing rituals, and employing amulets and relics. Even the Buddhist movements of the Kamakura period (1185–1333), the Pure Land, Zen, and the Nichiren sect, have an essen-tially magicometaphysical ideology that provides salvation or enlighten-ment in an expedient manner at variance with the original Hinayana teachings. In an overall sense, Japanese Buddhism has emerged more as a world-affirming than a world-denying outlook.

Buddhism entered Japan with the introduction of writing and Chinese culture and prospered through its strong alliance with the state and politi-cal machinery. Like universalistic missionizing religions in general, it sought to replace indigenous cult centers. But due to its gentler nature and greater ability to adapt and coexist, the result in Japan has been the erection of Buddhist temples at preexisting shrines and, rather than obliterating them, to consider these shrines as the dwelling place of the protecting spirit of the temple area. A good example of this adjustment is the stupendously grand Senso-ji or Asakusa Kannon temple of Tokyo on a raised area adjacent to the Sumida River. Facing the temple, one finds to its rear right the Asakusa shrine, popularly known as the Sanja-sama, which translates as the "shrine of the three gods." These are explained as three fishermen who found a tiny statue of Kannon in their nets while fishing in the river. But while the legend is interesting, it suggests simultaneously the kind of reworking of local legends that one often encounters in Christian Europe. For instance, the iconography of St. George and the Dragon may be seen as a transformation and survival of Zeus's battle with Typhon, as one of Zeus's epithets is *georgos* (the farmer, literally the earth worker).[113] An important feast day of Zeus's Roman equivalent, Jupiter, is the Vinalia of April 23, ecclesiastically dedicated today to St. George.

Apart from the identity of old folk deities as Buddhist deities, other assimilative procedures of Japanese Buddhism are the development of the "shrine-temple" (or *jingū-ji*) constructed in Shinto precincts.[114] These are designed as places in which Buddhist priests perform ceremonies, including chanting sutras, with the aim of securing the enlightenment of the *kami*. Moreover, various Buddhist-Shinto syncretic sects came into being, such as Ryōbu Shinto, Sannō Shinto, and Yoshida Shinto.[115] The former two took root in the philosophical concept of *honji-suijaku* in which the *kami* came to be considered as secondary manifestations of certain Buddhas or bodhisattvas understood as the primary entities.

The Japanese term for the incarnation of a Buddha or Buddhist divinity as a Shinto deity is *gongen*, a word also used to describe a Shinto sanctuary style developed during the Edo period (1600–1868) when Shinto shrine types were strongly influenced by Buddhist architecture.[116] Yoshida Shinto stresses that the *kami* are the fundamental phenomenon from which the Buddhistic beings sprang. Collectively, this Buddhist-Shinto fusion is known as *shimbutsu shūgō*, although the two religions were officially separated during the Meiji period (1868–1912).[117] I found in Kyoto near the Yasaka shrine a good example of a shrine that adopted elements and paraphernalia belonging to both sects, here combining features of Kannon and Amaterasu worship. Such trends ameliorated the adaptive fusion of imported Buddhism with indigenous Shinto. But along with the traditional political suppression of Christianity, they allowed in Japan the preservation of such pagan forms of expression as Shinto, Shingon, and other forms of Buddhism in a manner virtually unparalleled elsewhere in the world.

## Christianity

After Hinduism and Buddhism, the next major world religion, chronologically and numerically speaking, is Christianity.[118] In its bid for power, the Christian Church annexed and incorporated many of the pagan elements belonging originally to its indigenous rival faiths throughout Europe and Latin America if not elsewhere as well.[119] Martin Luther's Protestant "rebellion" was in part a revolt against the compromising and pagan adoptions of the Roman Catholic Church. The Church of Rome is the largest single religious organization in the world, and together with the Eastern Orthodox Churches, much if not most of their combined cultic behavior may be seen as pagan.

Unlike Protestantism, Catholicism appears more gentle, plastic, and compromising, with its emphasis on pilgrimage to holy places, veneration of saints, use of reliquaries (receptacles for containing relics), Mariolatry, and so forth. In short, we find many of the familiar elements of pagan/cultic behavior, notwithstanding their engrafting onto an ideology that, like Judaism and Islam, fundamentally denies validity to animistic perception. With Christianity, however, the concept of the godhead in three persons appears to be an influence of or concession to pagan sentiments of multiplicity, at least compared with Judeo-Islamic unitarian doctrines. The anthropomorphic and avian representations used for these persons, in spite of the injunction against such by the Ten Commandments of the Old Testament, bespeak the natural and often irresistible iconological tendency by humankind in general.

Roman Catholic and Orthodox Christianity, on the one hand, may be compared with Hinduism and Mahayana Buddhism to the extent that it has incorporated into the official faith itself the natural propensity toward countercult veneration. Protestantism, on the other hand, exists largely in a situation comparable to Theravada in which cultic behavior, although still present, is largely external to and separate from official theological practice. Because this kind of counterresponse often takes the coloring of secularization, I will discuss it more fully under the heading of agnosticism. Within the more dominant Christian form of Catholicism, we find that despite the position of the authoritative tradition itself, the cultic needs and this-worldly concerns of adherents have been fully accommodated.

The fringe identities of Christianity take many forms, and certainly the Christian polytheism of the Church of Jesus Christ of Latter-day Saints is among the more interesting.[120] The basic impact of the Mormon pantheon of deities differs little from the corpus of saints and martyrs venerated by the Roman Catholic Church. In practical terms, these offer a full panoply of variation to allow for individual concerns and personal approaches to the godhead.

In its historical development, the company of Catholic saints came to include numbers of heathen deities in the ecclesiastical attempt to reduce paganism to a manageable yet useful status (e.g., Brighid, George, Dennis).[121] Many a local deity was incorporated in this manner and thereby became a functional bridge through which the indigenous religiosity was assimilated into the Church Triumphant. But the process works both ways. Practitioners of such pagan religions as Santería or voodoo have been able to retain the venerational expression of their own *orissa* or *lua* figures under the guise of—or at least in association with—Christian iconography.[122] In addition, the atavistic earth mother of native Mexican peoples is said to survive today as Our Lady of Guadalupe.[123]

The cult of saints is close to pre-Christian pagan worship. The marketing of sacred objects, talismans, holy water, and the like and the organization of pilgrimage institutions focused on revered figures are reflective of pagan behavior. These became part of the age-old cultivation process that stemmed from and still constitutes cultic or pagan worship. The sacred manifests and becomes accessible through the physical. Despite its nonpagan theology and antipagan animosity, the bulk of actual Christian practice can be accurately assessed as behaviorally pagan.

In its historical development, the Judeo-Christian God began as a polytheistic figure by being one god among many. Over time, he succeeded in gaining the unmitigated allegiance of the Israelites by forbidding "his" people's worship of his rivals. The monotheistic notion of Yahweh developed, as Eilberg-Schwartz shows, through the contingent necessity stemming from homosexual implications to keep the body (and phallus) of God veiled.[124] As is still the case for the Mormons, God for the earliest Israelites was corporeal. He had a body. But with this body kept hidden, it could be "theologically" forgotten, and the doctrine of a transcendent, incorporeal creator could be—and was—developed. Although the spiritualization of the Old Testament God is an involuted and complex process, at the base of the resultant Christian Supreme Being is a physical deity that psychoanalytically appears to suffer with schizophrenic delusions of grandeur and paranoid jealousy but is nevertheless fully at home in a pagan milieu.

We must remember that Christianity is *not* a pagan religion as such and that its ultimate values and aspirations are not this-worldly. Moreover, physical creation occupies an ambivalent position.[125] As a "gift" from God, physical creation must be cherished and respected, but it always remains in some sense secondary and something, as in Hinduism and Buddhism, to escape. The concomitant pursuit of pleasure is an uncertain and sometimes even false undertaking; it is never central. Most important, human beings—apart from the doctrinaire instance of Jesus Christ—never share in the godhead. They always are separate, and the primary purpose of their life is atonement, or release from original sin.[126] The Christian world is a ruptured one and not the pagan's organic realm of unbroken growth and continuity. The pagan road may be a bumpy one, but it always remains integrally complete, along which humanity traverses its endless spiraling into the future. It does not include a cosmic fall from grace but instead leads continuously toward a variable horizon of perpetual rapture. Paganism has neither a primordial moment of disobedience to a preconceived divine plan nor an omega point of ultimate attainment.

Although Christianity is a nonpagan religion, much of its Roman Catholic and Orthodox practice is pagan. The eucharistic "eating of God' that constitutes the pivotal sacrament of communion is a development from, if not a parody of, pagan rites of sacrifice and theophagy.[127] The very notion of transubstantiation is pure magic. And while Christian holy sites (churches and pilgrimage centers) have been constructed over former shrines and temples understood as sacred to pagans,[128] Christianity has likewise appropriated pagan holidays for its own ecclesiastical calendar. Behind the Christian celebrations of Christmas, Candlemas, Easter, and the Feast of St. John the Baptist, among others, we find earlier heathen festivals.[129]

Many of the celebrations of the Christian religion may be seen as age-old continuations of pre-Christian commemorations. Moreover, while the particular foci have been changed, many of the times and locations of Christian practice are still those that once were recognized by indigenous and ethnic communities that we can identify as pagan. So even though it was not my intention to argue that Christianity is pagan, many of its practices and features, particularly among its Roman Catholic and Eastern Orthodox variants, clearly are.[130]

## Islam

Islam is the religion of approximately one-fifth the world's population, totaling, according to the Jidda (Saudi Arabia)-based *Motamar Alam-i-Islam* gazeteer, more than one billion believers.[131] As a missionizing religion like Buddhism and Christianity, Islam has spread considerably beyond its linguistic Arab locale of origin to the point that Indonesia holds more than 140 million Muslims; India, 130 million; Bangladesh, 76 million; and Pakistan, 75 million.[132] In China, more than 65 million people are Muslims; in the former Soviet Union, about 60 million are. Islam has also made great inroads into Africa, where Nigeria alone has more than 50 million believers. In Europe, the Muslim concentrations are in Turkey, Bulgaria, Macedonia, and Albania, which has approximately 2.2 million Muslim adherents.

The only Arabic Muslim countries I have visited are Morocco and Egypt, Morocco in 1961 and again ten years later, and Egypt in 1985. Beyond this, my experience of the Islamic world is restricted to Macedonia when it was still part of the Yugoslav Republic, Turkey, Pakistan, and Bangladesh—and, of course, India. The Turks, along with the other members of the common Turkic branch of languages—the speakers of Uzbek, Azerbaijani, Tatar, Kazakh, Uighur, Turkmen, and Kirghiz—are Altaic Muslims. Of the Western Altaic branch, only the Chuvash of the Bulgar group are Orthodox Christians. With the exception of the Dravidians of South India, the Muslims of India, Pakistan, and Bangladesh speak Indo-European languages, as do the Muslims of Iran and Afghanistan.

Islam contains one major sectarian divide separating the majority (approximately 85%) or orthodox Sunnites from the more intolerant and fanatic but perhaps more interesting Shiites.[133] The Sunni predominate throughout most of Turkey, the Near East, Africa, Afghanistan, Pakistan, India, Bangladesh, Malaysia, and Indonesia. Shi'ism is primarily a Persian variation of Muhammad's teachings. Its stronghold is Iran, but the majority of the Iraqi population are also Shia, although ruled by Sunnites (whereas, by contrast, the government of Sunnite Syria is Shiite). The most important shrines of Shi'ism, those of Kerbela (containing the tomb of Hussein, Muhammad's grandson) and Nejef (with the tomb of

Ali, Muhammad's son-in-law and fourth successor to the Prophet), are in Iraq.[134] Other Shiite communities are located in Yemen, Oman, and Pakistan.

The only politically significant modern separatist Sunnite sect is the puritanical and reforming Wahabi, whose members include the ruling Saud family of Saudi Arabia.[135] African Islam, although Sunnite, exhibits a much greater variety of practice than is otherwise the case with traditional orthodoxy. Most sectarian developments, however, are Shiite.[136] Their point of departure is the rejection of the Ijma, or "consensus" of Sunna, and acceptance instead of the authority of the Hidden Imam who is believed to descend from Muhammad's son-in-law Ali and his descendants as a virtual incarnation of the godhead. Emerging also from Shi'ism as a semimonastic mystic order is Sufism, which ostensibly forms a third branch of Islam.[137]

In its monotheistic fundamentals, Islam, like Judaism, is strictly opposed to the kind of veneration involved in worshiping the *anima* and *animus*. Formulating a straightforward yet rigid concept of Allah as well as the mode and time of prayer, there is little orthodox scope for venerative variation. Nevertheless, throughout much of the Muslim world has developed a rich cult of saints whose tombs become centers of pilgrimage and whose *urs*, or death dates, are especially commemorated.[138]

Particularly in Shia is an extreme exaltation of Fatima, Muhammad's daughter, wife of Ali, and mother of the martyrs Hassan and Hussein.[139] In certain sects, Fatima is known as the masculine *Fâtir*, or creator, and hailed as the Source of the Sun and the Mother of Her Father. The countercult tendencies of Shia may go even further, for I have seen from Iran a religious medallion bearing a portrayal that its owner insisted was of Muhammad, in blatant contradiction to the orthodox prohibition against any depiction of the Prophet.[140]

The most ironic aspect of Islam is that despite its antipagan continuation of the Judeo-Christian heritage, its most sacred point of focus—the direction of all prayer and praise of Allah and the orientation of every mosque—is the Kaaba, or cubic building of Mecca, a rectangular stone structure dating to pre-Islamic times as the shrine of the god Hubal whose image it contained along with other sacred objects as well as the famous Black Stone.[141]

Most likely of meteoric origin, the Black Stone was regarded as the pivot and unifying force among the Arabian tribes before the time of

Muhammad, and this archaic stone cult is still today the central object at the heart of all Muslim devotions.[142] The Kaaba holding this aerolith is kept covered with a black cloth annually renewed by the Egyptian government. At the time of its renewal, the old cloth is cut into small pieces and sold as sacred relics.

It is in the cult devotion of saints that one perceives that automatic sense of the miraculous and special that is like the veneration of the *anima* and *animus*.[143] In India alone are found as greatly revered Muslim shrines the tombs of Kwaja Mohinuddin Chisti in Ajmer, of Masud Ghazi in Bahraich, of Zinda Shah Madar in Makanpur, of Hazrat Nizamuddin Aulia Chisti near New Delhi, of Banda Nawaz Chisti in Gulbarga, and, in southern India, of St. Quadirwali Sahib at Nagore in the Thanjavur district.[144]

These tombs have developed a national if not wider recognition, but they are similar no doubt to many other more purely local shrines honored by the Muslim community and, as is frequently the case in India, by Hindus as well—particularly such shrines as those of Mohinuddin and Quadirwali. In Kashmir, at Srinagar on the shores of Lake Dal, is a shrine that possesses a glass bottle containing a brown hair from the head of Muhammad. Usually kept locked in a cabinet, the flask is exhibited to pilgrims only during important Islamic festivals.

The shrines of saints are usually illuminated during the commemoration of the *urs*, or death anniversary, of their enshrined figure.[145] The death anniversary is typically celebrated with the preparation of special foods or cakes that are first surrounded by lamps, then consecrated through the recitation of Qur'anic verses over them, and finally distributed among the pilgrims for consumption. At the shrine of the soldier-saint Masud Ghazi, the *urs* ritual is known as Kanduri-ki-Fatiha, or "blessing of the food on a napkin." This takes place during the month of Rajab. Here, in keeping with making a vow or expressing thanksgiving, it is customary to make a flour image of a horse that is then boiled in syrup while a blessing in the name of the saint is repeated over it. The pastry is then shared with other devotees and consumed at the shrine itself.

On the eve of the seventeenth of Jamadi-ul-Awwal, the *urs* of Shah Madar, the protector of children, special collars of gold or silver are placed within a circle of seventeen lamps and dedicated in the name of the saint. These are then placed on children in the belief that they will henceforth be protected from the *jinn*, or evil spirits. The ceremony of Dhammal Kudna, or fire walking, takes place at this shrine and suggests that many of Islam's miracle-working holy men are derived from the various semimonastic dervish or fakir orders with their reputation for magical tricks and feats of skill. Shah Madar holds the title of Zinda, "living," because of the belief that Muhammad granted him the ability to survive without breathing and hence, although entombed, he remains alive. Women are excluded from his shrine.

In Pakistan, while visiting the Indus Valley civilization sites of Mohenjo-daro and Harappa, at the latter I encountered the locally but highly venerated shrine of Nûshah, reckoned to be an Arabian saint whose dates are no longer known. The presumably pre-Aryan Indus Valley civilization that flourished roughly between 2500 and 1500 b.c.e. had its most spectacular achievements in these two cities. The contrast between the two in subsequent history could not be more striking. To the south, Mohenjo-daro (the mound of the dead), although situated in a flat, low-lying area subject to flooding, has never been resettled save for the erection of a Buddhist monastery and adjacent stupa, whose ruins form the site's most conspicuous archaeological feature today. Nor has the area been used for burial. Harappa, however, contains a contemporary settlement that partially overlaps the ancient site. The shrine of Nûshah is on what is called the citadel (mound AB) of the former metropolis of Harappa and is surrounded by numerous latter-day Muslim tombs, which is a typical Islamic custom, that is, burial near the grave of a holy man. Adjacent to Nûshah's open-air shrine are the ruins of a mosque. The sarcophagus itself is exceedingly long—maybe twelve or more feet—which was explained to me as due not to his having been such a tall man but having been such a great one.

The paraphernalia of oil wick lamps and other offerings, identical to those employed in Hindu shrines in India, were in abundance in the enclosure of Nûshah's tomb, and in fact, it was the recognition of this similarity of the countercult practices of both Hinduism and Islam that generated the idea for this book. Throughout the day, there was a steady trickle of visitors to the sacred area from the village of Harappa and its surroundings. I could not help but wonder whether, as is so common in Europe, this was again an instance of the survival of a cult predating to pagan times.

According to the strict injunctions of Islam, worship is solely of Allah without the use of intermediaries, simile, or anthropomorphic symbols. Islam is monotheistic and, as such, is fundamentally opposed to polytheism, which deifies attributes of life, nature, or the godhead; differentiates various phenomena among different gods; or venerates metaphorical qualities and entities.[146] Apart from the exclusive adoration of Allah, Islamic worship to seek reward or benefit, remove misfortune, or protect from adversary differs little from most countercult aspirations. This basic celebration of life is reflected in such festivals as the mid-July Utchal or the late-September Phool harvest celebrations or the midwinter Chowas commemoration in such places as the Chitral valley of Pakistan and most likely were originally formulated before any Islamic reinterpretation of them.

The revering of sacred objects such as the hair from the head of Muhammad or the veneration of saints is itself a survival or reassertion of countercult propensities. Muslims' widespread use of graves as a mantic/cultic point of reference is clearly understandable in a religious ideology that does not officially recognize the numinous, despite the Black Stone's dichotomous hold on all believers. It is as "good Muslims" that the various saints have been able to find their place in the canons of official acceptance, but it is through the wondrous and potentially miracle-working quality of their memories and tombs that venerational attention toward them is engendered.[147]

It is this revered superhuman quality that is the *anima-animus*. This potentiality remains fluid and elusive—being manifested spontaneously or at least felt—at any time or in any place. But once its presence has been perceived, it may then become regularly honored, at the particular time of its perception as an annual festival, at the particular place of its initial perception as a visited shrine, or both. In other words, the recognized manifestation of the *anima-animus*—whether through a person, object, or event—occasions temporal and/or local veneration.

The Muslim veneration of saints is, of course, different from the *anima-animus* found in such male-female dualities as the Japanese *dōsojin* or the Hawaiian *ku* and *hina*. The Hawaiian duality is an acknowledgment of an aura more like the early Latin understanding of *anima* as vaporously intangible—be it the wind or breeze, the physical breath, or the life soul. As the breath of life, the *anima* is the vital principle, and as such, it was believed by the Romans to maintain an independent existence after death, that is, as the soul, *manes*, or shade of the lower world.

The *animus*, by contrast, refers to the consciousness, the mind, and hence the spirit or soul. It may originally have been a development of the *anima*, and although there is no surviving early Roman evidence of the fact, it too came to be regarded as continuing after the death of the body, most likely as what in many so-called primitive societies is designated as the free soul or dream soul.[148]

The common and animating denominator of the concepts of soul dual-ity, the male-female, the *anima-animus*; that is, the vaporous yet activating and sentient force lurking throughout all nature is centered at the core of humanity's sense of the supernatural in whatever its forms and veneration of it. Quite simply, this is the life force, but one perceived in the inanimate world perhaps as much as it is in that of the animate. Worship is usually the appreciation of special instances of this life force, generally those bor-dering on the miraculous. This is where the Islamic cult of saints is found.

Once again, Islam is not a pagan religion. In fact, of virtually all major world religions, it is perhaps the most diametrically opposed to paganism. Its unforgivable sin is *shirk*, the "association of Allah with another."[149] Baldick sees early Islam as an attempt "to produce a simple, lowest-com-mon-denominator religion."[150] Nevertheless, we still can find in Islam various pagan elements and behaviors. Horrie and Chippindale describe the veneration directed toward the imams in the Ithna-'Ashariyah (the Twelvers) or dominant Shiite sect as making them into "godlike" figures despite the injunctions against *shirk*, or the polytheistic linking of God with any other.[151] In fact, Twelver subsects, especially those in Central Asia and North Africa, "often reflect the resurgence of [pre-Islamic] tribal pa-ganism and shamanism."[152] Moreover, the use of talismans (*ta'widh*) throughout much of the Muslim world to avert the "evil eye"—as well as the belief in *jinn* and magical powers in general—"implies that supernat-ural powers do not ultimately derive from God."[153] While this position may be heretical, it belongs to the animistic substratum that persists de-spite the official theology. "Islam absorbed [practices] of earlier religions to a far greater extent than is conceded by contemporary Muslim authori-ties," revealing a syncretism that even here accommodates countercult behavior.[154]

## Agnosticism, Atheism, and Secularism

In the non-Catholic realms of Western Christendom, especially the pri-marily Protestant domains of northern Europe and North America, the countercult veneration of the *anima-animus* exhibits a radically different form than is found elsewhere. The almost universal practice of pictorializ-ing, along with the cult of saints, is probably strongest in such Roman Catholic areas as Latin America, Poland, or southern Europe as well as the

Europe of the Eastern Orthodox Church. Here, such ostensibly pagan behavior has been largely successfully integrated with Christian practice. In
more secular or Protestant cultures, cultic practice has different guises and
is often separate from recognized religious exercise itself. In the former
Communist world where various forms of Marxism became the official
theology, the Christian Church itself often assumed the semblance of a
stubborn, irremovable, and perennial countercult. In the "modern," Protestant Western world in which scientific empiricism now vies for the position of the official creed, countercult veneration persists, albeit in unfocused—and hence generally unrecognized—forms.

The disenchantment that began with Christianity and its ascendancy
over the magical world of paganism infused with the perception of the
*anima-animus* progressed even further with the Protestant Reformation.[155]
This development is often referred to as secularization, and while there are
several different understandings of what is meant by the term, *secularism*
describes in general the loss of religion as a social force.[156] The diminish-
ment of religious influence in Western society relates to several factors,
one of which concerns the devaluing or lack of interest in the godhead
however it is conceived. Both atheism and agnosticism represent a non-
commitment to the supernatural. Atheism denies its existence completely;
agnosticism postpones any decision regarding ultimate reality or denies
the possibility of doing so. Both atheism and agnosticism may be seen
as forms of secularism inasmuch as they are modes of thought or ways
of viewing the world in which the supernatural or spiritual does not play
a role.[157]

Protestantism is not, of course, either atheistic or agnostic, but it helped
pave the way for the Western ascendancy of secularism. It is a step further
away than Roman Catholicism from pagan enchantment. Protestantism is,
consequently, more at home with the rationalism and concentration on
the purely ethical that is increasingly associated with secularism. The mystical, magical, numinous, or even rapturous have little place in the non-
Evangelical Protestant and/or secular thought of the modern West.

This atheistic/agnostic attitude tends to find a corollary in the rise of
humanism.[158] The emphasis on secular concerns that began with the Renaissance has traditionally been understood as the exaltation of reason
and the rejection of supernaturalism. More broadly, humanism refers to
any doctrine, way of life, or attitude that takes human interests and values
as central.[159] Rational humanism itself assumed the form of Deism during
the Age of Enlightenment. It accepted God as creator of the universe and

humanity but saw no active role for God in the subsequent maintenance of the world. It also denied the need or possibility of revelation.[160]

Both Deistic and atheistic notions have probably always been present in paganism. Epicurus, for instance, taught that the gods were irrelevant. Even if they did exist, they would not have any interest in the material world. The notion of a *deus otiosus* who creates the world but then distances himself completely from it is found throughout African pagan religions and such Afro-Atlantic offshoots as Santería. Likewise, contemporary Western paganism holds that belief itself is not of primary importance. According to Margot Adler, it is the *doing* of paganism—the performance of rituals, the celebration of festivals, the commensurate geocentric activities—that is important, and not necessarily the affirmation of supernatural reality.[161] Apart from any concern with otherworldly dimensions, naturism (worship of nature) and humanism are two strands found variously throughout paganism in one form or another. Consequently, contemporary atheism and agnosticism—especially in their more humanistic (and humanitarian) expressions—exhibit a resonance fully commensurate with paganism as a major theological option. Pagan humanism itself has a venerable continuity that includes classical Greco-Roman religion from the Mediterranean and Confucianism from China. The very pagan notion that the supernatural cannot be directly apprehended except through religious metaphor is itself a quasi-humanistic and/or quasi-atheistic position, one that offers a possibility of bridging the gap between the dichotomy between religion and science.

Regardless of whether pagans and secularists make good bedfellows or whether paganism may be seen, from certain perspectives, to embrace humanism, atheism, and/or agnosticism, I am not concerned here with paganism as a religion per se but with paganism as a form of behavior. Apart from either the pagan dimensions of humanism or the humanistic dimensions of paganism, I am interested here with pagan survivals or countercult activities that persist in the face of a dominant secular and/or Protestant status quo. My contention is that along with various subcult conscious formulations, unfocused forms of venerating the *anima* and *animus* can be found throughout modern Western society as subliminal behaviors or reflexes.

Several persistent atavisms are found in the West that could be interpreted as vestiges of a universal cultic reflex. Felicitas Goodman contends that in the long run, human beings are not capable of tolerating ecstasy deprivation,[162] and so such vestiges could be reclaimed as possible ways in which the increasingly secular West might be able to relocate a sense of enchantment. Specifically, the 1960s counterculture, Native American insights, voodoo practice, and the pursuit of Indo-European and Roman origins may offer routes to social reenchantment. My basic predicate is the reverse of three hundred years of scholarly anthropological-psychological thought, which is described by Rodney Stark as attempting to denigrate all religion on the basis that "primitive religion" is an intellectual aberration or mental malfunction.[163] With the collapse of the primitive mind thesis and the continual erosion of the irrationalist premise, we are freed to contemplate religious experience as a healthy and natural proclivity of being human. We also are in a position to understand the relativity of cultural programming or indoctrination and, therefore, the possibility that evolution need not always be linearly progressive but that valuable insights and understandings might be buried beneath the historic and archaeological accumulations of sociocultural change. To understand paganism is in part to retrieve a viable part of humanity's dialogue with the godhead.

Returning to the West after my relatively prolonged sojourn in the East, I was perhaps in a better position than I otherwise would have been to view various acts and behaviors as venerative despite their normally secular province. I found countercult no less a part of life in general but in what may be classified as nontheistic forms. To put it in another way, an unfocused veneration takes the place of the this-worldly, life-oriented formulations of worship found in Asia and Polynesia.

In its essential features, much of the basic venerative act remains the same, though without the conscious reflection or awareness of the act as such that frequently accompanies it in the East. The automatic quality is still present. People still go to the temple, although it is no longer called such. Hence, the nomenclature is often different. In addition, the deities themselves are largely absent, or else they are no longer designated as such. But in the fundamental affirmation of life and the use of ritualistic approach, the focused and nonfocused forms of veneration exhibit their common denominator.

The use of mind-altering sacraments reaches back into the core of shamanism. In Vedic times, the Indra cult used the psychotropic or entheogenic *soma* personified as the god Soma.[164] In the Indo-European tradition, the hallucinogenic aspect must have been ancient and reappears, for instance, with the Scandinavian *berserker*. At some point, however, due to the lack of availability or changing social conditions, alcoholic inebriation came to replace hallucinatory intoxication. In Europe, the god of wine, Dionysus, is perhaps the earliest figure connected with this development, at least in the classical tradition.[165] The legacy of this bacchic cult is the taverns, saloons, and pubs that have become local recreational social centers in so much of the West. The "watering place" is a normal venue for communal gathering, ritual behavior, mind alteration, and individual as well as group catharsis. Consequently, in the public house, despite the lack of conscious recognition of deity exemplified through deliberate prayer or the absence of adoration, many of the remaining features of devotional practice are nonetheless present.

In the West, it is the pub or neighborhood bar that has become the local shrine. As such, it is sectarian: people have their preferred locale, and many segments of the population do not frequent these establishments at all. Nevertheless, to the degree that a bar culture does flourish, its cult centers primarily on the sacramental substance of alcohol. The alternative name of "spirits" conveys perhaps more of the original provenance. "Devotees"—if we may so call the patrons of the establishment—usually revere a particular "spiritual being," perhaps that embodied by whiskey, gin, vodka, wine, or beer. In keeping with the regimented ways of Western capitalism, one's offering in the "pub shrine" is a fixed amount according to the deity of devotion. In America, the offering is usually presented first or at the time the *prasad* is presented; in Europe, the sacrificial gift is frequently made later or when the devotee leaves the shrine: in other words, when his or her bill is calculated. The altar of course has become the bar; the priest, the bartender.

Another feature of the Dionysian cultus is the theater. Today, in this we have in the secular West another surviving form of the temple. Historical diversification has separated the spirit cult of inebriation from the thespian cult of the stage, but in origin, tragedy can be traced to the spring festival of Dionysus Eleuthereus and the religious ceremony held in the theater attached to the god's shrine on the southern slope of the Acropolis in Athens. The Great Dionysia was nevertheless not an act of worship but dealt instead with myths and actions elucidating the relationship between humans and gods. In this way, tragedy differs from the dithyramb in which the chorus, representing the citizens, sang an ode of honor directly to the god. Tragedy, and hence drama in general, reveals instead an affinity with the divine possession of the worshiper that was an early feature of the wine cult and persists in many overt pagan religious expressions of today.[166]

I consider the theater and the concert hall as contemporary nontheistic shrines, structures that have deviated from the venerationally focused emphasis of their prototypes. In India, for instance, the typical stage theater always has a small shrine to the goddess Sarasvati as the patron of the arts. In traditional China, the theater is often combined with the temple, as it served to assemble the community for religious worship and for maintaining public recreation under religious auspices.

In the West, this connection of sanctum and stage has been lost, though not as completely as we might think. The movie theater reveals most clearly the traditional continuation. It is here that we go for *darshan* of our "screen idols." The technical capabilities have changed, and our symbolic icons are now in motion. Movie actors and actresses as well as those of the stage attract their own popular following and have emerged as "stars." In other words, we use the same term as the ancient Greeks or the Chinese did for their apotheosized hero/heroine, poet/poetess, or statesman/stateswoman. We have created an astral pantheon and, as fans, notwithstanding the denial of polytheism by our Christian heritage, have enthusiastically supported rock stars, musical virtuosos, operatic divas, athletes, dramatic performers or personalities, and occasionally even politicians. Moreover, today's iconography extends beyond the bounds of life and death. We can still adore James Dean, Gloria Swanson, or Marilyn Monroe as well as Natasha Kinski, Brad Pitt, Sandra Bullock, or Gwyneth Paltrow within the confines of our own residences. Although the theater, musical center, and sports arena, along with the temple of the Muses (or museum), have become our largest, most conspicuous, and opulent temples, through television, the *eidôlon*, or image, has reentered our homes. The *puja* is absent, but the idolatry so often associated with countercult has come full circle. We behold and venerate symbols that, fittingly for the twenty-first century, are now more often composed of reconverted electromagnetic waves rather than stone, wood, or metal.

Another modern equivalent of devotional phenomena is the popularity of present-day tourism. What does the tourist seek if not the *darshan* of art and historic or memorial monuments? In the American capital, the shrines of Presidents Washington, Jefferson, and Lincoln partake architecturally of classical or Egyptian religious styles. The physical act at these structures, however, consists of seeing them only, without presenting offerings or lighting candles and incense, but they serve nonetheless as foci encouraging reflection and appreciation. In one manner or another, this is what happens at most of the Western world's tourist attractions, whether a famous museum, a renowned architectural creation, a garden park, or a technological development. With all these, nontheistic veneration has taken the form of pilgrimage and the receiving of *darshan*.

Commemorative practice is not only to be found through travel but exists also in the town squares of the Western world in the form of public statues and memorial shrines. As with the Chinese system of the *tz'u*, cultural and political value structures are instilled in the community's awareness through such devices aiming to perpetuate the memory of its extraordinary citizens. On another level, we have an airport named after John F. Kennedy, an avenue after Princess Grace, and a museum after Georges Pompidou.

In this cult of our leading citizens, moral qualities, creativeness, and exemplary public service are especially honored. Perhaps the wreaths and flowers presented at shrines to the war dead come the closest to the kind of ritualistic offerings common in the East, although the public demonstrations of tangible gifts (flowers, photos, teddy bears, poems, and messages) occasioned by the death of Britain's Princess Diana constituted the largest expression in recent times of what Durkheim referred to as collective (religious) effervescence. But even with the war dead and other national heroes, if the state rather than the gods and goddesses of a particular pantheon becomes the focus, it is the centering process itself that unites all the manifestations of veneration.[167]

It is chiefly through the arts that the West has found a substitute for the viably emotional, ritualistic, and colorful part of religious life that is largely missing in its dominant Protestant theology. Through art, with or without its frequent incorporation of forms and themes borrowed directly from classical mythology, the focus becomes aesthetic or ideational rather than divine, but once again we have a quid pro quo for the passionate and sensational corpus of traditional devotion. Perhaps this focal response is no more clearly operative than through the Western phenomenon of operatic art. This innovative combination of stage drama and orchestral-vocal music has produced some of the most lavish and popular performances bordering on the rich pageantry of old-time religious ceremony and is equaled perhaps only by the public opera house itself, which in several Western cities has emerged as a more prominent monument than even its chief locus for official worship, the cathedral. The centrality of "operatic worship" over other leading art forms, like film, may be reflected in the designation for its prima donna as *diva*, or "goddess," which in traditional hierarchy has a higher rank than those apotheosized divinities, the stars.

Related to the opera and often deriving from it are such kindred music and drama syntheses as the *opera comique*, operetta, revue, and musical. With the development of cinematic musical comedies and the filming of grand opera for the movie hall or video, these two leading art forms have merged into yet another contemporary dimension. Nevertheless, in Western society, one of the highlights and sacrosanct celebrations of individual life is "a night at the opera," a live and gala performance.

In Germany, opera derived in part from the Latin or German moral and religious school play which included solo odes, choral pieces, and instrumental dances. This in turn developed from the medieval miracle play which also led to the passion and carnival plays later forbidden by the Church. Such local celebrations are direct descendants of earlier and sometimes pre-Christian commemorations surviving today, especially in Europe and in America as well. These include Mardi Gras, or Carnival, and Thanksgiving, as well as many of the fetes in honor of the local, patron saint.[168]

The chief occasions to be honored remain seasonal: the death of winter, the appearance of spring, the return of vegetation, the harvest, and the vintage. Sometimes these are superimposed by or augmented with various national or political anniversaries, but often they retain the veneer of official Christian observance. Bacchus has become St. Vincent or St. Denis; Gargantua, St. Christopher; and the summer solstice, the feast of St. John the Baptist. In France and Italy especially, the local fete includes costumed processions, the distribution of holy bread, traditional dancing, a communal feast, shooting contests, amusement park rides, gambling, and loud rock music usually provided by a live band. The typical celebration also includes the town mayor's or representative's attendance at Mass, after which the official presents a floral bouquet at the local memorial. All this can be viewed as a chiefly but not exclusively southern European form, among others, of contemporary venerational survival.

This need for ritual and celebration is even reflected in the assumption of ceremonial functions by the state under such a Protestant-like equivalent as Marxism. The local Palace of Festive Events replaced the church or temple, but elaborate rites nevertheless took place for such events as birth, marriage, and death. The performing officials wore special robes somewhat reminiscent of the black robes and white horsehair wig of attorneys and justices in the English court. The success of these state substitutions may not have been proved in the long run, but their incorporation into the people's lives in the first place undoubtedly stems from the identical impulse that led the Christian Church to adopt and/or tolerate many of the earlier pagan habits and traditions.

In the West, this same need has repeatedly given birth to such fringe sects as the witches' covens or druidic societies of Great Britain or the "piss and leather" / sadomasochism bars and their followings in the cities of North America. But such phenomena as the magical order of the nineteenth-century Golden Dawn and Anton LaVey's Church of Satan must be seen in the last resort more as subcults than as representing the countercult mainstream.[169] Countercult veneration, as we have seen, does not necessarily repudiate the official deity system but instead employs its own means of approach within the orthodox hierarchy to the Buddha or the godhead or even the *anima-animus*. These responses are usually unconsciously automatic, seminaturalistic, and anthropomorphically projecting. They tend to spring from deep-rooted collective habits that antedate any self-consciously created theological system. They may be pagan, but they are pagan behaviorally rather than pagan religiously.

The conventional bedrock of natural worship survives in such instinctive greetings as "Good morning," in spontaneous interjections like "Gesundheit," and in cultural reflexes like the nod of greeting or handshake. From this same impulsive complex comes the social ritual of toasting or dedicating one's drink to the health or honor of someone or something. Conceivably, the clinking of glasses, like the ringing of church bells, stems from the attempt to ward off negative spirits. And as with any offering in the Hindu *puja*, a toasting is always made with the right hand. Moreover, in Europe at least, when toasting another person, the accepted procedure is to make direct eye contact, thereby signifying that the "sacred act" of commemoration or celebration is symbolically a moment in which souls touch.

These automatic behavioral reflexes seen in toasting and greeting and found in the terminology and formats of many of our cultural institutions reveal that cultic ritual remains operative in at least some level of Western secular society. Although this ritual is often unconscious or unfocused, sometimes simply marginal as part of a new religious movement or New Age or Neopagan group, or otherwise incorporated into some mainstream service in which it is kept restricted and firmly controlled, the countercult or pagan impulse continues to be a part of organic human behavior. If it is repressed too strongly and not allowed to breathe and flourish, it risks psychocultural illness. Unlike many other cultures in the world, that of the West appears to flirt with being or becoming out of control. This is unhealthy not only for the West itself but also for the implications, through globalization, that the West has increasingly for the rest of the world.

With this perception in mind concerning Western and global unwholesomeness, I move now from a descriptive position to a more prescriptive one.

Despite my distinction between the subcult and the countercult, I consider the San Francisco–born phenomenon of the late 1960s a development of the countercult originating from a breakdown in the authority of the traditional value system in the face of the perception by many at the time that America was unjustifiably and vainly shipping the cream of its crop to the Vietnamese slaughterhouse. As with any nonorthodox movement, a countercult can become a vehicle for expressing political and social dissatisfaction.[170] Haight-Ashbury symbolized a rejection of orthodoxy through spiritual revaluation by resorting to fundamental techniques of shamanism, rites of nature, esoteric exploration, and gregarious experiment.[171] It was less an abandonment of traditional forms of the godhead as it was an incorporation or augmentation of a greater number of deiform manifestations from beyond the Jewish-Christian heritage. Despite being spontaneous, the hippy phenomenon was also largely deliberate and conscious.[172]

In its heyday, Haight Street was known as the "street of love," and it was certainly unlike anything the West had known either before or since with all the riotous color of an eastern bazaar, its euphoric "flower power" spirit, undercover drug peddling, and the overwhelming atmosphere of discovery in the thrill of love, brotherhood, newness, and change. This was a unique moment, and despite the subsequent repudiations by critics and historians, for most of us who knew it, it remains an experience we would never have wanted to miss.

In retrospect, Haight-Ashbury was perhaps too much a foretaste of something still belonging to the future. It was a localized countercult expression with international implications, but it was also premature, naively idealistic, too definitely a product of the immediate but changing, politically explosive social conditions, and, like countercults in general, totally unorganized in any institutional, orthodox churchlike sense. In time, Haight Street became quite literally a "street of hate" with specially installed street lamps allowing twenty-four-hour camera surveillance. It was marked by robbery, mugging, death, big-time underworld crime, and a preponderance of dangerous drugs. The fun had disappeared, and the street, with its boarded shop windows, took on the appearance of a wartime siege. The great mother had given her all.

When I returned to San Francisco many years later, I made the inevitable pilgrimage to the area between the panhandle of Golden Gate Park and Parnassus Heights, to "where it all began." Haight Street had undergone yet another metamorphosis and was now securely established in a respectable quiche culture with its boutiques and specialty food stores. Shop names typically and nostalgically evoked the former glory: Lost Horizons, Great Expectations, Forgotten Dreams, and the like. But despite the coming full circle from ethnic neighborhood and subsequently perpetual party to Mafia playground and now quasi-bourgeois memento, the mark of this grand street on history will remain, regardless of any periodic clouding of obscurity.

Besides San Francisco, another great North American pilgrimage center with special meaning for countercult venerational traditions—overlooking Hollywood as the birthplace and center of the film industry—is New Orleans. Here that twentieth-century American creation known as jazz was born. With its unique blend of French and black African culture, New Orleans offers the United States a vital root that, it may be argued, its puritanical origin sorely needs.

As a religion, voodoo occupies that fuzzy domain between a purely subculture sect and a countercult manifestation as Haight-Ashbury hippiedom did. As, however, a surviving approach to the perceptions and adorations of the *anima-animus*, it is not to be lightly dismissed or regarded merely as the practice of black magic spells. It may include this, as do certain elements of Hinduism, Taoism, Shinto, and *kahuna* magic, but it is primarily akin to shamanism in its use of trance to communicate with ancestral spirits, saints, and animistic deities. Being primarily an underground and secretive cult, voodoo's public shrines are preciously few but include in New Orleans the grave of Marie Laveau—a former voodoo queen—and the voodoo patron of St. Expedite in, for instance, the church of Our Lady of Guadalupe on Rampart Street (where it is, however, the statue of St. Jude that receives the most attention).[173]

I suspect that beside the exotic sources of Haight-Ashbury eclecticism and Franco-African voodooism as well as the contemporary nontheistic forms originating in the arts and society, the North American reencounter with veneration of the *anima-animus* might be met most successfully in its native Indian traditions. Hawaii's Polynesian connection offers a further viable root, but for the mainland itself, the indigenous pre-Western ideology derives from the various Amerindian cultures that once flourished before the arrival of the Europeans.

In fact, there are many similarities between the American Indian institutional approaches and the various expressions of voodoo and Santería. Both traditions are protective. The employment of charms, chanting, sacrificial gifts, and ritual performance is in each case a fundamentally defensive endeavor. But it has an active, offensive aspect as well, in that the practitioner may cast a spell on an enemy. The use of voodoo dolls and malevolent gris-gris is well known. The Pomo Indians of California made an image of the intended victim (called a *padok*); treated it with poisons collected from spiders, snakes, bees, and the like; and then performed a mock funeral for the effigy. This "darker" aspect of paganism also must be included if we are to understand this religious option fully. For example, several cursing tablets have been recovered from the thermal springs of Bath, England, which are dedicated to the goddess Sulis Minerva and condemn thieves or other antagonists. Pagans used their deities to secure balance and well-being, and equilibrium might occasionally necessitate rectifying a negative or, at other times, augmenting a positive.

Unlike the Pomo perception, however, the vast range of spirits, or *loa*, recognized by voodoo is not necessarily inimical to human individuals. Whereas in the voodoo ceremony, *loa* possession is passionately sought and occurs at random among one of the participants, in Indian ceremonial dances the gods are impersonated by previously selected cult members using various disguises and augmented by a large array of distinctive paraphernalia. Both the voodooists' and Amerindians' ceremonies reveal shamanistic roots; the creation of conditions of trance is the principal endeavor; and the objective is the magical concern with initiation, health, and prosperity. After the North American Indians were vanquished by the Europeans, they became primarily interested in spiritualism and communication with the spirits of the deceased. Both voodoo and Amerindian traditions are founded on the premise that spiritual realities exist apart from humanity and that, using the human body as the vehicle for expression of nonhuman spiritual forces, a positive and helpful communion with these basic animistic principles and personalities is possible.

If the indigenous animistic perceptions embodied in the American Indian tradition and in such phenomena as voodoo, Santería, and Polynesian belief can lead to a reawakening of theistic countercult veneration in North America, another potential means is the study of the original ideology embedded in our dominant languages. This applies equally to Europe where aboriginal cultural remnants have survived even less as separately identifiable elements.

The older European culture has incorporated more of the previous traditions into an integrated amalgam, although these are frequently no longer recognized as "extracultural," particularly in southern Europe. Nevertheless, a reexamination of the earliest linguistic level of belief and world outlook by both Americans and Europeans would not only reunite them with many of their Asian colleagues but would also open to them a rich, largely forgotten, and positivistic heritage.

The Indo-European ideology affords the unity and identity that the modern Western individual generally lacks. By revitalizing their indigenous roots, Western men and women might come to terms with their own place in the world and also replace both fear and insecurity with respect for their neighbors. Esteem for others begins with self-respect, which in turn rests on one's radical legacy.

The several theories regarding inceptive Indo-European mythology range from Max Müller's naturism to Georges Dumézil's tripartite concepts reflecting social division.[174] I am more inclined to accept an updated version of the former, although until recently, the latter has been more popular in academia. In any case, I believe that a careful comparative study of Vedic-Hindu, Greek, Roman, Germanic, and Celtic myths and the like reveals a substructure centering on a dual concept of the godhead and surviving in such figures as the Vedic Asvins, the Greek Dioscuri, the Roman Romulus and Remus, and deiform pairings like Indra and Agni, Apollo and Dionysus, and Mars and Quirinus.[175] In essence this duality symbolizes immortal and mortal humanity, the living human and his or her guardian spirit or after-death counterpart. In other words, Indo-European ideology is a humanism that transcends the immediate confines of life on earth.

Closely associated with the divine twins is a female figure giving rise to what is termed in modern parlance the *dioscuric triad*.[176] The dioscuric female generally approximates the goddess of the dawn, but continuing the neolithic heritage, the female archetype among the Indo-European daughter cultures is often understood in a triform manner: the Arcadian Hera as widow, wife, and maid; the underworld and/or upperworld manifestations of the *terra mater*; the celestial mistress embodied in the dawn, sun, or

moon; and the goddess of hearth and home. In mythology, the female relates to the dioscuric twins as mother, wife, or sister.

The twin gods and the female triad correspond to an essential Indo-European divine pentad, doubtless an understanding of "totality," that is, the
number five as the count of fingers that complete a hand.[177] It is apparent
that the early Indo-European worshiped the earth, heaven, sun, moon, and
dawn that, on one hand, included the divine twins but, on the other, were
augmented by them. The heptatheon, comprising the pentadic protopan-
theon plus the divine twins as something simultaneously *ex totum*, constitutes the central dynamic of original Indo-European religious perception
as it can now be reconstructed.[178]

In fact, perceiving the archetypal godhead in polytheistic terms, Indo-
Europeans were able to develop an extensive pantheon of gods that answered their various and growing needs for veneration. The greater number of deities may be understood as formations of the seven basic prototypes, regardless of their eventual emergence into such independent
figures as Shiva, Vishnu, Artemis, and Heracles. The personification of the
divine essence in all these theomorphisms is the Vedic Dyaus *pitar*, the
Greek Zeus *pater*, the Roman Jupiter, the Illyrian Deipatyros, and the Germanic Tîwaz (*vater*).[179]

In creedless, flexible paganism, the individual and community formu-
late their own pantheons, their particular understanding of divine manifestation that merits attention and honor. The eclecticism and all-inclu-
siveness of imperial Roman veneration belongs to the countercult tradition. The proto-Indo-European pagans, with their concept of gods and
antigods, *devas* and *asuras*, did not at first necessarily worship Chaos, the
dragon Vritra, and the like but may have eventually done so in much the
same manner as the California Indians who deemed it advantageous if not
mandatory to propitiate the inherently negative forces of nature.[180]

The unanswered question about the worship of the positivistic gods as
allies or the negative entities as potential bringers of woe or both remains
a part of the Indo-European legacy. The freedom and selection are left to
the individual and local level, and a favorite may be chosen from among a
recognized group, just as Catholics and communities today may have a patron saint. Unlike the ecclesiastical councils that attempted to dogmatize a
trinitarian pantheon for one and all, the number and particularity of
deities in the pagan and countercult traditions of popular veneration remain open and not predetermined.

There are likewise perhaps as many forms of worship in the Indian and European daughter traditions and their cousins as there are deities. Many have been lost through the ravages of time and authoritarian opposition. But many may be reconstructed through the comparison of both surviving literary records and living forms still operating amid the countercult practices of the world at large.

The West's fundamental devotional practices are those of the Romans. The Christian Church alone has incorporated a host of terms and institutions from the earlier pagan cult, including *religio, pietas, sanctus, sacramentum, ritus*, and *pontifex*. Therefore, to regain a sense of original forms of veneration for the early Western and Indo-European prototype, ancient Rome allows a viable approach. To the Romans, the key places of special and immediate significance were the house, spring, boundary, and tomb. These were also the portals to the otherworld, supplemented in time by the shrines and temples. The house, however, was the primary center whose heart was the hearth (*focus*), the locus of Vesta and the main economic and religious concerns. Nearby would have been the *penus*, or household receptacle for food storage, presided over by the two *di penates*. These three deities protected the material well-being of every home and were most likely the descendants or reinterpretations of the Indo-European dioscuric triad.[181] In fact, in later Roman times, the Penates were frequently represented by images of the Greek Dioscuri.

The formalized household shrine was called the *lararium*. Besides offering a portion of the *mola salsa*, or salt cake, from a special plate (the *patella*) during the midday meal to the hearth fire of Vesta, most families worshiped in front of the *lararium*, which may have included icons of the protecting *genius* of the *paterfamilias* and the *lar familiaris*, possibly a deified spirit or *genius* of an ancestor for whom bits of food that had fallen on the floor were burned. Especially in later times, the domestic chapel might include one or more statues of gods as specially selected patrons. The most popular were Jupiter, Mercury, Hercules, Fortuna, Mars, Silvanus, Aesculapius, Apollo, Liber, Diana, Venus, Mithras-Sol, Isis-Serapis, and Cybele.

In front of the *lararium* as well as in front of the worshiped image in the temple or shrine, the basic rite performed by the individual was the "kiss of adoration." Unlike the Greeks who paid homage to their deities with head uncovered, the Romans usually covered themselves as a means of increasing their concentration and lessening their distraction. With the thumb and middle finger of their right hand touching to form a circle, they held this hand against their lips and rotated themselves in clockwise fashion in front of the venerated idol.[182]

The Roman *focus* has been superseded by the modern kitchen range, no longer used as the primary source of heat but still the center of food preparation, and the television, replacing the fireplace as the evening's point of visual concentration or entertainment. Gone, however, is the conscious attitude of worship that was once considered integral to the *focus*. In other words, gone is the focus.

In our day, and not always necessarily negatively, we have abandoned many traditions of the past. For example, we regard marriage less and less as an institution in which one person belongs exclusively to the other, especially the female to the male. That is, marriage is becoming thought of as a voluntary and nonbinding partnership. It now incorporates the notion of freedom based on mutual respect. This in itself amounts to a major and, for some, a progressive social innovation.

At the same time, modern advancement need not be contingent on sacrificing a focus on the gods or providence. In fact, as even a casual perusal of customs around the world reveals, the establishment and use of shrines to domestic and nature spirits are natural, and their avoidance, by contrast, is artificial and hence unhealthy. Veneration may survive in the arts, but the arts in themselves do not meet all the needs of veneration. In India, where the number of films produced annually and movie theater attendance far exceed the greatest wishes of any Hollywood mogul, traditional veneration is not renounced in the process but flourishes simultaneously. There is no reason we in the West could not have the same.

# 3

# Paganism as Theology

In the development of a more complete and accurate understanding of what constitutes paganism, along with understanding paganism as religion and understanding paganism as cultic behavior, we must also understand paganism as a theological ideal type. But because of its peculiar nature when compared with other world religions, what is most appropriate to paganism is poly- and ad hoc definitions. A broad definition of paganism might see it as "an affirmation of interactive and polymorphic sacred relationship by the individual or community with the tangible, sentient and/or nonempirical." This explanation was offered on the Nature Religions list as part of the process distinguishing paganism and nature religion and the question of whether one includes the other. The definition allows not only humanism and naturism/naturalism (the worship of nature) but also traditional (poly-)theisms. Consequently, in this understanding of paganism, the two-way relationship that any person or community has with the physical world, with other humans or conscious beings, and/or with the supernatural, preternatural, or magical dimensions of reality is to be conceived of as a sacred, holy, or holistic relationship if it is a pagan one. At the same time, there is no single form to which this relationship must conform. Instead, many different forms are possible.

One critique of this suggested definition is that most religions would conform to it, because of the conjunction/disjunction *and/or* that was chosen to allow for the preference by some for a nonsupernatural nature religion as well as, for others, various transcendental gnosticisms. But at the same time, the definition also allows adherence to the old-school paganisms: for example, Greco-Roman classicism, Confucianism, Shinto, and Santería.

On the one hand, what distinguishes paganism from most other major and minor world religions is its extreme polymorphism. No canon or authority speaks exclusively for paganism. While there may be some strictly defined forms of paganism within the pagan category as a whole, its overall diffusion and variety exceed that found in Christianity, Buddhism, and even Hinduism. Aldous Huxley stated that "Christianity, like Hinduism or Buddhism, is not one religion, but several religions, adapted to the needs of different types of human beings,"[1] which is all the more true for paganism. The reason is that a pagan identity is locally determined, by both individuals and communities. Paganism has neither a central administration nor an ecclesiastical council. But paganism is polymorphic not only in its determination but also in how it perceives the divine. The sacred or spiritual itself can assume many different forms. This multiformity of the divine might be omniform or pantheistic, or it might simply be multiplex and polytheistic. At the same time, from a pagan perspective, the heterogeneity of divine reality may also be understood as subsumed within or as some kind of monistic unity. But even here, this is not necessary for a perspective to be pagan. In sum, paganism represents a celebration of variety that challenges the very limits of human conception and imagination.

Conversely, paganism suggests an interactive relationship among the different poles of reality: in one sense, the world, humanity, and the supernatural. Paganism takes neither the submissive attitude toward the godhead characterized by Islam nor the appropriative one toward nature as condoned by Genesis. Nor is its godhead so removed as is that of the Deist, neo-orthodox Christian, or Vedantist that it is unaffected by human behavior. The dynamic of paganism is such that instead, the world or nature is altered by humanity and the gods as much as they are by both it and one another. In paganism, the essential realms of reality, however conceived, are essentially codependent.

This interaction among divine realities furthermore precludes the theological notion of a sacrosanct One that emanates the Many but remains unperturbed, undisturbed, and untouched by the issuing plethora. This last is the theological understanding of gnosticism, a perception that sees divine reality as purely transcendent and matter as evil, something from which to escape.[2] The path of gnosticism is one of knowledge (*gnosis*) in which the individual apprehends "the true reality," detaches himself or herself therefore from the physical, and returns to the Source: whether Plotinus's One, Plato's Good or Idea, Shankaracharya's Brahman, or Buddha's Void. Gnosticism's *gnosis* is a particular kind of knowledge, understanding, or wisdom; it is definitely not the pagan cognition that tries to deconstruct dichotomous thought.

If paganism is a theological ideal type, gnosticism constitutes another. In fact, the basic divide between *all* religions may be seen to rest on pagan-gnostic distinctions. That is, virtually all religions may be divided between paganism and gnosticism or, at best, be seen as a blend of the two.[3] Following Albanese's distinction between those religions that see nature as real and those that understand nature as illusion, as an ideal category,[4] paganism posits the world or matter as real and valuable, while gnosticism sees the same as something to be penetrated, as something fictive or worthless or even evil.

The irony is that although paganism and gnosticism are, in essence, diametrically opposed ideal types, they are not enemies in their historic nominal manifestations. By their both being condemned by the church councils of rising Christianity, paganism and gnosticism have become natural allies. Moreover, albeit in different ways, both stress the need for learning and often textual study. This fundamental alliance between the two is reflected today in the affinity with, and even confusion between, the more gnostic-oriented New Age movement, on the one hand, and the Wiccan/Neopagan/Goddess Spirituality complex, on the other.[5] In their purer forms approximating the status of ideal types, both paganism and gnosticism have been and still are regarded by traditional Christianity as heresies or aberrations.

Ideal types, of course, do not exist. They are ideals often used by social scientists to measure a particular and related configuration. They become, and are used as, standards by which to study divergence as it appears in concrete instances. Consequently, as ideal types or generic categories, paganism and gnosticism are polar distinctions against which to measure and classify the world's actual religions.

Gnostic by category, as distinct from historic or nominal manifestation, would be official Hinduism with its Vedantic or Brahmanic theologies. Though often identified as monistic, speculative Hinduism entertains a dualism between *brahman* and *maya*, between the absolute and illusion, between true reality and phenomenal experience. Its metaphysics may be different, as are its mythological corpus and religious texts, but it parallels in pragmatic outcome the Manichaean teachings of Manes, which stress the release of spirit from matter through asceticism.[6] Manichaeanism is, in turn, a forerunner of Catharism, a group of Christian sects in the Middle Ages that, again, emphasized dualistic theology and ascetic practice.[7]

Manichaean and Catharistic *gnosis* is in itself closer to the wisdom tradition of Buddhism. As a more or less "Protestant" reform movement of Hinduism, Buddhism follows a closely similar stance, if not the same metaphysics. Theravada, for instance, regards the physical world as real and not *maya*, but its quest for release from rebirth is substantially the same. Its attitude toward matter is essentially the same as the Manichaean and Catharist. But in other respects, Theravada is more like atheistic materialism. Although it acknowledges the existence of the gods, it places no value in them. In this sense, it conforms also to Epicureanism,[8] but whereas this last is still pagan, Theravada, in its endeavor and goal, is gnostic. And while Mahayana Buddhism can seem so different in its ritual practice, its idealistic metaphysics, and its pantheon of deities, it still aims for the same nirvana, even if this is postponed until after the achievement of collective bodhisattvahood.

The categorization of gnostic and pagan religions is complicated by the inclusion of Pythagoreanism, Platonism, Neoplatonism, Cabalism, and even Theosophy as pagan religions. In the theological classification that I am suggesting, all of these are gnostic. They each postulate an ultimate source that at the same time becomes the ultimate goal. They identify an actual omega point and then identify it with the alpha point. Evolution or progress is not open-ended but is instead circular and returns to where it began. While this spiritual perspective frequently entertains the notion of reincarnation, the cycle of birth-death-rebirth is invariably something from which to escape, something from which to be released. Rebirth is not a product of a cosmic joie de vivre but a cause of Weltschmerz.

In this light, we must also distinguish between nominal and generic paganisms. In other words, we must learn to distinguish between those spiritualities that are pagan in name only or at least largely and those that are pagan in kind or actuality. A careful deconstruction allows us to elucidate the agendas and goals of any theological orientation and where it situates terrestrial existence in the overall cosmic picture. In some cases, such as Platonism, Orphism, or Theosophy, it becomes readily clear that although nominally pagan, these religions are transcendentally gnostic. Consequently, while polytheism is a common corollary to paganism, as a feature it is neither necessary nor sufficient. The presence of pantheonic conceptions of godhead in Apuleius' Isian Mysteries, in the Mysteries of Mithras, or in those of the Magna Mater does not preclude these faiths from conforming to a gnostic orientation. Likewise, despite its polytheism and the corporeal nature of its "Heavenly Father," the Church of Jesus Christ of Latter-day Saints is not pagan. The monistic biases of Stoicism and Epicureanism, the bitheism of Gardnerian and Alexandrian Wicca, and the monism if not monotheism of Dianic Wicca, however, do not invalidate the consideration of these as pagan religions.

The categories of gnosticism and paganism become more complex in regard to the Abrahamic religions or Zoroastrianism. Mazdaism, surviving today among the Parsis of India and the Irani Zoroastrians, is the remnant of a once flourishing religion reputedly founded by Zarathustra in Persia during the sixth century B.C.E.[9] Despite its polytheism and its cosmic dichotomy, as opposed to a spiritual-terrestrial dualism, it is not its puritanical ethics that render Zoroastrianism nonpagan—for we find similar notions of ritual pollution in Shinto—but its theological inversion. In Zarathustra's reform of Persia's ancient paganism, the gods, or *devas/daevas*, are transformed into devils, whereas the antigods, or *asuras/ahuras*, become exalted into the sacrosanct foci of worship.[10] Although in a strict sense, Zoroastrianism may not be classified as gnosticism, from the aboriginal Indo-European perspective from which it is derived, it represents a "pagan perversion." But if paganism is distorted enough, it ceases to be pagan and can be considered instead as a gnostic variant.

Judaism, Christianity, and Islam also are difficult to situate accurately between the gnostic-pagan theological divide. In some senses, each is a hybrid of the two ideal types. The ambivalence stems from the position of the created world. The physical is seen as a gift from God (Yahweh/Allah) and, as such, something to be cherished, not rejected.[11] The biblical injunction to subdue and dominate the world, however, does not make this a nonpagan position in itself. But inasmuch as all three religions radically oppose polytheism or any nonscriptural henotheism, they become antipagan. Their transcendental godhead, despite the physical nature of early Israelite religion or the semimaterial inference of Allah, is essentially a gnostic conception. In fact, fully deconstructing the Abrahamic theological position leads to an unquestionable gnostic understanding of its godhead, regardless of its personal or personified nature. Upon careful analysis, Christianity's distancing from and rejection of gnosticism may be seen as less a function of theological distinction as it is of political manipulation and an effort to secure an enduring power base. In short, Christianity's antignostic stance is political rather than theological.

Consequently, in understanding paganism, we must comprehend it not only as a religion and a behavior but also as a theology or theological category. The definition of paganism with which we began was designed to appeal to adherents of both nominal and generic paganism. But if we were to describe paganism in its full religious, behavioral, and theological senses, we would have to exclude nominal paganism. In other words, we would have to drop the *and/or* conjunction/disjunction from the definition so that it would read as follows: "Paganism is an affirmation of interactive and poly-morphic sacred relationship by individual or community with the tangible, sentient, and nonempirical." In this rewording, paganism is understood as endorsing the relationship between physical and supernatural realities as well as human (and possibly other forms of) consciousness. It may accept the supernatural as approachable only through metaphor (religious icons and symbols), or it may also accept that the supernatural appears and is accessible through the miraculous. But along with its supernaturalism or proclivity for the nonempirical, paganism's humanism and naturism/naturalism are equally weighted. In other words, even if paganism or particular pagan identities elevate the special or the numinously distinguishable over the whole, or the theistic or even polytheistic over the pantheistic, the divine or sacred will be found everywhere. Paganism, therefore, allows the divine to be manifested in and as the material, whatever else it may be. But paganism eschews any true hierarchy between the temporal and permanent, between the physical and spiritual, or between this-world and the otherworld. In paganism, all realms of being and possibly nonbeing partake in a dynamic partnership or colloquium of potential equals.

Along with the common misunderstandings of paganism as either devil worship or godless atheism, the possibility also exists that it is a religion with a particular theological understanding. There is, however, a disturbing further association with this spiritual option that cannot be dismissed out of hand but must be addressed and included in any consideration of the pagan orientation. If what I have described may be considered the essential nature of paganism, it is neither the atheism nor Satanism that it has been historically construed to be. Nevertheless, at several points in its trajectory, paganism has intersected with political exaltation of nation and race, resulting in the situation today in which, for many, paganism goes hand in hand with fascism. Fascism, being unquestionably convinced of its own correctness, strives for centralized autocracy, social and economic regimentation, and, in its worst excesses, the inhumane repression if not the elimination of opposition and difference. In its essentials, fascism may be understood as a particular kind of fundamentalism. And like any religion, paganism, too, can assume a fundamentalist orientation.

Peter Berger identifies fundamentalism as "any all-embracing system of belief held with rigid certitude and coupled with the moral assurance of one's right to impose it on everyone else."[12] For Caputo, fundamentalism is a form of confusion, a confusion between self-opinion and divine provenance.[13] But as Berger recognizes, whatever its theological position, fundamentalism is always the enemy of religious liberty, especially, as Barrett notes, when fundamentalists "of any religion gain political power, religious freedom disappears."[14]

At certain times, fascistic paganism or pagan fascism has become a reality. For example, the German Völkstumsbewegung promoted "Aryan" notions of eugenics and racial purity. It also spoke in terms of the "pagan" gods of the fatherland and the Teutonic peoples. Some of these ideas and practices survive, to be sure, in the contemporary Odinist and Asatru movements. But even these emphases remain largely minor and nonrepresentational in the full scope of the current Western pagan movement across North America, northern Europe, and Oceania. In fact, the contemporary pagan scene is generally center-left rather than right-wing conservative.

Paganism has endured a long association of being linked with fascist tendencies. None of these can be dismissed out of hand, and in certain instances, allegations of pagan right-wing behavior are true. Ken Wilber, for instance, lambastes the ancient pagan empires as dictatorial slave machines.[15] Closer to our times, paganism with its local bias shades indistinguishably into nationalism. *Völkish* ideas emerged at the end of the nineteenth century upon a foundation established by the Grimm brothers' monumental study, *Teutonic Mythology*, and by Richard Wagner's operas. The German nationalistic spirit was particularly influenced by the works of Guido von List and Jörg Lanz von Liebenfels, writers who developed the notion of Aryosophisme, or "Aryan wisdom." The popular Völkstumsbewegung, or "folk movement," embraced ideas that glorified both the fatherland and Pan-German tribalism. Racism and anti-Semitism were consequences of this Germanic folk movement and, in particular, its spiritual form designated by List as Armanism.[16]

In some instances, contemporary Odinist and Asatru movements have proclaimed an adamant belief in maintaining the tribal purity of the northern folk while denouncing mixed marriage and creolization.[17] But while typical of some groups, such fascist doctrines are rejected by others in the northern or heathen tradition let alone in contemporary Western paganism as a whole. Although more idiosyncratic than representational, these right-wing pagan groups remain natural chauvinist developments of paganism's preference for local manifestation, especially when tribal identity is perceived as racial and traditional or even pretraditional ways seem to be threatened.

Nevertheless, it is important to realize that fascist conservatism and tribal eugenics may become natural outgrowths of any religious orientation. The normally tolerant religion of Hinduism, for instance, has given birth in recent years to the extremist movements of the Vishna Hindu Parishad and the Bharatiya Janata Parishad. The collusion of the Roman Catholic Church with the fascist dictator Benito Mussolini and anticommunist factions in Eastern Europe also reveal conservative leanings toward the extreme right. The backing of Slobodan Milosevic by the Serbian Orthodox Church, the emergence of the Identity Movement and the Anti-Cult Movement from Christian fundamentalism, the Taliban in Afghanistan, and the Lakota protests in the United States all may be seen as illustrations of militant proclivity capable of any religion under conducive circumstances.

It is also important to realize that the German Völkstumsbewegung owed more to theosophical ideas than to indigenous pagan atavisms. Besides its roots in theosophy, Armanism is also largely shaped by Germany's Christian heritage. A close deconstruction and analysis, in fact, indicates little if any indigenous Germanic spirituality or any nonperverted traditional paganism. The extreme fascism in many of the ideas and writings of the theosophical spin-off, Alice Bailey, suggests ultimately that the inflexible and intolerant mind-set is at least as much, if not more, a product of gnostic than pagan thought. In either case, however, whether pagan or gnostic, the underlying notion of archetypes and inherited yet unconscious influences on human behavior can be attributed to cultural and linguistic resonance rather than hereditary genes and biological determination. Summarizing the contemporary and universal pagan consensus, the orator Isocrates, speaking of Athens, expressed the noneugenic propensity of pagan evolution when he proclaimed in his *Panegyricus*:

And so much did our city bequeath to the other peoples on matters of reason and speech that her disciples did in turn enlighten others, and the name of the Hellenes is now considered pertinent not to race but rather to spirit, to the point of calling Hellenes those partaking of our education rather than sharing our origin.

This emancipation from parochial and restricting ways of thinking and feeling is the full consequence of the pagan theological position that sacralizes the world, the cosmos, humanity itself, and the nonempirical reaches of the imagination.

*

In my own ongoing study of religion as religion, I increasingly find that besides whatever other purposes it can be applied to—social integration, validation of social hierarchy, political influence—from a psychological perspective, religion provides a gateway of emancipation from what can be perceived as empirical imprisonment. Religions open us to something beyond the here and the now, to something beyond what we can know only through our senses, and this remains the case even when a chief preoccupation of the religious mind-set is to become fully conscious of the here and the now. Religion takes us beyond the merely mechanical world of cause and effect; in a word, religion delineates purpose.

To understand paganism as a religion with a genuine theological base is part of a broader recognition that religions per se are about seeing and doing. Any religion gives us an operational framework through which we can interpret the world in ways that allow us to see and behave in a particular manner. A religion offers a hermeneutical structure that shapes how we see things and what we do as a result. In most cases, though not all, it is also "an attempt by human beings to symbolize the meta-human, the *other*."[18]

The panorama of the world's different major, minor, old, and new religions is a kaleidoscope of various worldviews that give their adherents a raison d'être. Through any study of the rich fabric comprising religions, we are constantly confronted with different perspectives, different ways of assessing significance, and different goals and objectives. If our world is becoming more homogenized through globalization and whatever other factors that reduce us to a logic of the same,[19] the transnational communication systems of our electronic age are at the same time allowing us to become more aware of difference. Our world as a whole is, in fact, becoming more cosmopolitan in which its pluralism is increasingly affirmed as a celebration of cultural and religious difference. Nevertheless, the amount of innovation and divergence from established norms and hegemonic models that we can tolerate is limited, at least as a regional and more local concern. Germany currently resists Scientology in a way since superseded in the United States, Canada, the United Kingdom, and Australia. The Assemblée nationale of France has enacted its comprehensive Rapport parlementaire sur les sectes et religions nouveaux in which, essentially, any religious nonconformity is automatically suspect and subject to state-sponsored harassment, even liquidation. And in the American state of Texas, the notorious siege of the Branch Davidians in Waco made us all the more aware of the consequences of nonconformity in a context of biased and limited understanding.[20]

To understand the full range of religion, it is helpful to know that most of the world's population subscribes to one of four broad religious positions, namely, the Abrahamic, dharmic, secular, and pagan.[21] Paganism, like the Abrahamic religions, is essentially or at least originally tribal in outlook. But at the same time, like both the secular and dharmic—especially the Buddhist—orientations, paganism encompasses the greater human collective in a nonintimidating and noncoercive manner.

Regarding "tribalism," nothing is inherently detrimental to its focus as long as it is able to be contextualized in the pancollective. But if any religious perspective cannot so situate itself, it must seriously question its fundamentals. In an increasingly shrinking and globalizing world, all peoples need to learn to live together as part of a freely associative and cooperative venture. In Corrington's words, this world could be described as a "postpatriarchal age . . . of natural justice and organic renewal."[22] The freedom of religion—of all religions—is a foundation for humans to work and live together constructively. For, as Berger eloquently stated, "the hidden purpose of religious liberty is to protect the possibility of laughter in this world."[23] We do not have to like or agree with the ways that others do what they do, but we have to find a modus vivendi in which we at least give the others their space.

Atheists, for example, have a right to deny the supernatural, but they have not yet been able to prove that the supernatural does *not* exist, and followers of the other traditions have not yet been able to demonstrate that it does exist. Atheism too, then, is a faith position. No less than any other, it must be accorded the freedom to operate as long as it does not restrict, unfairly intimidate, persecute, and/or violate those observing a different framework. The atheistic framework simply does not include the supernatural. We all oppose tyrannical systems—bureaucracies, colleges, cliques, cabals, and the like—that seek to impose their view on others. In this, paganism joins the other religions in affirming that people can be educated and acculturated into a particular hermeneutical framework, but all frameworks must be accepted only by invitation and not by coercion. Except for its perpetual and ongoing violations, our world stands on the brink of finding solutions to its environmental, economic, and political problems in ways that surpass the antiquated tribalisms that allow the excesses of anticollective behavior such as we witness in Israel and Palestine, Northern Ireland, Sri Lanka, and the Balkans.

As British Gardnerian Zachary Cox put it, pagans join all Christians, Muslims, Buddhists, Hindus, and others who as "People of Goodwill' are opposed to both "Fascists and Fundamentalists [who] have no contribution to make to a multiracial, multicultural plenum."[24] In this world colloquium, the pagan position emerges more clearly and identifiably. As Corrington explained it, "Within the vast sweep of nature's sacred folds, nature's intervals, nature's unruly ground, and nature's spirit, all gods and goddesses, however long-lived or powerful, are always enveloped in the end by the mystery of nature's abyss."[25] Call this abyss what we will and whether or not we conform to the "Feuerbachian notion of religion as a human projection," there is "no longer any excuse for theological ethnocentrism."[26]

Although I still believe that paganism is a religion in the sense that I have outlined, my current feeling is that it is less a religion as such than an internal dialogue among and within different but related religious frameworks, one that affirms organic roots in the distant past but is equally commensurate with the vanguard of contemporary growth, change, and discovery. Its very flexibility and ability to adjust make it as much at home in a nature largely untouched by human civilization or in the rural community as it is in an urban cosmopolitan metropolis, the unfolding parameters of cyberspace, or the expanding zones of cosmic imagination. Paganism is largely a dialogue of affirmation that reflects or develops from the rhythms and cycles of the natural world. It does not seek to escape or obliterate the great round of nature but to work within it and to celebrate it.

If there is a single concept or practice that encapsulates the essential orientation and identity of paganism, it is celebration. If the basic notion of Eastern spirituality is release and that of Christianity is preparation or salvation, pagan celebration is a festive rejoicing that also embraces service because service is likewise an affirmation of humanity, the world, and divinity. Paganism views humankind, nature, and whatever the supernatural may or may not be as essentially divine. It is this perception of the divine ubiquity or perpetual possibility that links the various individual expressions of pagan religiosities. In place of the increasingly obsolete but still entrenched position that doubts and rejects paganism as a religion, I argue that paganism is a "root religion." We could even call it "spiritual radicalism." Historically, all other religions are offshoots and/or counterdevelopments of the root religion. And I even argue that if we wish to understand any religion, we must also understand paganism as the root from which the tree of all religions grows. At the same time, this religion of the root or radix, this spiritual radicalism, represents in today's society and historical development a radical challenge to understand spirituality in both its primordial and most innovative dimensions.

Inasmuch as paganism is the root of religion, it confronts the earliest, the most immediate, and the least processed apprehensions of the sacred. This is the experiential level on which paganism in both its indigenous and contemporary forms wishes to concentrate. But while the very notion of the sacred raises theological and philosophical questions, it also presupposes the ethical. In fact, for pagans, the ethical heart of the sacral is what can best be termed *honor, trust,* and *friendship*. While all religions may share these goals, the concepts themselves date back to the earliest stages of human encounter, to the time when everyone was pagan. Whatever else these may be, honor, trust and friendship are pagan virtues, and they allow us to recognize that by virtue of its focus on the sacred, paganism is, by default, an ethical religiosity. The many varied routes of individual paganisms allow adherents different accesses to the experience of the sacred, and as the original custodians of ethical consciousness, paganism today as both a theological option and a religious practice is a spirituality prepared to engage with not only mother earth but also all her children, regardless of the differing and even opposing spiritual predilections that they may have. In the long run, pagans would wish to engage with the whole of cosmic nature and all forms of sentience, but the sacred planet and its "earthlings" who comprise the human community are now the task at hand. It becomes increasingly clear that the lack of ethical behavior in our world today stems from some fundamental rupture between us and a direct, noninstitutionalized, and unmediated encounter with the divine. It is my deepest hope that by re-recognizing a pagan understanding of our origins and the dynamics of culture, cultivation, and worship and by returning to a connection with our roots and origins, we might begin to reestablish a sacred immediacy as the foundation for an equitable, universal, and humane global society, one with its feet on the ground and its head challengingly but no less compassionately in the heavens.

# Notes

NOTES TO THE PREFACE

1. Peter Wood, "Strange Gods: Neo-Paganism on Campus," *National Review* online, 5 September 2001, http: www.nationalreview.com/comment/comment-wood090501.shtml.

2. Wood, "Strange Gods."

NOTES TO THE INTRODUCTION

1. Chuvin 1990:8ff. See also Jones and Pennick 1995:1.

NOTES TO CHAPTER 1

1. Barrett 1982:848. The following distribution has been tabulated from the figures given by the world's regions, adding together "members" of the same traditions across the various regions and computing respective percentages against the world population as a whole. In the *World Christian Encyclopedia*, Barrett breaks down the major religions of the world under the heading "World Religions," each of which in 1980 had more than 2 percent of the world's population: Christianity, 32.6%; Islam, 16.5%; Hinduism, 13.3%; Buddhism, 6.3%; Chinese folk religion, 4.5%; and Asiatic new religions 2.2%. The encyclopedia includes as worldwide quasi religions both agnosticism (16.4%) and atheism (4.5%). It excludes primal and tribal religions (2.4%), since these are local and not universal expressions.

2. This is a term used by Paul Tillich in his *Christianity and the Encounter of the World's Religions* (1963) to describe the secular systems that have arisen from the Judeo-Christian tradition and are antagonistic to it as well as other religions in general. See Barrett 1982:836, 840.

3. Barrett 1982:829.

4. Barrett 1982:72.

5. Barrett 1982:72.

6. Barrett 1982:846.

7. Barrett 1982:72.

8. Barrett draws his understanding of Afro-American spiritism from Simpson

(1978). He estimates the number of global adherents as 1,777,100 in 1970; 3,100,400 (in 21 countries) in 1980; and 3,810,300 in 1985.

9. Separate categories that Barrett (1982:71ff) includes under Roman Catholic Christians and not included in my compilations for pagans are Spiritist Catholics (Roman Catholics involved in organized spiritism, high or low, and including syncretized spirit possession cults) and Christo-pagans (Latin American Amerindian Roman Catholics who have syncretized folk Catholicism with organized traditional American Indian religion). Barrett (1982:820) lists the number of Christo-pagans as 12,919,700 in 1970; 15,698,900 in 1980 (in 16 countries); and 17,131,400 in 1985.

10. Chuvin 1990:7–9; Fox 1987:30ff; Hutton 1999:4.

11. Chuvin 1990:10.

12. Fung [1948] 1960. In his foundational six-volume study of Chinese religion, de Groot (1892–1910) emphasizes the animist religion of the people rather than the three religions of Buddhism, Taoism, and Confucianism. Bloomfield (1983:36) refers to "the mélange of animism, Tao-Buddhist scraps and patches, folk-myth and magic and long centuries of supernatural practices that is now the religion of the Chinese."

Figures for the numbers of Chinese folk religionists are difficult to ascertain. After the establishment of the People's Republic of China in 1949, public worship was discouraged, and the vernacular faith was no longer considered a religion. "It is clear that many aspects of popular or diffused religion in China, such as reverence for ancestors, family and even communal festivals, and belief in local deities and spirits continue to survive, albeit in restricted forms in the rural areas of mainland China" (Hinnells 1984:83). While Barrett's (1982) figures include Taiwan and Hong Kong and also indicate a decrease from 1980 to 2000, Chinese folk religionists range between 130 million and 215 million people.

13. Some key works on classical Chinese religion are Adler 2002; Baity 1975; Day 1940; Eberhard 1967; de Groot [1892–1910] 1964; Jochim 1986; Maspero 1978; Smith 1971; Thompson 1979; Wolf 1974; and Yang 1967. For an overview of Taoism both past and present, see Kohn 2001. Also Blofeld 1978; Liu 1979; Welch 1965; and Welch and Seidel 1977.

14. Recognizing the prime significance of local deities for the villagers or people at large, Bloomfield (1983:40) finds that these "include spirits which inhabited any natural feature of the land which people felt to have a special possessing spirit, such as unusually shaped rocks and boulders or very ancient trees, as well as fields, streams and roads." See further Werner 1922/1984.

15. Michael Saso in Hinnells 1984:349–55.

16. There are many reference materials on Chinese geomancy (feng-shui "wind-water'). For a representational overview, suggested works include Birdsall 1997; Morris 1985; Skinner 1989; and Walters 1995. See further Feuchtwang 1974 and Wu 1964.

17. Bloomfield 1983:65.
18. Young 1995:182.
19. E.g., Bloomfield 1983:41ff.
20. Chamberlain 1987:23ff.
21. Chamberlain 1987:37.
22. Somme 1997.
23. *She,* "powers of the land," and *ji* "powers of the growing crops."
24. Chamberlain 1987:25.
25. Apart from the *ch'i* inherent in nature, there is the *shen* residing in the in-dividual and in other aspects of nature. The *shen* of the individual is the male soul after death; during one's lifetime, this is known as the *hun,* or "cloud soul." The fe-male or *yin* soul is the *p'o* (the material soul) which after death becomes the *kuei,* or "ghost." There appears to be an intimate relationship between *shen/hun* and the vital energy (*ch'i*) and refined essence (*ching*) of the individual. Daniel Overmyer (Crim 1981:167) describes the *kuei,* which "are everywhere, in houses, along roads, in fields, mountains, and forests. Some, particularly spirits of the dead, may be based in purgatory, from which they emerge occasionally to seek redress." Bloomfield (1983:42, cf. 151ff) refers to the two components of the human soul: "the *hun,* or higher soul, and the *bor,* or lower soul. The spiritual elements under-lying both *hun* and *bor* are known as *shen* and *gwei*." These last are also recognized as ghosts or demons that cause problems to humans.
26. Chamberlain (1987:41), however, considers that "all spirits of the dead eventually revert to the status of *Kuei* in the afterlife (with the exception of the founder of the family)." Nobles were worshiped as *shen* for two generations and thereafter were venerated, like the spirits of common folk, as *kuei.*
27. For an excellent presentation of Chinese deities, see Stevens 1997. The most popular include Shang Ti, Huang Ti (the Yellow Emperor), Yu Huang (the Jade Emperor), Kuan Ti (embodiment of integrity and loyalty), Pak Tai (overlord of the Yellow Springs of the dead), Tin Hau (queen of Heaven), Hsi Wang Mu (queen of Western Heaven), Tsai Shen (god of wealth), K'uei Hsing (god of litera-ture), Lu Pan (patron of builders), Lei Kung (god of thunder), Tien Mu (goddess of lightning), and Kuan Yin, Na Cha.
28. Somme 1997.
29. The common titles granted to deities in their trajectories of apotheosis (deification) and promotion are "*Shen* (spirit), *Hsien* (fairy, immortal), *Sheng* (sage, holy one), *Kung* (lord), *Kuan* (ruler), *Hsing* (star), and *Ti* (emperor)" (Chamberlain 1987:43).
30. Chamberlain 1987:93.
31. The Taoist pantheon is also headed by a triad of various deities, the most common being the Three Pure Ones, that is, the Jade Emperor accompanied by Lao-Tzu and Tao Chun ("the rule of *yin* and *yang*").
32. Crim 1981:167.

33. Somme 1997.

34. On Confucianism in general, see Berthrong and Berthrong 2000. For Confucianism along with Taoism, Buddhism, and popular/folk religion in China and Taiwan, see Adler 2002.

35. Chamberlain 1987:117.

36. Bloomfield 1983:38.

37. Bodhisattvahood is a preliminary state in which the candidate who has qualified to become a Buddha postpones nirvana and chooses instead to work for the salvation of all beings.

38. The soul of the individual that disintegrates with the body is known as the *p'o*. The individual's spirit, or *hun*, lives on as a *shen* or nonmalevolent *kwei*.

39. Bloomfield 1983:58.

40. Bloomfield 1983:75. On religious leadership and specialists, see Overmeyer in Crim 1981:167 and Saso in Hinnells 1984:360.

41. On Chinese forms of divination, see Bloomfield's chapter "Reading Fate: Chinese Methods of Fortune Telling" (1983:119–45). "Fortune-telling," for the Chinese, "is the seeking of guidance from the gods and spirits who, because they are beyond the limits of time and space and matter, know what will come" (121).

42. Hori et al. (1972) present an accessible overview and survey of the varieties of religious traditions coexisting in contemporary Japan: Shinto, Buddhism, Confucianism, Christianity, new religious movements, and folk religion. As in China, because of the diffusion of religion and blending of practice among the different traditions in Japan, it is difficult to ascertain accurate figures for the numbers of Shinto followers. According to Carpenter (1991:321), "Estimates of the number of practicing adherents of Shinto range between 3,400,000 and 35,000,000. Over 90,000,000 Japanese are said to belong to the Shinto 'community' but have no active allegiance to the religion."

43. For a discussion of *shimbutsu shūgō* and the subsequent dissociation of Shinto from Buddhism, see York 1999.

44. Young 1995:210. The Japanese terms for imperial, shrine, sect, and folk worship are, respectively, *kōshitsu, jinja, kyōha,* and *minkan*.

45. Two significant works on Japanese folk religion are Otto 1963 and Hori 1968. See also Hitoshi Miyake, "Rethinking Japanese Folk Religion: A Study of Kumano Shugen," in Kornicki and McMullen 1996:120–34, esp. 120–22. David Reid (Hinnells 1984:371) describes *shugendō* as an endeavor to attain magicoreligious powers through asceticism in the mountains: "A blend of folk Shinto, esoteric Buddhism and *yin-yang* Taoist magic, this tradition traces its origin to the legend-surrounded shaman En-no-Gyoja of the Nara period (710–94)." See also Yusa 2002.

46. Miyake Hitoshi in Hori et al. 1972:124.

47. Harris 2001:17ff.

48. Noteworthy works on Shinto include Aston [1905] 1974; Bunce 1982;

Creemers 1968; Earhart 1983, 1984; Ellwood and Pilgrim 1985; Holtom [1938] 1965; Kitagawa 1987; Muraoka 1964; and Yamamoto 1987. See also Watson 1981.

49. Hori et al. 1972:31ff.

50. Nigosian 1994:237.

51. As David Reid (in Hinnells 1984:379) explains, "In a rough division of labour, the *kami* altar is generally associated with life and with the avoidance of whatever impedes vitality and productivity, the buddha altar with death and the veneration of those who are becoming or have become ancestors. On both, offerings of food and drink are reverently presented at the beginning of each day." On the *kamidana*, see also Lowell [1894] 1990:128.

52. Hori et al. 1972:18.

53. Nelson 1996:238.

54. According to Nelson (1996:265), in Shinto, "*tama* [means] 'soul' or 'spirit,' which has both benevolent and malevolent aspects." See Blacker 1992:43–47, 324, n. 11.

55. Blacker 1992:43.

56. At the same time, "some indication of the inscrutability of the *kami* may be inferred from Motoori's statement, 'I do not yet understand the meaning of the word *kami*'" (Blacker 1992:323, n. 1).

57. Harris 2001:14.

58. "*Kami* can be broadly classified into two categories, (1) 'nature *kami*,' and (2) 'culture *kami*' having a close relationship to human life." (Havens and Inoue 2001:3). The nature *kami*—the supranormal elements in natural objects or phenomena—can be either "celestial" (deified heavenly bodies, meteorological phenomena) or "terrestrial" (deified "geological forms, physical processes, and plants and animals.") Culture *kami* are community (belonging to particular social groups), functional (relating to specific human professions or aspects), and human (apotheosized human beings) (4).

59. The key designations involving the *miya* or Shinto shrine are the *yorishiro*, the demarcating ring of stakes, trees, or rocks; the *shimenawa*, ropes of pleated straw; the *shiki*, the consecrated flat and empty area; and the *iwasaka*, the sacred pile of rocks. For the *iwasaka* and *shimenawa*, see Nelson 1996:256, 264. On the *yorishiro*, see Blacker 1992:38–40; also Harris 2001:224, cf. 15, in which the *yorishiro* is explained as a "prepared place or object, such as a tree, stone or anthropomorphic image, in which the spirit of the *kami* resides and which is venerated as a representation of the *kami*." Harris compares this with the *himorogi* as the place or object serving as a temporary residence for the *kami*.

60. On the development of the *shinden*, see Harris 2001:134ff.

61. The seat of the deity in the main sanctuary is known as the *shinza*. The inner sanctum of the *honden* is the *gonaiden*, which houses the sacred object (*shintai*). In this last dwells the *kami*'s divine spirit, or *shinrei*.

62. Nelson 1996:265. The ritual purification wand, *haraigushi*; the folded

cloth, *yufu*; the phallic elder or willow rod, *kezurikake*; and the baton bearing *shide* or paper strips, *gohei*.

63. Harris 2001:223.

64. Lowell ([1894] 1990:128ff) refers to the *gohei*, wand, and its place in the *tokonoma*, the *kamidana* (gods' shelf), or even the temporary shrine.

65. Harris (2001:23–26) describes the Japanese shrine complex in general as well as the Grand Shrine at Ise and the Izumo shrine in particular.

66. The worship hall, *haiden*; the covered passageway, *ishi no ma*; and the two-story gate, *romon*.

67. Harris 2001:14.

68. Nonhuman spirits, *mi*; august spirits, *goryō*; demons, *mono*; and the quasi-personified calamitous influences, *tatarigami*. For Ueda Kenji (in Hori et al. 1972:41), "another dimension of *kami* belief . . . is the idea that *kami* power has, in addition to its positive side, a negative, destructive aspect. Thus, for example, belief in *kami* that inflict calamities (*tatarigami*) and in vengeful, malevolent spirits (*goryō*) has long occupied an important place in Shinto." Only the *kami* with human characteristics are those toward which shrine worship is directed. "Other divinities, classified as spirits (*mi*) or demons (*mono*) are ranked below the anthropomorphic *kami*" (38).

69. The three cosmogonic deities are Ame-no-Minakanushi, Takami Musubi, and Kami Musubi. Amaterasu's brother Susa-no-o has also been "Buddhasized" as Emperor Gozu. The war-god Hachiman is a composite figure of Ōjin, his wife Himegami, and his mother Jingū.

70. On Japanese phallicism and *dōsojin* worship, see Czaja 1974.

71. Harris 2001:89.

72. As explained to me in a personal communication from Dr. Keishin Inaba, Centre de recherches sur le Japon, École des hautes études en sciences sociales, Paris (January 29, 2002), *sae* (or *sai*) indicates "obstructing" or "keeping out." The designation Sae/Sai-no-kami (*kami* of the border) suggests therefore the function of obstructing or keeping out evil spirits. See also Hori et al. 1972:125.

73. Czaja 1974:29ff; cf. Lowell [1894] 1990:274. Ugadama is the deity enshrined along with Amaterasu at the Ise shrine. Saruta hiko is also known as Oda no Mikoto; Uzume, as Oichi hime. See also Watanabe 1974.

74. Harris 2001:15.

75. Onamochi (Okuni nushi, the "master of the great land") is the son of Susa-no-o.

76. On Inari, see Czaja 1974:257–60, *passim*.

77. Czaja 1974:140. As Inaba explains, *dōsojin* have no connection with institutional religion. Therefore, Shintoists' reaction to *dōsojin* is varied. Some people do not pay much attention to such shrines, but others have a feeling of reverence. "In general, the majority of Japanese treat religious ceremonies at shrines as if they were simply social customs. Thus, some people do not even consider things

like *hatsumode* (the New Year's visits to shrines or temples) to have any religious significance." Nevertheless, many Japanese enjoy participating in *hatsumode* and some of the other observances.

78. *Jichinsai*: "Land-calming and land-claiming rituals held before the construction of buildings" (Nelson 1996:256, also 182–84, 194ff).

79. Hori et al. 1972:123. Mountain *kami: yama no kami*; field *kami: ta no kami*.

80. Cf. Harris 2001:12ff, 30ff, 160ff.

81. The human soul (*tama* or *mitama*) is known as the *seirei* for living people but as the *shirei* for the dead.

82. Malevolent *kami: yakushin*; malevolent spirits: *jashin jarei*.

83. The "rough soul": *ara mitama*; the "gentle soul": *nigi mitama*; the "luck soul": *saki mitama*; and the "wondrous soul": *kushi mitama*.

84. Blacker 1992:45.

85. The invocation, *kami oroshi*; and its counterpart, the ritual farewell, or *kami age*.

86. Festivals in honor of the local *kami* are known as *ujigami matsuri*; shrine commemorations are called *reitaisai*. According to Inaba (personal communication, 2002): "Festive celebrations to *dōsojin* are widely observed throughout Japan on *dondo*, the ritual burning of the New Year's ornaments on 14 and 15 January. The burning of large erect pillars signifies the exorcism of pollutions from within the community via the purifying element of fire, simultaneously drawing into this world new powers of life. The Meiji government's policy of introducing modern Western civilization and enlightenment led to the prohibition of *dōsojin* festivals in some areas due to their status as superstition."

Inaba also observes that "Shinto is closely tied to annual celebrations and ceremonies marking various stages in life such as *hatsumiyamairi* (the presentation of a newborn), *shichigosan* (the visit by three-, five-, and seven-year olds), and *seijinshiki* (coming of age), and as such it has played an important role in binding the community together. Recently, however, the nature of the community itself has been changing, so the social functions of Shinto have weakened" (personal communication 2002). See also Bauer and Carlquist 1980.

87. For introductory works on oral/tribal/indigenous religions in general, consult Campbell 1970; Eliade 1959; Gill 1982; Lewis 1989; Turner 1969; and Van Gennep 1989. For a compilation of classic and recent writings concerned with contemporary indigenous religions, see Harvey 2002.

88. Cunningham 2000 gives an overview of traditional Hawaiian spirituality. See also Grey 1970 on Maori mythology and tradition.

89. Geertz 1993:90.

90. Olupona 1991:26.

91. For classical anthropological studies that touch on aspects of individual ethnicities, see Durkheim [1912] 1976 on the Australian Aborigines; Malinowski 1982 on the Trobriand Islanders; Evans-Pritchard 1937 and 1956, respectively, on

the African Azande and Nuer; Turner 1957 on the Ndembu of Africa; and Tambiah 1985 on the Azande. On the Yamana, see Gusinde 1961; on Muntu, see Jahn 1961; on the Lugbara, see Middleton 1960; on the Dinka, see Lienhardt 1961; on the Gikuyu, see Kenyatta [1938] 1953; on the Yoruba, see Awolalu 1979; and on the Nyakyusa, see Wilson 1959. Carmody and Carmody (1993) present a student-accessible work on the oral traditions of North, Central, and South America; Africa; Australia; and New Zealand. Benjamin Ray (2000:2–22) provides a survey of the various perspectives on African religions. For more contemporary coverage of African traditional religions, see Booth 1977; Davidson 1969; Hackett 1996 and Olupona 1991; Idowu 1973; Mbiti 1969; Olupona 2000; Parrinder 1969; Ranger and Kimambo 1972; Taylor 1963; Thomas 1985; Willis 1974; and Zuesse 1979. Somé (1993) discusses ritual in his native West African village in Burkina Faso. For a comprehensive and pictorial coverage of the deeply rooted spirituality of sub-Saharan Africa, consult Christoph, Müller, and Ritz-Müller 1999. See also Eyo and Willet 1982; Parrinder 1967; and Trowell 1954.

Although I have not had a direct encounter with Aboriginal spirituality, some recommended firsthand accounts include Bell 1990; Bourke, Bourke, and Edwards 1994; Brock 1989; David 2002; Ellis 1994; and Morphy 1991. See also Mudrooroo 1994.

92. For a discussion of the difficulties and problems encountered by Western academics in studying the oral histories and traditions of Native Americans, see Angela Cavender Wilson's "Power of the Spoken Word: Native Oral Traditions in American Indian History," in Fixico 1997:101–16.

93. Cf. Ray 2000:19, 48ff, 55ff.

94. E.g., Ray 2000:103.

95. Cooper in Vecsey 1990:68.

96. On rites of passage, see Ray 2000: 58–70, 118–121.

97. "Witches owe their ability to harm to an innate quality, 'witch power,' which is often passed down in certain families and becomes stronger with increasing age. . . . They act by instinct, sometimes unconsciously, but always in secret, often in association with other witches whom they join on the witches' sabbath for orgiastic dancing." "Unlike sorcerers, witches tend to have no understandable motive for their misdemeanors" (Christoph, Müller, and Müller 1999:499, 138; see also 138–41, 154–65).

98. Ray 2000:102.

99. E.g., Ray 2000:4–12. "There are myths in all parts of Africa which mention that death was not originally in the world. Humans are created immortal, and succumb to death through the fault of a messenger, generally an animal, who either brings his message too late or mixes it up. . . . Or death, which existed in the background of the universe from the very beginning without God's knowledge, sneakily makes its way among human beings" (Christoph, Müller, and Müller 1999:170).

100. In discussing Aboriginal culture, Morphy (1991:62) explains that "one of the signs of a natural death as opposed to death at the hands of a sorcerer is that the dying man has had sufficient time to explain his wishes to the living," such as how to produce the clan's ceremonial sacred paintings.

101. E.g., Underhill 1965:88ff.

102. For the Yoruba *ashe*, see Ray 2000:137.

103. Olupona 1991:28.

104. For *wakan* or Wakonda and the interrelationship with the supreme being and/or "the Above, the Below, Darkness, Sun, Moon, Morning Star, and Thunder," see Underhill 1965:202.

105. For the Fon *arsen*, or idols, see Ray 2000:134ff.

106. The Sanskrit/Hindu *tirtha*, literally a "ford" or "crossing," is the generic for "shrine" or "holy place."

107. The classic work on pollution and purity is Douglas 1966.

108. David Edwards (in Bullock, Stallybrass, and Trombley 1988:625) considers polytheism as "the worship of many gods often connected with natural phenomena such as mountains, rivers, or storms," which is different from the more rationalist pantheism that "rejects both the transcendence and the personality of gods or God."

109. For instance, the deities of West Africa may be divided into three groups: gods associated with natural phenomena (earth, sky, storms, water); those connected to a specific place (town, spring, rock) or a related group (clan, lineage); and deities, often originally magical powers, introduced from outside (Christoph, Müller, and Müller 1999:262).

110. For African understandings of a supreme god, refer to Smith 1950 and Shorter 1975 as well as Nigosian 1994:39; Shorter in Hinnells 1984:428; Young 1995:50; and Zuesse in Crim 1981:6ff. According to Christoph, Müller, and Müller (1999:124), in Africa, "'God' means the god of the heavens, known and admired by nearly all African peoples: 'The Big One In The Sky' (*Njadenga*) or simply 'The One Up There' (*Wokumusoro*) as he is called by the Shona in Mozambique as well as by many other tribes." Likewise, Native Americans believe in a Great Spirit (Morgan [1851] 1995:144). For such Amerindian supreme beings or creator deities as the Pomo Kuksu, Cheyene Maheo, Algonquian Great Manitou, Northern Wintu Olebis, Yuki Taikomol, Maidu Kodoyanpe, and Pawnee Tirawahat, see Feest 2000:449ff, 458. On Chingichngish, the high god of the eighteenth-century religion that developed among the Ipai, Tipai, Luiseño, and Chumash peoples of southern California, and the Bole-Maru religion centered on dream instructions from the Creator (a fusion of the Kuksu cult and the Ghost Dance) that began in northern California in 1872, also see Feest 2000:443ff. Taylor and Sturtevant (1996:380) described the Algonquian Great Spirit, Manitou or Kitche Manitou, "as a remote, mysterious and omniscient being, playing no role in traditional myths and not represented or personified in ceremonies." As a *deus otiosus*, remote from

everyday Amerindian affairs, "the Supreme Being is often only vaguely outlined and plays little role in immediate religious concerns" (Cooper in Sutherland et al. 1988:875).

111. Ray 2000:27.

112. Olupona 1991:27ff.

113. Unlike witchcraft whose powers in Africa are used for evil, "magic is far more accessible, as it is not a special innate power but principally a technique for dealing with things, which can be learned by anyone . . . for good as well as evil. Magic powers can be found in minerals, rock formations, plants, animals, and human beings—in fact, everywhere in nature" (Christoph, Müller, and Müller 1999:142).

114. Abimbola in Olupona 1991:57.

115. There are virtually countless works on shamanism, both traditional and contemporary Western. The classic seminal works are Shirokogoroff [1935] 1980; and Eliade 1989; also Lewis 1989. On Siberian and Finno-Ugrian forms of shamanism, consult Casanowicz 1924; Czaplicka [1914] 1969; Diószegi 1968; Diószegi and Hoppál 1978; Hajdu 1975; Hatto 1970; Hoppál 1984; Lehtinen 1986; Pentikäinen 1998; and Siikala 1978; among others. Pentikäinen (2001) retains the same focus but extends it to include Hungarian, Greek, and modern, nontraditional invented forms. In the extension of the term to similar practices, on North American forms, see Jilek 1982; LaBarre 1938; and Park 1938; on South American expression, consider Douglas Sharon in Furst 1972:114–35; Langdon and Baer 1992; and Taussig 1980; on Korean shamanism, see Kim 1981; and Kister 1997; on Japanese shamanism, the classic work is Blacker 1982; on Nepalese shamanism, see Furer-Haimendorf 1974; Hitchcock 1968; Hitchcock and Jones 1976; Peters 1978, 1981; and Watters 1975; and for Mongolian shamanic religion, see Heissig 1980. A general portrayal of shamanism and its role in the evolution of religion can be found in Rutherford 1986. Flaherty 1992 discusses eighteenth-century Europe's initial encounter with shamanic peoples and practices and how they influenced the intellectual mainstream. For contemporary Western expressions of (neo-) shamanism, see Castaneda 1968, 1972; Drury 1978, 1982; Furst 1972; Harner 1973, 1986; and Noel 1976. Works covering both traditional and new shamanisms include Halifax 1982; Nicholson 1987; and Noel 1997.

116. Watkins (1969:1190) traces the Tungus term *saman* to the Tocharian *samâne* and ultimately the Sanskrit word for "ascetic," *sramanás*. See also Eliade 1989:495ff; and Jeanne Achterberg in Nicholson 1987:113. Rutherford (1986:15) mentions Diószegi's consideration of a derivation from an Indo-European root *sa: "to know," which suggests the shaman as "one who knows."

117. Feest (2000:456) considers the shaman "a person who, in an intentionally induced state of ecstasy, interacts with supernatural beings by sending his soul to the other world, by summoning his spirit helpers, or by being possessed by them."

118. The former view is Eliade's; the latter, Shirogokoroff's.

119. As Eliade (1989:17; following Shirogokoroff [1935] 1980:350ff) puts it, "Recognition as a shaman is bestowed only by the whole community and only after the aspirant has undergone the initiatory ordeal." In this context, Pentikäinen's observation that "one of the most important criteria in the choice of a new shaman was certainly the expertise in the ideological traditions of the culture," is relevant (1998:64). Note, further, the shaman's oath among the Buryat recorded by Ludmila Kuzmina and cited by Pentikäinen (1998:63).

120. On the issue of whether the shaman is "psychologically insane," see Pentikäinen 2001:5, 60ff; and Richard Noll's "The Presence of Spirits in Magic and Madness," in Nicholson 1987:47–61. In this context, Eliade (1989:498) notes that in Mongolia "the lamas advise the mentally unbalanced to become shamans."

121. Eliade 1989:237.

122. Shirogokoroff [1935] 1980:346ff.

123. Eliade 1989:28.

124. Nicholson 1987:56.

125. Eliade 1989:64ff; Pentikäinen 1998:51.

126. Rutherford 1986:38.

127. See Hoppál in Nicholson 1987:89, who refers to a paper by Ivan Kortt presented to the 1981 Bányai symposium, "Shamanism in Eurasia." Also see Eliade 1989:59, 62ff, *passim*.

128. Eliade 1989:63.

129. Cf. Baldick 2000; Halifax 1982:74; Hoppál in Nicholson 1987:121.

130. E.g., Chuner Taksami in Pentikäinen 2001:13–18; and Rutherford 1986: 44–51. On the shaman's drum as a cognitive map, see esp. Pentikäinen 1998: 26–48.

131. Baldick 2000:70.

132. Rutherford (1986:120) links soul flight with the Gnostic aim to liberate the soul from the body. In this connection, see Robert Ellwood's chapter, "Shamanism and Theosophy," in Nicholson 1987:253–63. Whereas the Gnostic seeks to emancipate the soul, the shaman tries to return it to the body.

133. Hultkrantz 1953.

134. Saso in Hinnells 1984:352.

135. According to Jeanne Achterberg (Nicholson 1987:108), "The Shamanic state of consciousness (SSC) is the very essence of shamanism, and critical to the premise that the shaman is the past and present master of the imagination as healer."

136. Eliade 1989:301; Shirogokoroff [1935] 1980:313.

137. E.g., Eliade 1989:182; Rutherford 1986:56ff.

138. Rutherford 1986:93. Eliade (1989:456) refers to "an endemic phenomenon of spontaneous pseudoshamanism, which is difficult to classify but whose most important characteristic is its *easiness*" (italics in original).

139. Turner 1969.

140. See Eliade in Nicholson 1987:17–26.

141. Eliade 1989:120ff. See also Hoppál in Pentikäinen 2001:85ff.

142. Eliade 1989:125, n. 36, 168, *passim*.

143. E.g., Rutherford 1986:152ff; Joan Townsend in Pentikäinen 2001:257–64; York 1995b:164–67. Some of the standard neoshamanic works are Andrews 1981; Castaneda 1968; Harner 1986; and Sun Bear 1984.

144. On the issue of appropriation, see my articles "The World Parliament of Religions, Chicago, 1993," *Religion Today: A Journal of Contemporary Religions* 9 (spring 1994): 17–20; and "New Age Commodification and Appropriation of Spirituality," *Journal of Contemporary Religion* 16 (October 2001): 361–72.

145. See, e.g., Noel 1997.

146. Among a host of publications conveying a New Age version of modern urban shamanism, two typical works are King 1990 and Telesco 2000.

147. Rasmussen 1930:120ff.

148. For a history of governmental and corporate violation against the "First Nations" in the United States, refer to Weyler 1992. He mentions Fools Crow's comment that "if white people wanted to help the Indians, they should find a place to live, settle down, look after the land where they live, and forget about running all over the planet trying to save it" (15). For an insight into twentieth-century Indian history and the emergence of the Red Power movement as well as the emergence of Indian gambling establishments, see Parman 1994. Nagel 1996 explores the modern emergence of American Indian ethnic identification. See Josephy 1994 for a sober assessment of Euro-American treatment of the North American indigenous peoples.

149. Some of the classic and/or recommended investigations into Native North American spirituality and culture include Fixico 1997; Hultkrantz 1953, 1979, 1983, 1987; Hurdey 1970; Kroeber [1925] 1976; Nagel 1996; Parman 1994; Radin 1956; Silko 1996; Sullivan 2000; Taylor and Sturtevant 1996; Underhill 1965; Vecsey 1990; and Vogel 1990. For a study of religious identity from a contemporary Native American Christian perspective, see Treat 1996. An illustrated yet detailed presentation of North American Indian cultures, refer to Feest 2000. See also Jocks 2002.

150. Vogel 1990:14.

151. Vogel 1990:31, italics in original.

152. See, e.g., Young 1995:68ff and, for the Oglala Sioux or Lakotas, 77– 81.

153. Vogel 1990:256.

154. See Hultkrantz's comments, "Studies of Rituals and Ritual Patterns," in Vecsey 1990:182–84. Feest (2000:459) defines the vision quest as "the purposeful attempt by an individual to bring about a vision of a supernatural being (guardian spirit) by fasting and other forms of castigation, in order to acquire from the being special skills and a promise of future assistance."

155. Vecsey 1990:154.

156. Albanese 1990:20, *passim*; also Hultkrantz 1953:483–97.

157. Morgan [1851] 1995:144–46.

158. As Morgan ([1851] 1995:147) sees it, the Iroquois—typically of Native Americans in general—"could not fully conceive of the omnipresence of the Great Spirit, except through the instrumentality of a class of inferior spiritual existences, by whom he was surrounded."

159. Feest (2000:447) describes the circular *hogan* with corbelled doomed-roof vault as female and the conical form with earth-covered roof as male. Taylor and Sturtevant (1996:136) explain that "designs on [Plains Indian] tipis were believed to secure for their owners protection against misfortune and sickness."

160. Louis A. Hieb in Crim 1981:529; Nigosian 1994:63. On the Hopi in general, see Waters 1977.

161. See especially Louise Lamphere, "Symbolic Elements in Navaho Ritual," *Southwestern Journal of Anthropology* 25 (1969): 279–303.

162. Other leading Aztec deities include Tezcatlipoca (smoking mirror), Huitzilopochtli (the solar war-god), and Coatlicue (Snake Skirt, the earth mother). The warrior Tezcatlipoca, the priestly Quetzalcoatl, and the agricultural Tlaloc constitute a triad of major Mesoamerican gods. See, e.g., Brotherston in Sutherland et al. 1988:896.

163. On Sedna, see Cooper in Sutherland et al. 1988:876; Sonja Lührmann in Feest 2000:57, cf. further 456; and Taylor and Sturtevant 1996:429.

164. "The most prominent role in native American mythology generally is filled by the Trickster-transformer-culture-hero" (Cooper in Sutherland et al. 1988:875).

165. Hultkrantz 1953:343ff.

166. Nigosian 1994:62.

167. Taylor and Sturtevant 1996:50.

168. E.g., Bender and Feest in Feest 2000:410ff, 445; Taylor and Sturtevant 1996:85.

169. Hultkrantz 1953:351ff, 492.

170. The Sun Dance is the most important ceremonial ritual belonging to the Plains people. Outlawed by the U.S. government in 1881 ostensibly because of the self-infliction that it sometimes involved, it has nevertheless made a comeback since the 1960s. The purpose of the Sun Dance, which takes place in specially built lodges and sometimes in the "medicine wheel" (a circular outline of piled stones flattened on one side), requires personal sacrifices and vows made by the dancers to supernatural beings who are thought to help the performers as well as the entire tribe (Liane Gugel in Feest 2000:203, 209, 226ff, *passim*; Taylor and Sturtevant 1996:162ff). "The Sun Dance spread from the Plains region to the Shoshone and the Ute, who believe it to be a powerful healing ceremony." Even more ubiquitous are the "medicine societies" dedicated, especially after rampant diseases had been introduced by the Europeans, to curing the ill as well as preventing disease and for

spiritual regeneration. In the Great Lakes region, the culture hero Nanabozho, the "Great Hare," although a trickster, "finally founded the "Medicine society' for the benefit of the people" (Henry Kammler in Feest 2000:333, 131). The ceremonies could last several days and were conducted in specially built wigwams.

171. Note in particular Sullivan 2001 for essays providing not only profiles of individual cultures of Central and South America but also discussions of the religious views belonging to the pre-Columbian Aztecs, Mayas, and Incas. See also Carmody and Carmody 1993; McEwan et al. 2001; Osborne 1968; and Steward and Faron 1959.

172. Louis Faron in Crim 1981:704.

173. Crim 1981:705.

174. "The Inca state religion was largely concerned with organization, particularly that of the food supply, and ritual, rather than with mysticism and spirituality" (George Bankes in Alexander 1994:55). See also Brotherston in Sutherland et al. 1988:899–904; and Faron in Crim 1981:706.

175. Faron in Crim 1981:706.

176. Faron in Crim 1981:706.

177. In considering the power of names and words, Cooper (Sutherland et al. 1988:874) states that "songs, prayers and myth-telling are viewed as spiritual forces which directly affect the world, giving it form and meaning and effecting changes."

178. "Conceptions of time among native Americans are cyclical and concerned with reciprocal relationships, such that ritual becomes not mere re-enactment of mythic events, but rather the mythic event re-occurs in the present" (Sutherland et al. 1988:874).

179. Nigosian 1994:64.

180. Young 1995:68. According to Cooper (in Sutherland et al. 1988:880), "The afterlife was commonly seen as a happier continuation of this life, behaviour in this life having little effect on one's fate after death."

181. Nigosian 1994:72.

182. Cooper in Sutherland et al. 1988:876.

183. Halifax 1982:90ff.

184. La Barre 1972; Mooney 1896. The Ghost Dance movement originated with the Piaute prophet Wovoka and ultimately culminated in the massacre of Wounded Knee of 1890. "It was, none the less, a significant attempt to posit a positive future for peoples whose ways of life were being destroyed" (Cooper in Sutherland et al. 1988:881).

185. La Barre 1938. Spreading northward from Mexico into the Plains Indian area toward the end of the nineteenth century, the hallucinogenic peyote cactus cult "clearly provides a means of gaining power for the dispirited and, by combining Christian (the use of the Bible, Christian prayers and ethics) and traditional (singing, drumming, visions and the incorporation of indigenous spirits) ele-

ments, it provides a new ritual form which is distinctly Indian, but which allows accommodation to a changing world" (Cooper in Sutherland et al. 1988:881). See also Young 1995:84 and esp. Slotkin 1956.

186. The literature on Afro-Latin religion is highly controversial. Practitioners argue that the spirituality cannot be learned through books but only through apprenticeship to godparents. The stress is on the lengthy training that precedes initiation. Written works, especially those by academics, are condemned. One of the first to appear was Gonzalez-Wippler 1981 [1973], which is routinely rejected on Afro-Latin electronic lists. Some other source books, all tentatively presented in deference to practitioners' sentiment, include Barnes 1997; Bastide 1978; Brown 1994; Gleason 1987; Goodman, Henney, and Pressel 1974; Herskovits 1941; Hunt 1979; Mason and Edwards 1985; Murphy 1988; Simpson 1978; Thompson 1984; and Verger 1954. Among these, Gleason has been "initiated to Oya"; Murphy has been "made to Obatala"; Thompson has been "cut in Palo"; and Mason is a *babalocha*. The *Journal for the Scientific Study of Religion* contains two relevant articles: LeFever 1996 and Pérez Y Mena 1998. Two vernacular pamphlets that are typical of the popular mass market are Donna Rose, "Santeria: The Cuban-African Magical System," Mi-World, 1980; and Anna Riva, "Devotions to the Saints" (Los Angeles: International Imports, 1990). In Spanish, there is Tomás Fernández Robaína, *Hablen Paleros y Santeros* (Havana: Editorial ciencias sociales, 1997). Further suggestions are Awolalu 1979; Badejo 1996; Ecun 1989; and other works on African religion itself.

Among works specifically devoted to voodoo/vodun, Hurston [1938] 1990 and Deren [1953] 1970 are among the earliest. Other sources include Chesi 1981; Cosentino 1995; Huxley 1966; Laguerre 1980; Metraux 1959; and Mintz 1972. See also John Q. Anderson, "The New Orleans Voodoo Rituals, Dance, and Its Twentieth Century Survivals," *Southern Folklore* 24 (1960), online http:lllibweb.sfasu.edu/etrc/COLLET/MANUSCRIPT/PERSONAL/AndersonJohnQ/andmain.html; Carole Devillers, "Haiti's Voodoo Pilgrimages of Spirits and Saints," *National Geographic*, March 1985, 395–408; and Michael Ventura, "Hear That Long Snake Moan," *Shadow Dancing in the USA* (New York: St. Martin's Press, 1985), 103–62.

187. The literature on Afro-Latin, Cuban, and voodoo altars is extensive. See in particular Cosentino 1995; Drewal and Mason 1998; Drewal, Pemberton, and Abíódún 1989; Dupré 1970; Galembo 1993; and Verger 1954. Note also Thompson 1993.

188. On the comparison between Afro-Atlantic and European altars, see Thompson 1993:24–26.

189. See Randy Conner, "In the Land of Laddo: Gay People and the Yoruba Spiritual Tradition," *The Advocate*, March 3, 1987, 28–31; Glenn L. Sitzman, "Wedded in 'Santeria,'" *RFD: A Country Journal for Gay Men Everywhere* 64 (Winter 1990–91): 30–32.

190. González-Wippler [1973] 1981:21. On the words *santo* (saint or *orisha*),

*santero/santera* (priest, initiate), and *Santería* (the way of the saints or where one gets the saints), see Clark 2001:32–36. For Drewal and Mason 1998:278, n. 3, "*Santeria* describes the system of worshipping, caring for, making, and selling saints."

191. "Despite its lowly origins translated to the Cuban refugee community in Miami, [Santería] has become a flourishing middle-class movement." Peter Clarke (Sutherland et al. 1988:832) also finds the same urban popularity for Umbanda in Brazil. See in particular Brown 1994.

192. E.g., Bascom 1969:77. Murphy (1988:12) claims that "the Yoruba recognize as many as 1,700 *orishas*, though only a few have achieved renown throughout the country."

193. Herskovits 1937. See also, e.g., Ecun 1989:*passim.*

194. See LeFever 1996:323; and González-Wippler [1973] 1981:103–23.

195. On the *orisha* system, see Badejo 1996:55–62.

196. E.g., González-Wippler [1973] 1981:30, 107. González-Wippler (1985:30) states that Eshú in Brazil, "where he is better known as Exu, . . . has been syncretized with the devil."

197. Pérez Y Mena 1998. For Santería as a "counterhegemonic strategy," see LeFever 1996:327, where he cites A. Apter's claim that rather than the use of Catholic saints as a means of masking the *orishas* from official detection, Santería Catholicism was "the religion of the masters, revised, transformed, and appropriated by slaves to harness its power with their universes of discourse." Clark (2001:21, *passim*) distinguishes West African religion from its Catholic elements and refers to the latter as "decorative and nonessential."

198. Clark 2001:25; LeFever 1996:320; Murphy 1988:7ff; and Abimbola in Olupona 1991:53.

199. "The difference between the Orishas and Olodumare," according to Ecun (1989:18ff), "is that Olodumare is the supreme being and therefore represents a more abstract concept of nature and human qualities." Moreover, "this deity has no temples nor directly consecrated priests."

200. On the *fundamentos*, "tools" or "stones," that constitute the god objects or residence of the *orishas* on Santería altars, consult Clark 2001:28ff, 31, 36ff.

201. Among others, see Badejo 1996:63. In referring to Santería offerings, LeFever (1996:321) states that "what is important is the reciprocal nature of the offering—the *orishas* are fed and, in return, the devotees share in the *orishas'* ashe. Drewal and Mason describe the Yoruba cosmos as divided into two distinct yet interrelated worlds: "the *òrun* (the invisible, spiritual realm) of gods, ancestors, and spirits, and the *ayé* (the visible, tangible world) of the living." The two "halves" of the cosmos are understood as a unity composed of mutually dependent parts. And while the predominant emphasis in Yoruba-derived spirituality is this-worldly, Drewal and Mason cite a traditional proverb: "Life in the world is a journey, the otherworld is home," distinguishing the transitory from the eternal (1998:21).

202. LeFever 1996:321: "A specific drum rhythm and dance posture is associated with each *orisha*." See also Georges Niangoran-Bouah's "The Talking Drum: A Traditional Instrument of Liturgy and of Mediation with the Sacred," in Olupona 1991:81–92; also Murphy 1988:92–100.

203. Clark 2001:38. Clark considers the trance moment as "the height of somaticity," and she sees matter being set into opposition not to spirituality but to the human body that "in and of itself seems to lack ultimate signification." The more usual understanding of divine ubiquity is expressed by Drewal and Mason (1998:278) when they report, "All . . . beings, from cockroaches to humans, were selected by God to exist and, therefore, are sacred and worthy of respect."

204. Eliade and Couliano 1991:14.

205. E.g., on *emi* and *ashe*, see Young 1995:55ff. Also LeFever 1996. According to Murphy (1988:8), "Ashe is present in the human line of continuity with the past." For other discussions of *ashe*, refer to Drewal, Pemberton, and Abíódún 1989; and Verger 1954.

206. Drewal and Mason 1998:279, n. 26; also Young 1995:56.

207. E.g., Badeju 1996:*passim*; LeFever 1996:321; Murphy 1988:62–69, 160ff. According to Eliade and Couliano (1991:13), "*Ifa* divination is a form of geomancy stemming from the Arabs."

208. Murphy 1988:*passim*.

209. LeFever 1996:323.

210. On Exú or the Exús, see Brown 1994:*passim*, esp. 74ff, 77.

211. Deren [1953] 1970:54–57, 294, n. 8. Deren found that her Haitian informants "transpose their concepts to Christian equivalents without being aware of discrepancies between them" (17).

212. On Rada and Petwo (Petro), see, e.g., Cosentino 1995:432ff; and Deren [1953] 1970:60ff, 64, 82–84.

213. On Kardecism as a social and intellectual manifestation in Brazil, see Brown 1994:15–25. Brown includes a discussion on cosmology and ritual. See also Smart 1989:545.

214. There are an ever increasing number of written works on contemporary Western paganism. Two of the classics are Adler 1986 and Simos 1979. Other important works on the modern pagan scene in the West and/or its antecedents include diZerega 2001; Greenwood 2000; Griffin 2000; Harvey 1997; Harvey and Hardman 1995; Hutton 1999; Jones and Pennick 1995; Luhrmann 1989; Pearson, Roberts, and Samuel 1998; Pike 2001; and York 1995b. On Wicca and contemporary witchcraft, five standard works are Crowley 1989; Davies and Lynch 2001; Farrar 1981; and Farrar and Farrar 1981, 1988. More recent works are Berger 1998; Harrow 1999; and Heselton 2000; but see also Valiente 1973, 1978. Note Scarboro and Luck 1997. On contemporary shamanism, see Castaneda 1968, 1972; Harner 1986; Serge King 1990; and Telesco 2000, among others. For the more psychonautic expression of contemporary shamanism or paganism, see

McKenna 1992; and Stevens 1989. On Hawaiian Kahuna, see Beckworth 1971; Cunningham 2000; and Steiger 1982. On Asatru/Northern Heathenism, see d'Apremont 1999.

215. The terms *neopagan, recopagan,* and *geopagan* are my own. The last might be akin to Gordon Melton's "cosmological religiosity" (Melton, Clark, and Kelly 1991:345) that he describes as the belief that the natural world is "ensouled," that spiritual powers are manifest in natural phenomena, that communication with the deceased is possible, and that certain persons are capable of furnishing divine revelation. Wesley Carr (1991:102, 137) considers the same as "ecological mysticism" or "cosmological naturalism" and rejects it for not affirming a transcendent God. But if Melton and Carr are touching on the more theological articulations of geopaganism as a practice and/or behavior in itself, natural or "folk" paganism is nonetheless largely subconscious and automatic, something more akin to Catherine Albanese's "broad popular mentality' that spiritualizes—even romanticizes— nature. Her "term nature religion is my own name for a symbolic center and the cluster of beliefs, behaviors and values that encircle it" (1990:7). Perhaps the essential element of geopaganism is relational activity that is grounded on an implicit if not explicit assumption of the material world as a holy place in which ecological harmony becomes the controlling ethic. See also Corrington's "ecstatic naturalism" (Corrington 1997).

216. Apart from its reconstructed and neopagan forms, contemporary Western paganism's more immediate and conscious geopagan expression is essentially similar to the way of life of "Amerindian peoples [who] lived symbolically with nature at center and boundaries. They understood the world as one that answered personally to their needs and words and, in turn, perceived themselves and their societies as part of a sacred landscape. With correspondence as controlling metaphor, they sought their own versions of mastery and control through harmony in a universe of persons who were part of the natural world." And today, "like seventeenth-century Indians, contemporary Native Americans and their fellow travelers counter Euro-Christianity with a religion of their own" (Albanese 1990: 25, 156).

217. While as a rule, geopaganism is often less conscious and more instinctually reflexive, its fundamental "nature religion" orientation is what tends to infuse much of contemporary Western paganism as a whole, including Neopaganism Wicca, Witchcraft, Goddess Spirituality, and recopaganism like Druidry. Peter Beyer (in Pearson, Roberts, and Samuel 1998) considers the "nature religion" that dominates paganism in the West today as a critique of contemporary global society. It affirms, in contrast, both locality and pluralistic difference, and much of this sentiment is allegedly witnessed behind the current Starhawk-led protests against the World Trade Organization and multinational corporate hegemony. Nevertheless, see Hutton 1999:415 for a discussion that questions a strict identity between "nature religion" and contemporary Western paganism.

218. Describing the contemporary pagan resurgence of North America in the last third of the twentieth century, Adler (1986:233) claims that "outside of the various Witchcraft traditions, the most prevalent forms of Neo-Paganism are groups that attempt to re-create ancient European pre-Christian traditions." Adler lists the Church of Aphrodite, Feraferia, the Sabaean Religious Order, the Church of the Eternal Source, as well as Odinism, Asatru, and Norse Paganism (233–82).

219. For elucidation of the contrast between Gardnerian and Alexandrian Wicca, see Crowley 1989. She describes "Wicca [as] a form of worship, a spiritual system and also a system for developing and using psychic power" that draws chiefly on the tradition of the original fertility cult, the occult traditions in general, and the pagan mysteries (11). On the proliferation of Wiccan lineages (Gardnerian, Alexandrian, Hereditary Craft, and others), see also Hutton 1999; and York 1995b.

220. See in particular Farrar and Farrar 1981, 1988. On the "wheel of the year," see Simos 1979:169–84. For the Goddess and Goddess Spirituality, see Christ 1997; Christ in Olson 1990:231–51; Christ and Plaskow 1979; Crowley 1989: 162–82; Eller 1993, 2000; Raphael 2000; Simos 1979:76–92; and Sjöö and Mor 1987. Melissa Raphael's focus is specifically on Goddess feminism, which includes Goddess worship but also "opposes patriarchal structures of religions and social power" while being "critical of the abstracted qualities of masculinist rationalism" (Raphael 2000:12, 22).

221. On ceremonial magic, see Bonewits 1979; Crowley 1991; Greenwood 2000; Francis King 1975, 1990; Lévi [1913] 1982; MacGregor-Mathers 1948; and Regardie 1969.

222. E.g., Greenwood 2000; Kelly 1991; and Luhrmann 1989. The seminal works for the modern witchcraft/Wiccan movement are Gardner 1954, 1959; and Murray 1921, [1931] 1970.

223. "In antiquity, magic was itself a religious ritual which worked on pagan divinities. It was not a separate technology, opposed to religious practice" (Fox 1987:36).

224. Nevertheless, Vivianne Crowley (1989:16) can say that "we have now entered the Age of Aquarius, the age of humanism, in which the divine as God and Goddess will be found in all men and women." See also York 1995b:118, 130.

225. Adler 1986:4, 23, 179f; York 1995b:127ff, 136.

226. According to Crowley, Wiccan "rites always take place within a sacred and consecrated space called 'the circle'" (1989:83; see also 83–110). Prudence Jones (in Jones and Matthews 1990:41–54) discusses the pagan ritual circle as "cosmograms," icons, and mandalas. Adler (1986:108ff, 159) distinguishes the ritual circle as employed by ceremonial magicians, on the one hand, and by witches and pagans, on the other, whereas Greenwood (2000:41) recognizes that the intentionality of specially created space separates pagan magic from what otherwise remains unfocused and undirected.

227. As Halbertal and Margalit (1992:40) patristically explain, the "idol is one of the manifestations of the god—sometimes his place of residence like the soul in the body and sometimes a direct concentration of his powers." They distinguish it from the fetish as an object to which people attribute nonexistent or imaginary powers (42). However, in any perusal of books on contemporary Western paganism and their indexes—for example, Adler 1986; Crowley 1989; Greenwood 2000; Hutton 1999; and Pennick 1992—the words *idol* and *idolatry* as subjects or entries never appear.

228. Jones (in Harvey and Hardman 1995:37) explains that for modern pagans, "the divine, transcendent powers seem to be present within Nature itself, and by deliberate ritual and contemplation the devout Pagan can make contact with these." She concludes that paganism is a religious outlook that is "Nature-venerating, polytheistic and recognisant of the Goddess" (45). See also Jones and Pennick 1995:2, 81, 219. As Simos (1979:8) phrases it, the Goddess "is the world, and all things in it: moon, sun, earth, star, stone, seed, flowing river, wind, wave, leaf and branch, bud and blossom, fang and claw, woman and man." Beyer (in Pearson, Roberts, and Samuel 1998:11–21) identifies "nature religion" as an individually oriented, institution-resisting, this-worldly emphasis on the natural that places the determination of truth or validity on personal experience, rejects hierarchical structure, and stresses an optimistic, holistic reality and future inclusive of humanity. Nature as idolon is further conveyed in Hutton's assessment of "nature religion" as a legitimation that "regards nature as the embodiment of divinity or sacredness" (1999:414).

229. Starhawk: "The Goddess has infinite aspects and thousands of names— She is the reality behind many metaphors" (Simos 1979:8). For Jones and Pennick (1995:220), "other goddesses and gods are seen as 'aspects' of [the Great Goddess and the God]."

230. See, e.g., Adler 1986:273–82; Harvey in Harvey and Hardman 1995:62; York 1995b:124–27.

231. Rather than my Neopaganism, for Hutton (1999:415ff), "paganism, including pagan witchcraft, . . . occupies the ground at which nature religion, postmodern religion, and revived religion intersect."

## Notes to Chapter 2

1. See also Berger's statement: "The fundamental religious impulse is not to theorize about transcendence but to worship it" (1990:98).

2. Adler 1986:25.

3. Corrington 1997:10.

4. See York 1995b:323ff.

5. General introductory works on Hinduism include Brockington 1981;

Dubois 1953; Flood 1996; Kinsley 1993; Klostermaier 1994; Lipner 1994; and Shattuck 1999. Undergraduates might want to consider Knott 1998.

6. On the demotion of Indra and the mythological variants of this motif, see O'Flaherty 1976:*passim*. Sullivan (1997:48) explains that the "English spelling 'Brahmin' is a corruption of the Sanskrit word Brahamana."

7. On "the brahmanification of India," see York 1995a:401–7.

8. "Such a person would be 'Brahmana' meaning 'one who has Brahman,' descriptive of the fact that the Brahmin embodies Brahman-power in the form of his knowledge of Veda and ritual" (Sullivan 1997:48).

9. The *ghats* accepted as particularly meritorious are those of Dashashvamedha, Manikarnika, and Panchaganga. These were always the most crowded during morning worship. See Vidyarthi et al. 1979.

10. Most devotees consumed this amount of liquid immediately, but because it was often directly from the Ganges or mixed with water from the river and because I did not have the same resistance as did the locals, drinking the water usually presented a slight dilemma to me. I would feign consumption as best I could, but sometimes the potion would inadvertently land in my mouth all the same. I was often plagued with dysentery and nausea during my Indian sojourn, but when I returned home, these symptoms disappeared on their own within a few months.

11. See Flood 1996:209; Mookerjee 1985:169.

12. On *puja* in general, see Flood 1996:208–11; Hardy in Sutherland et al. 1988:619, 621; Sullivan 1997:168ff; Tyberg 1970:140–42. The two basic modes of *puja* are the *panchopachar pujan*, which is more informal and includes only five articles as offerings, and the *shodashopchar pujan*, which in Kashi occurs only at the temples of Vishwanth, Naya Vishwanath, Sankatamochan Hanuman, and Annapurna and includes sixteen articles of oblation. For Vishwanath, these consist of *akshata* (sun-dried rice), *bibhooti* (sacred ashes), *durba* grass, *belapatra* leaf, and *dhatura* flowers. Vishnu, his avatars, and circle are worshiped only with flowers and *tulsi* leaves. More elaborate forms of the Rudrabhisheka are the *sarvanga ekadashi*, which employs eleven priests rather than merely one; the *laghu*, twelve priests; the *maha*, 1,331 priests; and the *ati*, 1,463.

13. The four occasions for priestly *arati* are the *mangala*, or waking *arati*, usually occurring between 3 and 3:30 A.M.; the *bhoga*, sometime after noon in which various food dishes are offered and the doors of the shrine are closed for the god's lunchtime privacy; the *shringara*, or decorating of the deity with flowers, sandal paste, scents, and various clothes and/or ornaments after first bathing the idol: the Vishwanath *lingam* is washed with the five offerings or *panchamrita*; and the *shayana*, or retirement *arati*, at about 11 P.M. in which nighttime items such as a bed and chamber pot are placed near the deity and the temple doors are closed until the following morning. During each of these ceremonies, one or more *arati* are waved round the idol, always with the right hand, to the accompaniment of

mantra recitation, the ringing of bells, and/or the playing of various musical instruments such as the *damru* or ritual drum. On *arati*, see Mookerjee 1985:169; Weightman in Hinnells 1984:218ff.

14. The votive rite includes the *mundan* ceremony, or shaving of a boy's head for the first time in front of Shiva; the *dudhadharia*, or pouring of milk over the sacred *lingam*; the costly *tuladana* in which the performer donates the equivalent of his body's weight in gold or silver; the rain-procuring *jaldalai*; the *chandi thokana*, in which silver coins are engraved within the temple precincts; the Satyanarayan *katha*, or organized worship of the god Vishnu in which stories are narrated and *prasad* distributed to those present in Kashi, usually taking place at the Dashashwamedh ghat; the *aar-par* rite for newlywed couples; coconut offerings as part of *Gangapujan*; the *godan* ritual in which the devotee grabs hold of a cow's tail on emerging from a holy bath; and the *jan ke badale jan charaibo* rite in which a newborn child or one that has recovered from illness is put into the Ganges at midstream, retrieved by a boatman, and finally returned to the parents. For a general discussion on Hindu rites of passage, see Weightman in Hinnells 1984:216–18.

15. Clothey in Crim 1981:627. See also Thomas 1971.

16. On *upas*, see Tyberg 1970:77, 119; on *darsana*, Flood 1996:211ff, 224; and Sullivan 1997:64. The Hindu festival of Siva Ratri occurs with the Hindu month of Marga, but Flood incorrectly associates this last with November/December rather than, correctly, with January/February.

17. Flood 1996:212; Nigosian 1994:108; Sullivan 1997:96. In an allusion to the carnivalesque associations of the end of winter and beginning of spring, Sullivan states, "Inversion of caste-based hierarchy is a common feature of Holi" (1997:96).

18. Mookerjee 1985:107.

19. Sullivan (1997:75) recognizes that the rituals of the Durga Puja Dasahra, Dussehra, and Navaratri are not Vedic in style and may indeed be pre-Vedic commemorations.

20. Mookerjee 1985:124, 129.

21. Mookerjee 1985:57ff, 63.

22. The Durga Puja shrines of Banaras are Shailaputri, Brahmacariti, Citra Ghanta, Kushmanda at the Durga temple; Bagashauri or Skandamata, Katyayani, Varahi Devi/ Kalaratri, Mahagauri, and Siddhidatri.

23. Flood 1996:212; Nigosian 1994:107ff.

24. The Sanskrit *rasa* refers originally to the sense of taste and then, by extension, aesthetic experience as the transformation of emotion (Flood 1996:141) or the "essential delight-giving quality of all experience" (Tyberg 1970:102). As the accumulation of all experiential essence, it becomes the supreme gift that humans can offer to the gods and also the motivation for both growth and rebirth (Tyberg 1970:198).

25. The weekdays *varas*, beginning with Sunday, are governed, respectively, by the sun, Ravi; the moon, Chandra or Soma; Mars, Mangala or Karttikeya; Mer-

cury, Buddha; Jupiter, Brihaspati; Venus, Shukra; and Saturn, Shani. In addition, Mondays belong especially to Shiva; Tuesdays and Saturdays, to Devi, Bhairava, and Hanuman; and Fridays, to particular *devis* or goddesses like Sankata Devi and Santoshi Mata.

26. On the *tirtha*, see Eck in Crim 1981:306; Flood 1996:212. For the annual cycle of festivals, see the comments of Weightman in Hinnells 1984:221.

27. For the seven sacred cities, see Flood 1996:213 and, on pilgrimage in general, 212–14; and Eck 1998:63–75. On Banaras/Varanasi as the preeminent *tirtha*, note particularly Eck 1982:39–41.

28. Eck 1998:65, on Puri, 53ff, *passim*.

29. On the *pithas*, see Flood 1996:192ff.

30. In this connection, Weightman (in Hinnells 1984:223), in contrast to metaphysical speculation and elaborate ritual, refers to the more pragmatic and practical concerns of the majority of Indian villagers who seek "to attain ends in this world—a son, a good crop, recovery from illness etc.— . . . as much a part of Hinduism as any other aspect." See also Flood 1996:17ff.

31. For these and other deities of the Hindu pantheon, consult, e.g., Bhattacharji 1970. Knott (1998:57ff) cites the conversation from the Brihadaranyaka Upanishad 3.9.1 that expresses a monistic reduction of the 300,306 Hindu deities to one. While the ultimate purport of this passage is Vedantic, it nevertheless expresses an interplay between a pantheon of key figures and a pagan proliferation into a multitude of local and departmental varieties.

32. On the *pañcayatanapuja*, see Sullivan 1997:213ff. See also Flood 1996:113; Sanderson in Sutherland et al. 1988:662; and Weightman in Hinnells 1984:207ff. On the Hindu gods and goddesses in general, see Hardy in Sutherland et al. 1988:610–18. See further Eck 1982; Martin 1972; Sastri 1974; and Stutley 1985. For the deities of Nepal, both Hindu and Buddhist, see Detmold and Rubel 1979.

33. On the nuance between such "nonhuman beings" as *yaksas, ganas,* and *nagas,* on the one hand, and *devas,* "gods," and *devis,* "goddesses," on the other, see Hardy in Sutherland et al. 1988:619ff. Moreover, Hardy finds this local animism paralleling "a trend to give concrete form to being believed to be permanently present in a given place." For Hindu iconography itself, see Eck 1982; Pal 1981; and Rao 1971.

34. E.g., Chatpatimata, Pattuguru, Khokhidevi, Sati Sthan, Agiyabir, Lahurabir, Daitrabir, Karamanbir, and Harasubarahm. See in particular, Chattopadhyaya 1973.

35. Eck 1982 offers a discussion of these folk or demotic figures of indigenous veneration.

36. In Banaras, for example, the rite known as *bhuta jharana* is frequently performed at the shrines of the *birs* and *satis* to get rid of or avoid any ghostly influence on the *bhuta-pishach.* It also occurs at the Pishachamochan *kund*, a Kashi center for the *pinda dan*, or ancestor rites. See Vidyarthi et al. 1979.

37. Eck 1982; Weightman in Hinnells 1984:217ff. For death rituals in general, see Mookerjee 1985:143–51.

38. On both animism and animatism, see Richard Brandt's article, "Primitive Religion," in Ferm 1945:608ff.

39. Eck (1998:36) obliquely refers to the *anima-animus* substratum dynamic in discussing Shiva's aniconic and/or phallic symbol: "We suspect the interpretations of the 'eye of the beholder': The *linga* consists of two parts: the vertical stone shaft, which may be seen as the male component, Siva, and the circular horizontal base, called a *yoni* or *pitha*, which is the female component, Sakti."

40. The *bir* stone can perhaps best be described as of the nature of the *svayambhuva-lingam*, or a natural shape; the *ganapa-lingam*, a conical or cylindrical shape; the *arsha-lingam*, a spheroidal shape; or the *daivika lingam*, a flame shape. When compared with the *manusha-lingam* or those sculptured according to the rules prescribed by the *Agamas*, all these are described as having no shape and no measurement. For another classification of *lingams*, see Tagare 1996: 22–24, 112ff. In contrast to Tagare's denial of Shiva's symbol as the human penis, Flood 1996:29 refers to "'phallic'-shaped stones [that] have . . . been found [at Indus Valley sites], suggestive of the later aniconic representation of Siva, the *linga*." Elsewhere, Flood (1996:151) explicitly states that the "linga represents a phallus within a vulva."

41. Weightman (in Hinnells 1984:225–27) discusses the *grama devata*. See also Eck 1998:34.

42. See Eck 1998:39, 53ff.

43. Shucindra, Kanyakumari, the Meenakshi-Somasundarar temple of Madurai, Rameswaram, Brihadeeshwarar in Thanjavur, Swamimalai, and the Nataraj temple of Chidambaram. See in particular Padmanabhan 1979.

44. Lipner (1994:278ff) discusses the Hindu temple. See also Harshananda 1979; Sullivan 1997:226ff; Weightman in Hinnells 1984:206; and Wu 1964.

45. Braden in Ferm 1945:770; Weightman in Hinnells 1984:206.

46. Sullivan 1997:103ff. For Hindu festivals overall, see Thomas 1971.

47. On the Brahmanas, see Bhattacharji 1970:5, 7–9, *passim*; Hardy in Sutherland et al. 1988:578–80; Lipner 1994:31ff, 36, *passim*; York 1995a:402–5.

48. See Flood 1996:42ff; Mookerjee 1985:34ff, 38; Sullivan 1997:24, 258ff. See also Ashby in Crim 1981:307ff.

49. See, *passim*, York 1995a:401–20.

50. "The greatest regular assemblies of human beings on earth are those of pilgrims" (Westwood 1997:18). In the case of India, the entire land forms a sacred geography (Eck 1998:65). Flood (1996:212) recognizes that in connection with Hinduism, pilgrimage is "integral."

51. In fact, "the more profound our study, the more difficult it becomes to distinguish Buddhism from Brahmanism" (Coomaraswamy n.d.:45). For some introductory works on Buddhism, see Cush 1994; Gethin 1998; Harvey 1990, 2001;

Lopez 1995; and Williams 2000. Further recommendations are Armstrong 2000a; Gyatso 2001; Keown 2000; Powers 2000; and the 2000 reissue of Conze 1980. Gombrich 1988 explores the social history of Theravada Buddhism, and Williams 1989 presents not only the doctrinal foundations of Mahayana Buddhism but also much of the devotion and iconography connected to it. See also Hawkins 1999.

52. See Conze 2000:22ff. Hardy (in Sutherland et al. 1988:596) mentions the transience of all empirical phenomena.

53. Note Powers 2000:36. Apart from the deference they receive, the Theravada *bhikkhus* have little similarity to the Hindu brahmins. The Hinayanist priesthood is open to all, and in fact, in Thailand, virtually every male once past the age of twenty is ordained as a monk during a monsoon season for a minimum period of three months. The life they lead is austere, and they must eschew all entertainment and luxuries, including a comfortable bed, worldly goods, sexual intercourse, and any physical contact with women, money, gold, silver, and even food and drink that has not been expressly offered to them. They take but two meals per day, the second to be completed before noon, after which they abstain from further consumption until the ensuing daybreak. The priest's duties include reciting morning and evening prayers and giving sermons on the days of full, new, and quarter moons as well as assisting in the performances of special rites, for example, blessing ceremonies, rituals of paying homage to teachers, marriages, funerals, state functions, and even exorcisms of haunted houses.

54. On Buddhist temples in general, both Theravada and Mahayana, see Harvey 1990:170–72.

55. Strictly speaking, the Buddha's enlightenment signified the "death" of his self, his becoming the "Tathagata, one who had, quite simply, 'gone.'" But it was not his "final nirvana," *parinibbana*, that came with the physical death of the body. Before that, he was a person who "had learned to manipulate his psyche in order to live without egotism" (Armstrong 2000b:112).

56. On the Three Treasures, see Conze 2000:18–25.

57. Conze (2000:21) speaks of the indestructibility of the bony parts of the Buddha's body which, upon cremation, "were not reduced to ashes" but were distributed as relics.

58. "In the region of modern Thailand, a mix of Mahayana and Saivism was present from the tenth century" (Harvey 1990:145). Afterward, the demotic populations were converted to Theravada by Mon missions beginning in the twelfth century. The royalty had converted to Theravada by the fourteenth century, but undoubtedly the earlier substratum persisted as well.

59. Armstrong 2000a:84-86.

60. Conze 2000:86–89; Reynolds in Crim 1981:142–45.

61. Keyes in Crim 1981:321ff; Powers 2000:21.

62. Describing Theravada in general, Cousins (Hinnells 1984:313) asserts, "Buddhism has had little difficulty in accommodating a large number of local

beliefs concerning various gods, spirits and the like." Keyes (in Crim 1981:322) speaks of the subordination and integration of "folk Brahminism" to Buddhism among the Thai and Lao. For Thai Buddhism, see Jumsai 1980.

63. See Tambiah 1970.

64. On the *preta* as a constantly hungry ghost, see Harvey 1990:33ff and Powers 2000:168.

65. The four Buddhist festivals are those of Thailand's Magha, considered the third lunar month; Vaishakha, the sixth month; Ashadha, the eighth month; and Ashvina, the eleventh month. The Thais call the first one Makha Bucha and celebrate the day on which 1,250 disciples spontaneously but also coincidentally arrived to hear the Buddha preach. On this "All Saints' Day," worshipers carry lighted candles three times around the *bot*. The Wesak Bucha of Vaishakha, however, is the most special day of the year for Buddhists, as it is not only Buddha Jayanti, the birthday of Sakyamuni, but also both the day on which he received enlightenment and the one on which he died. Again, devotees circle the *bot* three times with lighted tapers. Asalaha Bucha of Ashadha commemorates the Buddha's first sermon after attaining enlightenment, which he gave to the five ascetics in the Deer Park of Sarnath, a suburb of Banaras. It also signifies the Buddhist "Lent," which begins the following day. This corresponds to the rainy season during which all priests are must remain inside their monasteries and not travel. The investiture of *bhikkhus* is held at this time, including the ordination of most Thai youths after the age of twenty as temporary monks. Villagers make a large "Lenten" candle—sometimes even taller than the height of a person—and in a colorful procession it is taken to the temple and presented to the *bhikkhus*. The candle is then used to light the image of the Buddha during the monsoon. The Atthami Bucha of Ashvina marks the day of the Buddha's cremation. It also signifies the end of this "Lent" as well as the presentation of new robes to the priests, which the people bring to the temple, again in a bright procession with musical accompaniment and dancers. Properly speaking, only uncut white cloth is offered, and the monks are required both to dye the material and to sew it into their vestments before the next daybreak. The people must first ritualistically offer their gifts using the ancient Pali language of the Buddha before the priests can accept the offered Kathin cloth, new utensils, and presents. For the Thai Buddhist homage to teachers, see Yupho 1970.

66. On the contrasts between Theravada and Mahayana, see Chen in Crim 1981:126–30; Cousins in Hinnells 1984:295, *passim*; and Young 1995:214–16.

67. In speaking of the changes to original Buddhism as it traveled from India through Central Asia to China and Japan, Hori et al. (1972:49) signal the emergence of salvation through faith and belief in magic. The concept of Amitabha's Sukhavati, or Pure Land, as a Western Paradise inhabited by gods and humans culminates with the Jōdo shū and Jōdo shinshū of Japan (Hori et al. 1972:59–61). See also Harvey 1990:126ff. Powers (2000:57) traces this emphasis on "other-power"

(Chinese: *t'o-li*) in the Ch'ing-t'u tsung, or Pure Land school, to fourth and fifth century C.E. China. On the "other worlds" in general, see Conze 1959:221ff.

68. Chen (in Crim 1981:129) contrasts the "cold and passionless" *arhat* of Theravada with the selfless Mahayana bodhisattva. Harvey (1990:92ff) describes the "subtle pride" of the *arhat* from the Mahayana perspective.

69. For the Mahayana pantheon, see Harvey 1990:129–33; also Conze 2000: 47ff. On the *dharma* body of the "great being," or *tathagata*, consult Harvey 1990: 127ff, 261ff.

70. See Coleman (in Crim 1981:780ff). *Tathagatha* itself is a Buddhist epithet that signifies the attainment of the transcendental state of awakening.

71. Powers (2000:251) discusses the *yi dam*, or tutelary, in connection with tantric visualization practice. See esp. Harvey 1990:261–64. Hardy (in Sutherland et al. 1988:620), speaking of the classical religions of India, claims that "once the cults of the epic and puranic gods, and indeed, Gods, had gained prominence, a complex interaction with . . . folk-religious cults began."

72. The Contemplative school, which embraces the once operative *dhyana* sects of India as well as Ch'an in China and Zen in Japan, is based on concentrated mental meditation and inner enlightenment through sudden intuition. In contrast, the Rational school (Chinese: T'ien-t'ai, Japanese: Tendai) emphasizes both logical study, particularly of the Lotus Sutra of the Mysterious Law and meditation in which the object is not successive detachment from desire and the material realm but the discovery of truth as innately given. Like Zen and the purely Japanese nationalistic reform movements founded by Nichiren, the Pure Land school (Chinese: Ching-t'u, Japanese: Jōdo and Jōdo shin) began in Japan as an offshoot of Tendai that stresses salvation through faith in the merciful compassion of the Dhyana Buddha of the West, Amitabha (Japanese: Amida). This is a purely emotional form of Buddhism centering on a savior cult rather than an ascetic denial aiming for enlightenment. It is the least monastically oriented of all the various forms of Buddhism. In fact, Jōdo shinshū priests marry and live otherwise secular lives.

73. On Mantrayana/Vajrayana Buddhism, see Cousins's discussion of "Northern Buddhism" (Hinnells 1984:333, 335–39). Conze (1980:75ff) historicizes three phases of tantric Mahayana development that he terms Mantrayána, Vajrayána, and Sahajayána, culminating with the tenth-century syncretistic and astrological Kálacakra, or "Wheel of Time" text, and initiation ceremony. For Vajrayana in general, see Rhie and Thurman 1991. For Shingon, note Yamasaki 1988. The Tibetan variety of Vajrayana is known as Lamaism, but in Tibet a more traditional Mahayana Buddhism continued to coexist with what became known as the "Short Path," exemplified by the Yellow Hat, or reformed sect, whose leader is the Dalai Lama. For Tibet and Tibetan Buddhism, see David-Neel 1958; Jigmei et al. 1980; Maraini 1952; Reynolds 1978; and Zwalf 1981.

74. The Japanese Shingon sect calls Vairocana or the Adi Buddha, Dainichi; the Tibetan Red Hat (rNying-ma-pa) tradition terms the same, Samantabhadra.

75. E.g., Rhie and Thurman 1991:228ff.

76. There are, of course, countless variations of the cosmic diagram, but in the Nepalese version of the *vajra dhatu* mandala that one sees throughout the Kathmandu Valley and on the votive stupas, the *tathagathas* are recognized by color as well as *mudra*, or hand position. It also is easy to identify Amoghasiddhi of the north because of his distinctive canopy formed by the hood of a seven-headed cobra. At the important Buddhist centers of Svayambunath and Bodhanath, Vairocana, or the Adi Buddha, is depicted on all four sides of the *torana*, the square top-piece surmounting the *chaitya* dome, as a pair of "all-seeing" eyes. See Detmold and Rubel 1979.

77. On Tara, see Conze 1980:78, 111; Harvey 1990:137; Powers 2000:216.

78. E.g., Harvey 1990:263; Rhie and Thurman 1991:16, esp. 51.

79. Powers 2000:62, 252; Rhie and Thurman 1991:390.

80. Rhie and Thurman 1991:370ff.

81. Note Cousins in Hinnells 1984:327; also Rhie and Thurman 1991:34. In describing the Bön contributions to Tibetan Lamaism, Wing-tsit Chan (Ferm 1945:93, 101ff) mentions the "great deal of the indigenous animistic, phallic, necromantic, devil-dancing, and demon-worshiping" elements of that "Shamanist" religion, while Harvey (1990:172) includes shrines dedicated to various gods as well as nature spirits as a typical part of the Buddhist temple.

82. Hori et al. (1972:53) mentions the "traces of magic" from the earliest Buddhism of India that became increasingly augmented by folk beliefs with the advent of Tantrism. On merit in general as well as its possible "transference," see Harvey 1990:42–44. Powers (2000:170) discusses the same under the entry "punya."

83. Rhie and Thurman 1991:136–38, 322–30; Wing-tsit Chan in Ferm 1945: 92ff.

84. Cousins in Hinnells 1984:336; Harvey 1990:126; Powers 2000:152ff, 204. See also Skorupski in Sutherland et al. 1988:796ff.

85. See Conze 1980:51ff on the three bodies of the Buddha.

86. In some respects, the *tulpa* is similar to the *nirmána-káya*, or phantom body of the Buddha (Conze 1980:51; Powers 2000:152ff). See also Hitching 1978: 241.

87. See the articles on "apotheosis," "deification," and "hero worship," respectively, by Newnan, Morrison, and Haydon in Ferm 1945:34, 221, 334.

88. E.g., L. S. Cousins in Hinnels 1984:331–39; and Skorupski in Sutherland et al. 1988:779–805. See Powers 2000:126 for a rejection of the term Lamaism.

89. On Bon-po, see Harvey 1990:145ff; Powers 2000:42; Rhie and Thurman 1991:21ff, 26; Skorupski in Sutherland et al. 1988:805–10; and Yamasaki 1988:14.

90. Skorupski (in Sutherland et al. 1988:782) mentions the "lesser or mundane deities *laukika*" of the Tibetan pantheon and their ability to absorb the pre-Buddhist local deities. See also 802, *passim*; and Spence 1960:413.

91. Note Skorupski in Sutherland et al. 1988:805. In Tibetan, the portable amulet case is known as a *gahu.*

92. Harvey 1990:172ff.

93. E.g., Béguin 1977.

94. On the sculptural icons, see Thurman in Rhie and Thurman 1991:37; also Detmold and Rubel 1979.

95. On the range of offerings in Buddhism in general as well as northern Buddhism in particular, see Harvey 1990:172–76; also Béguin 1977.

96. Bharati in Crim 1981:737. On the rNying-ma, or Red Hat school, see Harvey 1990:145ff; and Powers 2000:180. On Vajrabhairava and meditation on his image, see Rhie and Thurman 1991:36, also 282–87.

97. On the Buddhism and indigenous shamanism of Mongolia, see Baldick 2000:92–125; Conze 1980:138ff; Fontein 1999; and Siklós in Sutherland et al. 1988:811–17. For *mani* stones as well as rudimentary piles of stones as elementary stupas, or *chöten;* see Thurman in Rhie and Thurman 1991:34.

98. Bernbaum in Swan 1993:108. Stone offerings in Tibetan are *chöd do;* in Mongolian, *obo.*

99. See Béguin 1977:*passim.* The Nepalese round stones are known as *mai.*

100. Baldick 2000:116ff; Hessig 1980.

101. On the Buddhist festival calendar in general, including those of the Southern, Northern, and Eastern traditions, see Harvey 1990:191–95.

102. These range from Maha Shiva Ratri; Holi; Naga Panchami; Janai Purnima Raksha Bandhan, the full moon of Shrawan; Krishna Jayanti; and Ganesh Chaturthi; to Durga Puja, Diwali, and Basant Panchami.

103. See Dhar and Dhar 1985; Deep 1993; and Lall 1991.

104. See also Majupuria and Kumar 1998.

105. E.g., Baldick 2000:112,116. While I have linked Qoormusta functionally with Indra, Baldick points out that nominally and historically, he is clearly Indra's Iranian opponent, the supreme god Ahura Mazda. Siklós (in Sutherland et al. 1988:812) identifies Khormusta with the Zurvanite Ohrmazd and the Mazdean Ahura Mazda and refers to the "Mongolian shamanic synthesis" comprising "the various Iranian, Taoist, Manchu-Tunguz shamanist and, later, Buddhist ideas." On Samantabhadra, see Rhie and Thurman 1991:198.

106. E.g., Béguin 1977; also Hessig 1980:84–91.

107. Hessig 1980:25f, 49ff.

108. The Vedic Prithivi or Bhumi; the Mongolian Etüen Eke. The waters as deities are depicted as *nagas,* or snake gods.

109. Hori et al. 1972:65.

110. The Buddhist edifices of Kyoto range from the dominating Higashi and Nishi Honganji temples that are, respectively, the headquarters of the Shinshū ōtaniha and Jōdo shinshū sects. There are also the superbly magnificent Kiyomizu temple and the Tōji temple, Shingon's central seminary of Mikkyō, or Esoteric

Buddhism. Among the Zen centers, we have here the Myōshinji temple with its majestically rustic structures; the Ryōanji temple with its famous fifteen-stone rock garden; and the Daitokuji temple whose compound more or less reminded me of an immaculate and prosperous Beverly Hills. On the other hand, the Rinzai Zen Kenninji temple, with its incorporation of Tendai and Shingon teachings, appeared to attract a great profusion of Shinto-Buddhist shrines in its immediate area.

111. Czaja 1974:266ff; Yamasaki 1988:53ff; also Hori et al. 1972:124.

112. Hori et al. 1972:53.

113. York 1995a:99.

114. Hori et al. 1972:17ff; Powers 2000:105.

115. Conze 1980:102, 124; Harvey 1990:162; Hori et al. 1972:18; Lowell [1894] 1990:33ff, 166–69; Reid in Hinnells 1984:376ff.

116. Havens and Inoue (2001:3, 13) refer to the word *gongen*, a Buddhist term for *avatar*, used for the *kami* who were "interpreted as temporal manifestations of the eternal Buddha." They also mention the designation *banshin* for imported deities that could likewise be used to indicate the Buddha (5ff).

117. Hitoshi in Kornicki and McMullen 1996:120ff; Hori et al. 1972:17ff; Yamasaki 1988:48, 52ff.

118. An introduction to Christianity is presented by Wilson 1999. See also Walls in Hinnells 1984:56–122; and, on the history of Christianity, Sutherland et al. 1988.

119. E.g., Hutton 1991:284ff: "During the sixth century it became more common all over the former Roman world to transform pagan buildings into churches." Note in particular Fox, who finds in the religious procession that "the impact of a pagan cult can still be sensed in the journeys of the Christian images." He does not see these, however, as pagan survivals but as "similar expressions of religious honour" (1987:68).

120. See Jackson 2000. Jackson lists the rejection of the ecumenical creeds as among the chief differences between the Church of Jesus Christ of Latter-day Saints and general Christian faith. Another is the Mormon belief that God has a finite, material body. Finally, citing the "Relations with the Church of Jesus Christ of Latter-Day Saints and Its People: Position Paper" issued by the Presbyterian Church's Presbytery of Utah in Salt Lake City on January 21, 1995, Jackson concludes that "Mormon theology is tri-theistic rather than Trinitarian. . . . It would be more accurate to classify Mormon theology as polytheistic rather than mono-theistic" (58). On Latter-day Saints, see Clark and Burgess in Ferm 1945:431ff; Lippy in Crim 1981:423–25; Melton in Hinnells 1984:460; Melton 1986:29–38 and 39–44. On the fundamentalist or polygamy-practicing groups, Lippy states, "Some strands of Mormon thought posit a plurality of deities, giving the religion a poly-theistic cast" (424).

121. The classic work that presents this development is Frazer 1911–14. Hut-

ton (1991:153–56) discusses the transformation of genuine pagan deities into characters of early Christian and Celtic vernacular literature. Hutton (1991:166ff) also mentions the "Christianization" of pagan sacred springs and how their rededication to a Christian saint allowed their continued use, but see esp. 284 where Hutton names examples of the "direct continuity" of images of the former deities the Italian Black Madonnas, the Virgin of Chartres, and the Madonna and Child or Ceres and Proserpina of Enna in Sicily. Turcan (1996:336) in reference to the durability of the local and rural pagan cults, claims that "bishops had to come to terms with these popular devotions by Christianizing them under the patronage of the saints." See also Ferguson 1970:239–42.

122. Brenner 1929. Speaking of La Virgen de la Caridad del Cobre, the patron saint of Cuba, De La Torre 2001:838 informs us that "this same image is venerated by the practitioners of Santería, the repressed religion of Cuba, as Ochún, brought to the island by African slaves." See also González-Wippler [1973] 1981.

123. See Eric R. Wolf, "The Virgin of Guadalupe: A Mexican National Symbol," *Journal of American Folklore* 71 (1958): 35–39; reprinted in Lessa and Vogt 1979: 112–15. Devine 1982:183 identifies Our Lady of Guadalupe as the lunar water-mother Tontantzín Cuahtlalpancihuateotl, "with roots deep in the Aztec substratum of Mexican culture"; see also xix.

The key Marian centers include Fatima, Lourdes, Guadaloupe, Ballinspittle, and Madjugorje. The literature on Mariology and Mariolatry in general is enormous and varies from apologetic to academic. For some representative works, see Begg 1985; Benko 1993; Boss 2000; Daniélou 1949; Johnson 1994; Miller and Samples 1992; and Preston 1982. Note in addition *Maria: Journal of Marian Studies*, first published by the Sheffield Academic Press in August 2000. On Walsinham, Lourdes, Guadalupe, Fátima, Czestochowa, and Medugorje, see also Westwood 1997:208, 210–13.

124. Eilberg-Schwartz 1994.

125. For a radical Christian argument that seeks to avoid the difficulties of panentheism and pantheism in understanding traditional Christian theology, see John Macquarrie's discussion of Grace Jantzen, who speculates "that God and the world constitute a single reality, within which the world or physical universe can be considered as the body of God" (Macquarrie 1988:438). Jantzen argues that a God who is separate from worldly suffering is "morally questionable."

126. On the neo-orthodox position associated with Karl Barth concerning the transcendence or "wholly otherness" of God, see, e.g., Piper in Ferm 1945:57ff. In reaffirming the position of classical Christianity, Barth stresses "the discontinuity between creator and creature" (Leith in Crim 1981:755). In a 1970 lecture, Joseph Campbell stated that in the West, "God and his creatures are *not* to be conceived of as in any sense identical" (Campbell 1972:97). In place of an experience of *identity*, which is heretical, the Judeo-Christian tradition allows only a religious *relationship* to God. See also Berger 1990:43, 56ff, 134ff.

127. Ferm 1945:783.

128. See Hutton 1991:253. Hutton also discusses the ambivalence of much of the evidence in connection with Britain (e.g., 1991:260, 271). See also York 1995a: 437.

129. Ferguson 1970:238ff; Frazer 1911–14; Hutton 1991:285ff.

130. In summing up the final contest between Christianity and Greco-Roman paganism, Ferguson (1970:242) concludes, "Christianity won, but it had changed in the winning."

131. As an Arab creation, Islam represents numerically the dominant ideology of the Hamito-Semitic linguistic family which itself covers 4 percent of the earth's population. The Hamito-Semitic or, as it is sometimes called, the Afro-Asiatic family, includes languages spoken by more than one million speakers: Arabic, Berber, Amharic, Hausa, Galla, Tigrinya, Hebrew, and Somali. The Arabs account for by far the greatest number, with roughly 80 million speakers. Some suggested source references on Islam are Afkhami 1995; Armstrong 2000b; Bloom and Blair 2002; Elias 1999; Horrie and Chippindale 1991; Rippin 2000; Ruthven 1997; and Walton 1993. See also the Islam section edited by Peter Clarke in Sutherland et al. 1988:305–529; as well as Welch in Hinnells 1984:123–70.

132. Baldick (in Sutherland et al. 1988:326ff) argues that contrary to popular opinion, conversion to Islam was not universally achieved through military intimidation but, rather, through discriminatory taxation.

133. For Baldick (in Sutherland et al. 1988:321), Shi'a resembles Roman Catholicism in contrast to the Sunni majority, which is more like Protestantism.

134. Horrie and Chippindale 1991:166. Bloom and Blair (2002:201ff) also mention Mashhad in Khurasan, burial site of Reza, the eighth imam, as the holiest Iranian Shiite site, complemented by Qom, burial place of Fatima, the sister of Reza, and now the Shiite theological center. See also Armstrong 2000b:37, 57, 147ff.

135. See MacEoin in Sutherland et al. 1988:458–62.

136. E.g., Horrie and Chippindale 1991:125–37. Shiite sects include Assassins, Druses, Fatimites, Ismailis, Karmathians, and Zaidiyah.

137. On Sufism, see Armstrong 2000b:62ff, *passim*; Baldick in Sutherland et al. 1988:323ff; Bloom and Blair 2002:57ff, *passim*; Elias 1999:54–60, 103ff; and Horrie and Chippindale 1991:139–44;. Armstrong, however, calls Sufism "the mysticism of Sunni Islam" (2000b:62); but Johnson (in Ferm 1945:742) identifies it as a "system of Mohammedan mysticism arising chiefly in Persia."

138. Bloom and Blair 2002:60ff; Elias 1999:58ff.

139. E.g., Baldick in Sutherland et al. 1988:321; Newby in Crim 1981:254.

140. Despite the affirmations of the medallion's owner, I am inclined to think that it depicted Muhammad's cousin Ali rather than the prophet himself (see Elias 1999:22). Horrie and Chippindale (1991:136) go as far to state that the Babylon-

ian cult of the god king and divine incarnation have survived as "'Ali-worship within Islam and Christ-worship within Judaism, since Christianity is sometimes described as a Jewish sub-sect."

141. On Hubal, see the unabridged 1944 edition of *Webster's New International Dictionary*, p. 1210, as well as Armstrong 2000b:10. See also Teixidor 1977:38ff, 71–76. Armstrong tells us that originally the Kaaba was dedicated to the Nabatean deity Hubal, with "360 idols arranged around the Kabah, probably representing the days of the year" (2000b:10).

142. See Elias 1999:31, 35, 71; Horrie and Chippindale 1991:14ff, 18ff; York 1995a:214.

143. Young 1995:362.

144. E.g., Nizami in Sutherland et al. 1988:374. Elias (1999:59) also mentions the shrine of Sayyida Zaynab, Muhammad's great-great-great-granddaughter, in Cairo.

145. For the Islamic calendar and the principal commemorative events associated with it, see Welch in Hinnells 1984:166.

146. The Arabic terms, respectively, for *worship, monotheism,* and *polytheism* are *ibadah, tawhid,* and *shirk.*

147. Elias (1999:59) identifies the miraculous charisma of the saint with *baraka,* a contagious propensity that enables "curative and mediatory powers."

148. Hultkrantz 1953.

149. Horrie and Chippindale 1991:23. According to Johnson (in Ferm 1945:501), "The Moslem faith *iman* rests first of all in the basic conviction of one God and no other." See also Smart 1989:282.

150. Baldick in Sutherland et al. 1988:327.

151. Horrie and Chippindale 1991:127.

152. Horrie and Chippindale 1991:136.

153. Elias 1999:59ff.

154. Horrie and Chippindale 1991:137. In fact, the "God is One" doctrine becomes so dominant in the later portions of the Qur'an that Welch (in Hinnells 1984:132ff) says, "It is easy to overlook the fact that earlier parts of the Islamic scripture do not reject the existence of other deities." He affirms that in vernacular Islam the belief persists in an elaborate spirit world comprising angels, *jinn,* Iblis or Satan, and other supernatural beings who affect this world and the other alike. On the three pagan goddesses of the *Satanic Verses,* see Gordon 1943:50ff; Horrie and Chippindale 1991:22ff; and York 1995a:73. Armstrong (2000b:148–52) briefly mentions the consequences of the Salman Rushdie / *Satanic Verses* affair.

155. "Thus Calvinism represented the culmination of the process which had been initiated by the Hebrew prophets and propelled by Hellenistic scientific thought . . . —the elimination of magic from the world" (Hill 1973:117, also 233, 264). Hill cites Peter Berger in allowing that in some respects, the Christian doctrine

of the incarnation amounted to a "re-enchantment of the world" in comparison to the strict monotheism of Judaism (264). Nevertheless, in regard to pagan Europe, even Catholicism represents a "disenchantment."

156. On secularization, see York 1995b:281ff; also 253f. See also Hill 1973: 228–51; and Wilson in Sutherland et al. 1988:953–66. For Berger 1990:29, the global trend of secularization means that a mass discovery of the supernatural "is not in the books."

157. In describing secular humanism, Mohabir (1992:115) claims, "It denies the existence of God and its greatest stronghold is in the affluent West." Writing from an apologetic and evangelizing perspective, Mohabir identifies this as "pagan ideas" that erode Christian values and influence. But for someone like Nakamura (1964:577), who extols "modern ideas and culture," "the weakness of the critical spirit of the Japanese people allowed the persistence of old ideologies that should have been abolished or modified by radical social changes." As Wilson recognizes, secularism is an "ideology [that] denotes a negative evaluative attitude towards religion." Nevertheless, Wilson sees this as a religious position in that it "adopts certain premises a priori and canvasses a normative albeit negative position about supernaturalism" (in Sutherland et al. 1988:954). But secularism may still embrace a mystical, if not supernatural, dimension. For "ecstatic naturalism," see Corrington 1997, along with Robert Cummings Neville's foreword, ix–xv.

158. Macquarrie (1988:181) suggests that humanism is the belief in progress through science, intelligence, and education rather than through religious insight. According to Mohabir (1992:115), secular humanism supersedes reason as "the sole arbiter of standards and controller of destiny."

159. As Carroll (1993:2) understands it, in tracing humanism's development from the Renaissance and Reformation through Nietzsche and Marx, humanism has sought "to replace God by man, to put man at the centre of the universe, to deify him." But see also Braden in Ferm 1945:349 on "religious humanism," in which the stress is on this-worldly and cooperative progress and, while generally nontheistic, may assume theistic forms as well. For a discussion of atheism and agnosticism, see Jeffner in Sutherland et al. 1988:52–60.

160. On Deism, see Enslin in Ferm 1945:221ff.

161. Adler 1986:20, 305, 307, 441. See also York 1995b:102.

162. Goodman 1988:171. For Berger 1990:84, "human life gains the greatest part of its richness from the capacity for ecstasy."

163. Stark 1999. Stark particularly lambastes (47) the primitive-mind thesis that formed the hermeneutic for the arguments of Comte, Spencer, Lévy-Bruhl, and Durkheim.

164. York 1995a:302ff, 305.

165. York 1995a:312ff.

166. On the connection between Dionysus and/or the Dionysian festivals and religious drama, see Bell 1790:vol. 1, pp. 243ff; Eastman in Ferm 1945:648; and

Smart 1989:228. Drama declined with the conquest of Greece by Rome, and "it was the Dionysism of the Hellenized East rather than that of Euripides' Bacchae which burst upon Rome in 186 B.C. with the affair of the Bacchanalia" (Turcan 1996:293). With the advent of the church, the theater was suppressed for a millennium. Its rebirth began in England during the ninth and tenth centuries with the institution of church-sponsored passion plays that also became popular on much of the European continent. With the eventual development of *pageants*, or "rolling platforms," by which the stage could be wheeled from the churchyard to the marketplace, plays became increasingly secular. In Italy, the Commedia del arte played a key role in the emergence of the modern theatrical performance.

167. Durkheim 1976:235–55, 479–87. See also Shilling and Mellor 1998.

168. For a concise history of the origins of opera, see Ewen 1963:355–60.

169. Founded by the occultist Samuel MacGregor Mathers in England in 1887, the Hermetic Order of the Golden Dawn (OGD) attracted such writers as William Butler Yeats, Bulwer-Lytton, and Bram Stoker as well as the magician Aleister Crowley, who was expelled in 1900. As a branch from the Rosicrucian Society and patterned after the Hermetic Society, the OGD became an influential occult secret society engaged in the practice of magic. An American offshoot is the Builders of the Adytum. Crowley proceeded to found his own Ordo Templi Orientis. Newport 1998:540 describes the OGD as a "magical and pseudo-Masonic community." See Barrett 1996:182–84. For the Church of Satan, founded in 1966 by Anton LaVey, continuing the tradition of Crowley, see Barrett 1996:168; and Newport 1998: 543–54. In regard to other groups associated with the Western Mystery Tradition, Barrett also discusses the Builders of the Adytum, Dion Fortune's Society of the Inner Light, the Servants of the Light, and the London Group (184–91).

170. Wilson 1973:12: "The sect may be regarded as a self-distinguishing protest movement, its protest . . . may be against the state, against the secular institutions of society. Or in opposition to or separation from particular institutions or groups within the society." See also Lofland and Richardson's typology of the religious movement organization RMO as a subtype, along with political movement organization PMO, and also of the social movement organization SMO, discussed in York 1995b:322ff. See also Beckford 1985:79.

171. See Stevens 1989:*passim*, esp. 393–415.

172. See, for example, Gustaitis 1969; Tipton 1982; York 1995b:37ff.

173. Note, e.g., Thompson 1993:292–95. For the indigenous practice of Hawaiian Kahuna, see Beckworth 1971 and Steiger 1982.

174. York 1995a:389–401.

175. York 1995a:231ff, *passim*.

176. York 1995a:249, 275–77, 286, 291ff 298ff, 519.

177. See Johnson 1995:C1; Menninger 1969:149; York 1995a:504ff, 574, n. 139.

178. E.g., York 1995a:522–30.

179. York 1995a:105, 525.

180. E.g., York 1995a:111, 533.
181. E.g., Blakeney 1920:389, 567ff; Newman in Ferm 1945:669; Rose 1926:82; York 1986:68, 1995a:243, 277, 299.
182. Bell 1790:vol. 1, pp. 13ff.

Notes to Chapter 3

1. Huxley 1937: 227.
2. For some of the key Gnostic texts, see Grant 1978 and Layton 1987. On Gnosticism itself, see Grant's introduction (13–19, *passim*) as well as Bloom 1996. See also Moehlman in Ferm 1945:300ff; and Smart 1989:240, 242.
3. For a third type of religion, which I have designated *astral* and is exemplified by Raëlianism, see my entry "UFO Religion and Nature" in the forthcoming *Encyclopedia of Religion and Nature* Continuum. Like paganism, astralism assumes the reality of the tangible or physical world, but it denies the reality of any supernatural horizon whatsoever. In an astral understanding, supernatural entities are translated into some sort of extraterrestrial space beings. However, if paganism and gnosticism can be seen as opposite ideal types, the opposite of astralism would be "infernalism," in which reality for the individual becomes locked in a private hell. This last would be a form of psychosis and not a religious understanding that could be shared with others.
4. Albanese 1990. See also York 2001:284.
5. On the contrasts, similarities, and overlaps between contemporary Western paganism and New Age, see York 1995b:145–77; also York 1997, 2001:285–88.
6. Smart 1989:214, 222–24; Sprengling in Ferm 1945:465-67.
7. On the Cathari or Albigenses, see, e.g., Buckler and Hausheer in Ferm 1945:9, 129; Russell 1946:464, 468–70; Smart 1989:271–73. An excellent exposé is O'Shea 2000.
8. See Stark 1999:52.
9. E.g., Baldick in Sutherland et al. 1988:552–68; and Boyce in Hinnells 1984: 171–90.
10. York 1995a:164–84.
11. Smart (1989:242) refers to Christianity's "positive attitudes to the world."
12. Berger 1990:175.
13. Caputo 2001:94.
14. Barrett 1996:285. For more on the history of fundamentalism, see Miller in Crim 1981:268ff; and Sweet in Ferm 1945:291ff.
15. Wilber 1996:321.
16. See Ardvisson 1999.
17. E.g., York 1995b:124–27.
18. Berger 1990:119.
19. Martin 1992:53, 59.

20. E.g., Lewis 1994.
21. See also York in Swatos and Tomasi 2002:143; and Berger 1990:101.
22. Corrington 1997:2.
23. Berger 1990:168.
24. In York 1995b:129.
25. Corrington 1997:166.
26. Berger 1990:51, 92.

# References

Adler, Joseph. 2002. Chinese Religions. London: Routledge.

Adler, Margot. 1986. Drawing Down the Moon: Witches, Druids, Goddess-Worshippers, and Other Pagans in America Today. Boston: Beacon Press.

Afkhami, Mahnaz, ed. 1995. Faith and Freedom: Women's Human Rights in the Muslim World. London: I. B. Tauris.

Ahern, Emily M. 1973. The Cult of the Dead in a Chinese Village. Stanford, CA: Stanford University Press.

Albanese, Catherine. 1990. Nature Religion in America from the Algonkian Indians to the New Age. Chicago: University of Chicago Press.

Alexander, Pat, organizing ed. 1994. The World's Religions. Oxford: Lion Publishing.

Andrews, Lynn V. 1981. Medicine Woman. New York: Perennial Library.

d'Apremont, Arnaud. 1999. Tradition nordique. Puiseaux: Pardès.

Ardvisson, Stefan. 1999. "Aryan Mythology As Science and Ideology." Journal of the American Academy of Religion 67 (June): 327–54.

Armstrong, Karen. 2000a. Buddha. London: Weidenfeld & Nicolson.

———. 2000b. Islam: A Short History. London: Weidenfeld & Nicolson.

Aston, William George. [1905] 1974. Shinto: The Way of the Gods. New York: Krishna.

Awolalu, J. Omosade. 1979. Yoruba Beliefs and Sacrificial Rites. London: Longman.

Badejo, Dierdre. 1996. Òsun Sèègèsí: The Elegant Deity of Wealth, Power and Feminity. Trenton, NJ: Africa World Press.

Baity, Philip Chesley. 1975. Religion in a Chinese Town. Taipei: Chinese Association for Folklore.

Baldick, Julian. 2000. Animal and Shaman: Ancient Religions of Central Asia. New York: NYU Press.

Barnes, Sandra T., ed. 1997. Africa's Ogun: Old World and New. Bloomington: Indiana University Press.

Barrett, David B., ed. 1982. Christian Encyclopedia: A Comparative Study of Churches and Religions in the Modern World A.D. 1900–2000. Oxford: Oxford University Press.

Barrett, David V. 1996. Sects, "Cults" and Alternative Religions: A World Survey and Sourcebook. London: Blandford.

Bascom, William R. 1969. Ifa Divination: Communication between Gods and Men in West Africa. Bloomington: Indiana University Press.

Bastide, Roger. 1978. African Religions of Brazil: Toward a Sociology of Interpretation of Civilizations. Baltimore: John Hopkins University Press.

Bauer, Helen, and Sherwin Carlquist. 1980. Japanese Festivals. Tokyo: Tuttle.

Beckford, James A. 1985. Cult Controversies: The Societal Response to the New Religious Movements. London: Tavistock.

Beckworth, Martha. 1971. Hawaiian Mythology. Honolulu: University of Hawai'i Press.

Begg, Ean. 1985. The Cult of the Black Virgin. Boston: Arkana / Routledge & Kegan Paul.

Béguin, Gilles. 1977. Dieux et démons de l'Himalaya. Paris: Réunion des musées nationaux.

Bell, Diane. 1990. Daughters of the Dreaming. North Sydney: Allen & Unwin Australia.

Bell, John. 1790. New Pantheon; or, Historical Dictionary of the Gods, Demi-Gods, Heroes, and Fabulous Personages of Antiquity. London: British Library.

Benko, Stephen. 1993. The Virgin Goddess: Studies in the Pagan and Christian Roots of Mariology. New York: Brill.

Berger, Helen A. 1998. A Community of Witches: Contemporary Neo-Paganism and Witchcraft in the United States. Columbia: University of South Carolina Press.

Berger, Peter L. 1990. A Rumor of Angels: Modern Society and the Rediscovery of the Supernatural. New York: Doubleday.

Berthrong, John H., and Evelyn Nagai Berthrong. 2000. Confucianism: A Short Introduction. Oxford: Oneworld.

Bhattacharji, Sukumari. 1970. The Indian Theogony: Brahma, Visnu and Siva. Cambridge: Cambridge University Press.

Birdsall, George. 1997. The Feng Shui Companion: A User-Friendly Guide to the Ancient Art of Placement. Rochester, VT: Destiny Books.

Bishop, Peter. 1993. Dreams of Power: Tibetan Buddhism and the Western Imagination. London: Athlone.

Blacker, Carmen. 1992. The Catalpa Bow: A Study of Shamanistic Practices in Japan. London: Mandala.

Blakeney, E. H., ed. 1920. A Smaller Classical Dictionary. London: Dutton.

Blofeld, John. 1978. Taoism: The Road to Immortality. Boulder, CO: Shambhala.

Bloom, Harold. 1996. Omens of Millennium: The Gnosis of Angels, Dreams, and Resurrection. New York: Putnam.

Bloom, Jonathan, and Sheila Blair. 2002. Islam: A Thousand Years of Faith and Power. New Haven, CT: Yale University Press.

Bloomfield, Frena. 1983.The Book of Chinese Beliefs: A Journey into the Chinese Inner World. London: Arrow Books.

Bocking, Brian. 1997. A Popular Dictionary of Shinto. Richmond, Surrey: Curzon.

Bonewits, P. E. Isaac. 1979. Real Magic. Berkeley, CA: Creative Arts Book Company.

Bonnefoy, Yves, comp. 1993. American, African, and Old European Mythologies, trans. Wendy Doniger. Chicago: University of Chicago Press.

Booth, Newell S. Jr. 1977. African Religions: A Symposium. New York: NOK Publishers.

Boss, Sarah Jane. 2000. Empress and Handmaid: On Nature and Gender in the Cult of the Virgin Mary. London: Cassell/Continuum.

Bourke, Colin, Eleanor Bourke, and Bill Edwards, eds. 1994. Aboriginal Australia: An Introductory Reader in Aboriginal Studies. St. Lucia, Queensland: University of Queensland Press.

Bowker, John. 1997. The Oxford Dictionary of World Religions. Oxford: Oxford University Press.

Brenner, Anita. 1929. Idols behind Altars. New York: Harcourt, Brace.

Brock, Peggy, ed. 1989. Women Rites and Sites: Aboriginal Women's Cultural Knowledge. London: Unwin Hyman.

Brockington, John. 1981. The Sacred Press: Hinduism and Its Continuity and Diversity. Edinburgh: Edinburgh University Press.

Brown, Diana DeG. 1994.Umbanda: Religion and Politics in Urban Brazil. New York: Columbia University Press.

Brown, Joseph Epes. 1988. The Spiritual Legacy of the American Indian. New York: Crossroad.

Bullock, Alan, Oliver Stallybrass, and Stephen Trombley, eds. 1988. The Fontana Dictionary of Modern Thought. 2d ed. London: Fontana / HarperCollins.

Bunce, William K. 1982. Religions in Japan: Buddhism, Shinto, Christianity. Rutland, VT: Tuttle.

Campbell, Joseph. 1970. The Masks of God: Primitive Mythology. New York: Viking.

———. 1972. Myths to Live By. New York: Viking Penguin.

Caputo, John D. 2001. On Religion. London: Routledge.

Carmody, Denise Lardner, and John Tully Carmody. 1993. Original Visions: The Religions of Oral Peoples. New York: Macmillan.

Carpenter, Clive, ed. 1991. The Guinness Book of Answers. London: Guinness.

Carr, Wesley. 1991. Manifold Wisdom: Christians in the New Age. London: SPCK.

Carroll, John. 1993. Humanism: The Wreck of Western Culture. London: Fontana.

Casanowicz, Immanuel Moses. 1924. Shamanism of the Natives of Siberia. Washington, DC: Annual Report of the Smithsonian Institution.

Castaneda, Carlos. 1968. The Teachings of Don Juan: A Yaqui Way of Knowledge. Berkeley and Los Angeles: University of California Press.

———. 1972. Journey to Ixtlian: The Lessons of Don Juan. New York: Pocket Books.

Chamberlain, Jonathan. 1987. Chinese Gods. Selangar Darul Ehsan, Malaysia: Pelanduk.

Chattopadhyaya, Debiprasad. 1973. Lokāyata: A Study in Ancient Indian Materialism. New Delhi: People's Publishing.

Chesi, Gert. 1981. Vodun: Africa's Secret Power. Wörgl: Perlinger.

Christ, Carol P. 1997. Rebirth of the Goddess: Finding Meaning in Feminist Spirituality. Reading, MA: Addison-Wesley.

Christ, Carol P., and Judith Plaskow, eds. 1979. Womanspirit Rising: A Feminist Reader in Religion. San Francisco: Harper & Row.

Christoph, Henning, Klaus E. Müller, and Ute Ritz-Müller. 1999. Soul of Africa: Magical Rites and Traditions, trans. Amanda Riddick, Neil Morris, Ting Morris, and Sabine Troelsch. Cologne: Könemann.

Chuvin, Pierre. 1990. A Chronicle of the Last Pagans, trans. B. A. Archer. Cambridge, MA: Harvard University Press.

Clark, Mary Ann. 2001. "No Hay Ningún Santo Aqui!. There Are No Saints Here!: Symbolic Language within Santería." Journal of the American Academy of Religion 69 (March): 21–41.

Confucius. 1969. The Unwobbling Pivot; The Great Digest; The Analects, trans. and commentator Ezra Pound. New York: New Directions.

Conze, Edward. 1959. Buddhist Scriptures. Harmondsworth: Penguin.

———. 1980. Buddhism: A Short History. Oxford: Oneworld.

Coomaraswamy, Ananda K. n.d. Hinduism and Buddhism. New York: Wisdom Library / Philosophical Library.

Corrington, Robert S. 1997. Nature's Religion. Lanham, MD: Rowman & Littlefield.

Cosentino, Donald J., ed. 1995. Sacred Arts of Haitian Vodou. Los Angeles: UCLA Fowler Museum of Cultural History.

Creemers, Wilhelmus H. M. 1968. Shrine Shinto after World War II. Leiden: Brill.

Crim, Keith, ed. 1981. Abingdon Dictionary of Living Religions. Nashville, TN: Abingdon.

Crowley, Aleister. 1991. Magick in Theory and Practice. Secaucus, NJ: Castle. (Originally published in Paris as Magick by the Master Theiron, 1929.)

Crowley, Vivianne. 1989. Wicca: The Old Religion in the New Age. Wellingborough: Aquarian Press. (Reprinted in 1996 as Wicca: The Old Religion in the New Millennium by Thorsons/Harper Collins.)

Cunningham, Graham. 1999. Religion and Magic: Approaches and Theories. New York: NYU Press.

Cunningham, Scott. 2000. Hawaiian Magic and Spirituality. St. Paul: Llewellyn.

Cush, Denise. 1994. Buddhism: Student's Approach to World Religions. London: Hodder & Stoughton.

Czaja, Michael. 1974. Gods of Myth and Stone: Phallicism in Japanese Folk Religion. New York: Weatherhill.

Czaplicka, Marie Antoinette. [1914] 1969. Aboriginal Siberia: A Study in Social Anthropology. Oxford: Clarendon Press.

Daniélou, Jean. 1949. "Le Culte mariale et le paganisme." Maria, Études sur la Sainte Vierge 1: 159–81.

David, Bruno. 2002. Landscape, Rock-Art and the Dreaming: An Archaeology of Preunderstanding. Leicester: Leicester University Press.

David-Neel, Alexandra. 1958. Magic and Mystery in Tibet. New York: University Books.

Davidson, Basil. 1969. The African Genius. London: Little, Brown.

Davies, Morganna, and Aradia Lynch. 2001. Keepers of the Flame: Interviews with Elders of Traditional Witchcraft in America. Providence, RI: Olympian Press.

Day, Clarence Burton. 1940. Chinese Peasant Culture: Being a Study of Chinese Paper Gods. Shanghai: Kelly and Walsh.

Deep, Dhurba K. 1993. Popular Deities, Emblems and Images of Nepal. Jaipur: Nirala Publications.

De La Torre, Miguel. 2001. "Ochún: (N)Either the (M)Other of All Cubans (n)or the Bleached Virgin." Journal of the American Academy of Religion 69 (December): 837–61.

Deren, Maya. [1953] 1970. Divine Horsemen: The Voodoo Gods of Haiti. London: Thames & Hudson.

Detmold, Geoffrey, and Mary Rubel. 1979. The Gods and Goddesses of Nepal. Kathmandu: Ratna Pustak Bhandar.

Devine, Mary Virginia. 1982. Brujería: A Study of Mexican-American Folk-Magic. St. Paul: Llewellyn.

Dhar, Somnath, and Asha Dhar. 1985. Nepal: Land of Gods, Goddesses and Demons. New Delhi: South Asia Books.

Diószegi, Vilmos. 1968. Tracing Shamans in Siberia: The Story of an Ethnographical Research Expedition. Oosterhout: Anthropological Publications.

Diószegi, Vilmos, and Mihály Hoppál, eds. 1978. Shamanism in Siberia. Budapest: Akademiai Kiado.

diZerega, Gus. 2001. Pagans and Christians: The Personal Spiritual Experience. St. Paul: Llewellyn.

Douglas, Mary. 1966. Purity and Danger: An Analysis of Concepts of Pollution and Taboo. New York: Praeger.

Drewal, Henry John, and John Mason. 1998. Beads, Body and Soul: Art and Light in the Yorùbá Universe. Los Angeles: UCLA Fowler Museum of Cultural History.

Drewal, Henry John, John Pemberton III, and Rowland Abíódún. 1989. Yorùbá: Nine Centuries of African Art and Thought. New York: Center for African Art and Harry N. Abrams.

Drury, Nevill. 1978. Don Juan, Mescalito, and Modern Magic: The Mythology of Inner Space. London: Routledge & Kegan Paul.

———. 1982. The Shaman and the Magician. London: Routledge & Kegan Paul.

Dubois, Abbé J. A. 1953. Hindu Manners, Customs and Ceremonies, trans. Henry K. Beauchamp. 3d ed. Oxford: Clarendon.

Dupré, Wilhelm. 1970. Religion in Primitive Cultures. The Hague: Mouton.

Durkheim, Émile. [1912] 1976. The Elementary Forms of the Religious Life. London: Allen & Unwin.

Earhart, H. Byron. 1983. Japanese Religion: Unity and Diversity. 2d ed. Belmont, CA: Wadsworth.

———. 1984. Religion in the Japanese Experience: Sources and Interpretations. Belmont, CA: Wadsworth.

Eberhard, Wolfram. 1967. Guilt and Sin in Traditional China. Berkeley and Los Angeles: University of California Press.

Eck, Diana L. 1982. Banaras: City of Light. New York: Knopf.

———. 1998. Darsan: Seeing the Divine Image in India. 3d ed. New York: Columbia University Press.

Ecun, Oba. 1989. Ita: Mythology of the Yoruba Religion. Miami: Obaecun Books.

Eilberg-Schwartz, Howard. 1994. God's Phallus—And Other Problems for Men and Monotheism. Boston: Beacon Press.

Eliade, Mircea. 1959. The Sacred and the Profane: The Nature of Religion, trans. Willard R. Task. New York: Harper & Row.

———, ed. 1987. The Encyclopedia of Religion. New York: Macmillan.

———. 1989. Shamanism: Archaic Techniques of Ecstasy, trans. William R. Trask. London: Arkana.

Eliade, Mircea, and Ioan P. Couliano. 1991. The Eliade Guide to World Religions. San Francsico: Harper.

Elias, Jamal J. 1999. *Islam*. London: Routledge.

Eller, Cynthia. 1993. Living in the Lap of the Goddess: The Feminist Spirituality Movement in America. Boston: Beacon Press.

———. 2000. The Myth of Matriarchal Prehistory: Why an Invented Past Won't Give Women a Future. Boston: Beacon Press.

Ellis, Jean A. 1994. Australia's Aboriginal Heritage. North Blackburn, Victoria: Collins Dove.

Ellwood, Robert S. Jr., and Robert Pilgrim. 1985. Japanese Religion: A Cultural Perspective. Englewood Cliffs, NJ: Prentice-Hall.

Evans-Pritchard, Edward Evan. 1937. Witchcraft, Oracles and Magic among the Azande. Oxford: Oxford University Press.

———. 1956. Nuer Religion. Oxford: Oxford University Press.

Ewen, David. 1963. Encyclopedia of the Opera. New York: Hill & Wang.

Eyo, Ekpo, and Frank Willet. 1982. Treasures of Ancient Nigeria. London: Royal Academy of Arts.

Farrar, Janet, and Stewart Farrar. 1981. Eight Sabbats for Witches. London: Robert Hale.

————. 1988. The Witches' Way: Principles, Rituals and Beliefs of Modern Witch-craft. Custer, WA: Phoenix Publishing.

Farrar, Stewart. 1981. What Witches Do. 2d ed. Custer, WA: Phoenix Publishing.

Feest, Christian F., ed. 2000. The Cultures of Native North Americans. Cologne: Könemann.

Feraca, Stephen E. 1998. Wakinyan: Lakota Religion in the Twentieth Century. Lincoln: University of Nebraska Press.

Ferguson, John. 1970. The Religions of the Roman Empire. London: Thames & Hudson.

Ferm, Vergilius, ed. 1945. An Encyclopedia of Religion. New York: Philosophical Library.

Feuchtwang, Stephan D. R. 1974. An Anthropological Analysis of Chinese Geo-mancy. Vientiane: Vithagna.

Fixico, Donald L., ed. 1997. Rethinking American Indian History. Albuquerque: University of New Mexico Press.

Flaherty, Gloria. 1992. Shamanism and the Eighteenth Century. Princeton, NJ: Princeton University Press.

Flood, Gavin. 1996. An Introduction to Hinduism. Cambridge: Cambridge University Press.

Fontein, Jan. 1999. The Dancing Demons of Mongolia. London: Lund Humphries.

Fox, Robin Lane. 1987. Pagans and Christians. New York: Knopf.

Frazer, James George. 1911–14. The Golden Bough: A Study in Magic and Religion. 3d ed. London: Macmillan.

Freedman, Maurice, ed. 1970. Family and Kinship in Chinese Society. Stanford, CA: Stanford University Press.

Frye, Northrop. 1970. The Stubborn Structure: Essays on Criticism and Society. London: Methuen.

Fung, Yu-lan. [1948] 1960. A Short History of Chinese Philosophy, ed. Derk Bodde. New York: Macmillan.

von Furer-Haimendorf, Christoph, ed. 1974. Contributions to the Anthropology of Nepal. Warminster: Aris and Phillips.

Furst, Peter T., ed. 1972. Flesh of the Gods: The Ritual Use of Hallucinogens. New York: Doubleday / Natural History Press.

Galembo, Phyllis. 1993. Divine Inspiration: From Benin to Bahia. Albuquerque: University of New Mexico Press.

Gardner, Gerald B. 1954. Witchcraft Today. London: Rider.

————. 1959. The Meaning of Witchcraft. New York: Samuel Weiser.

Geertz, Clifford. 1993. The Interpretation of Cultures: Selected Essays. London: Fontana.

Gethin, Rupert. 1998. The Foundations of Buddhism. New York: Oxford University Press.

Gill, Sam. 1982. Beyond "The Primitive": The Religions of Nonliterate People. Englewood, NJ: Prentice-Hall.

Gleason, Judith. 1987. Oya: In Praise of the Goddess. Boston: Shambhala Publications.

Gombrich, Richard. 1988. Theravada Buddhism: A Social History from Ancient Benares to Modern Colombo. London: Routledge.

González-Wippler, Migene. [1973] 1981. Santería: African Magic in Latin America. New York: Original Productions.

———. 1985. Tales of the Orishas. New York: Original Publications.

Goodman, Felicitas D. 1988. Ecstasy, Ritual, and Alternate Reality: Religion in a Pluralistic World. Bloomington: Indiana University Press.

Goodman, Felicitas D., Jeanette H. Henney, and Esther Pressel, eds. 1974. Trance, Healing and Hallucination. New York: Wiley Interscience.

Gordon, Cyrus H. 1943. "The Daughters of Baal and Allah." Moslem World 33: 50–51.

Grant, Robert McQueen. 1978. Gnosticism: A Source Book of Heretical Writings from the Early Christian Period. New York: AMS Press.

Greenwood, Susan. 2000. Magic, Witchcraft and the Otherworld: An Anthropology. Oxford: Berg.

Grey, Sir George. 1970. Polynesian Mythology and Ancient Traditional History of the Maori As Told by Their Priests and Chiefs. New York: Taplinger.

Griffin, Wendy, ed. 2000. Daughters of the Goddess. Walnut Creek, CA: Alta Mira.

de Groot, Jan Jacob Maria. [1892–1910] 1964. The Religious System of China. 6 vols. Taipei: Literature House.

Gusinde, Martin. 1961. The Yamana: The Life and Thought of the Water Nomads of Cape Horn [1932], trans. Frieda Schultze. New Haven, CT: Human Relations File.

Gustaitis, Rasa. 1969. Turning On. New York: Macmillan.

Gyatso, Geshe Kelsang. 2001. Introduction to Buddhism: An Explanation of the Buddhist Way of Life. 2d ed. Ulverston: Tharpa.

Hackett, Rosalind I. J. 1996. Art and Religion in Africa. London: Cassell.

Hajdú, Péter, ed. 1975. Ancient Cultures of the Uralian Peoples. Budapest: Corvina.

———. 1978. The Rite Technique of the Siberian Shaman. Helsinki: Folklore Fellowship Communications no. 220.

Halbertal, Moshe, and Avishai Margalit. Idolatry 1992. Cambridge, MA: Harvard University Press.

Halifax, Joan. 1982. Shaman: The Wounded Healer. London: Thames & Hudson.

Harner, Michael, ed. 1973. Hallucinogens and Shamanism. Oxford: Oxford University Press.

———. 1986. The Way of the Shaman: A Guide to Power and Healing. London: Bantam.

Harris, Victor, ed. 2001. Shintô: The Sacred Art of Ancient Japan. London: British Museum Press.

Harrow, Judy. 1999. Wiccan Covens: How to Start and Organize Your Own. Sacramento, CA: Citadel Press.

Harshananda, Swami. 1979. All about Hindu Temples. Mysore: Ramakrishna Institute of Moral and Spiritual Education.

Harvey, Graham. 1997. Listening People, Speaking Earth, Contemporary Paganism. London: Hurst.

———. 2002. Readings in Indigenous Religions. New York: Continuum.

Harvey, Graham, and Charlotte Hardman, eds. 1995. Paganism Today: Wiccans, Druids, the Goddess and Ancient Earth Traditions for the Twenty-first Century. London: Thorsons.

Harvey, Peter. 1990. An Introduction to Buddhism. Cambridge: Cambridge University Press.

———, ed. 2001. Buddhism. New York: Continuum.

Hatto, Arthur T. 1970. Shamanism and Epic Poetry in Northern Asia. London: University of London Press.

Havens, Norman, and Nobutaka Inoue, eds. 2001. An Encyclopedia of Shinto. Vol. 1, Kami, trans. Norman Havens from the original Shintō jiten, 1994. Tokyo: Institute for Japanese Culture and Classics / Kokugakuin University.

Hawkins, Bradley K. 1999. Buddhism. London: Routledge.

Heissig, Walther. 1980. The Religions of Mongolia. London: Routledge & Kegan Paul.

Herskovits, Francis, ed. 1966. The New World Negro. Bloomington: Indiana University Press.

Herskovits, Melville J. 1937. "African Gods and Catholic Saints in New World Negro Beliefs." American Anthropologist 39: 635–43. (Reprinted in Herskovits 1966 and as "African Gods and Catholic Saints in New World Religious Belief" in Lessa and Vogt 1979:541–47.)

———. 1941. The Myth of the Negro Past. New York: Harper Bros.

Heselton, Philip. 2000. Wiccan Roots: Gerald Gardner and the Modern Wiccan Revival. Chieverly Berks: Capal Bann.

Hill, Michael. 1973. A Sociology of Religion. London: Heinemann.

Hinnells, John R., ed. 1984. A Handbook of Living Religions. Harmondsworth: Viking.

Hitchcock, John T. 1968. "Nepalese Shamanism and the Classic Inner Asian Tradition." History of Religions 7: 149–58.

Hitchcock, John T., and Rex Jones, eds. 1976. Spirit Possession in the Nepal Himalayas. New Delhi: Vikas Publishing House.

Hitching, Francis. 1978. World Atlas of Mysteries. London: William Collins.

Holtom, Daniel C. [1938] 1965. The National Faith of Japan: A Study in Modern Shinto. New York: Paragon Book Reprint Corp.

Hoppál, Mihály, ed. 1984. Shamanism in Eurasia. Göttingen: Edition Herodot.

Hori Ichirō. 1968. Folk Religion in Japan: Continuity and Change, ed. Joseph M. Kitagawa and Alan L. Miller. Chicago: University of Chicago Press.

Hori Ichirō, Ikado Fujio, Wakimoto Tsuneya, and Yanagawa Keiichi, eds. 1972. Japanese Religion: A Survey by the Agency for Cultural Affairs, trans. Abe Yoshiya and David Reid. New York: Kodansha.

Horrie, Chris, and Peter Chippindale. 1991. What Is Islam? London: Virgin Books / Virgin Publishing.

Hultkrantz, Ake. 1953. Conceptions of the Soul among North American Indians: A Study in Religious Ethnology. Stockholm: Statens Etnografiska Museum/ Coslon Press.

———. 1979. The Religions of the American Indians. Berkeley and Los Angeles: University of California Press.

———. 1983. Belief and Worship in Native North America. Syracuse, NY: Syracuse University Press.

———. 1987. Native Religions of North America: The Power of Visions and Fertility. San Francisco: Harper & Row.

Hunt, Carl M. 1979. Oyotunji Village: The Yoruba Movement in America. Washington, DC: University Press of America.

Hurdey, John Major. 1970. American Indian Religions. Los Angeles: Sherbourne Press.

Hurston, Zora Neale. [1938] 1990. Tell My Horse: Voodoo and Life in Haiti and Jamaica. New York: Harper & Row.

Hutton, Ronald. 1991. The Pagan Religions of the Ancient British Isles: Their Nature and Legacy. Oxford: Blackwell.

———. 1999. Triumph of the Moon: A History of Modern Witchcraft. Oxford: Oxford University Press.

Huxley, Aldous. 1937. Ends and Means. London: Chatto & Windus.

Huxley, Francis. 1966. The Invisibles: Voodoo Gods in Haiti. New York: McGraw-Hill.

Idowu, E. Bolaji. 1973. African Traditional Religion: A Definition. Maryknoll, NY: Orbis.

Jackson, Kent P. 2000. "Are Mormons Christian? Presbyterians, Mormons, and the Question of Religious Definitions." Nova Religio: The Journal of Alternative and Emergent Religions 4 (October): 52–65.

Jahn, Janheinz. 1961. Muntu: An Outline of the New African Culture, trans. Marjorie Greene. New York: Grove Press.

Jigmei, Ngapo Ngawang, Khrili Chodra, Chapel Tsetan Phuntso, Na Zhen, Cai Xiansheng, Jampei Chinlei, and Dongge Luosantselie. 1980. Tibet. London: Routledge & Kegan Paul.

Jilek, Wolfgang G. 1982. Indian Healing: Shamanic Ceremonialism in the Pacific Northwest Today. Blaine, WA: Hancock House.

Jochim, Christian. 1986. Chinese Religions: A Cultural Perspective. Englewood Cliffs, NJ: Prentice-Hall.

Jocks, Christopher. 2002. Native American Religions. London: Routledge.

Johnson, George. 1995. "Linguists Debating Deepest Roots of Language." New York Times, June 27, C1.

Johnson, S. Lewis. 1994. "Mary, the Saints, and Sacerdotalism." In Roman Catholicism: Evangelical Protestants Analyze What Divides and Unites Us, ed. John Armstrong. Chicago: Moody Press.

Jones, Prudence, and Caitlín Matthews, eds. 1990. Voices from the Circle: The Heritage of Western Paganism. Wellingborough: Aquarian Press.

Jones, Prudence, and Nigel Pennick. 1995. A History of Pagan Europe. London: Routledge.

Jordan, David K. 1972. Gods, Ghosts and Ancestors. Berkeley and Los Angeles: University of California Press.

Josephy, Alvin M. Jr. 1994. 500 Nations: An Illustrated History of North American Indians. New York: Knopf.

Jumsai, M. L. Manich/Kulamanito. 1980. Understanding Thai Buddhism: Being a Compendium of Information on Buddhism As Professed in Thailand. Bangkok: Chalermnit Press.

Kelly, Aidan A. 1991. Crafting the Art of Magic. Book 1, A History of Modern Witchcraft, 1939–1964, vol. 1. St. Paul: Llewellyn.

Kenyatta, Jomo. [1938] 1953. Facing Mount Kenya: The Tribal Life of the Gikuyu. London: Secker & Warburg.

Keown, Damien. 2000. Buddhism: A Very Short Introduction. Oxford: Oxford University Press.

Kim, Taegon. 1981. A Study of Shamanism in Korea. Seoul: Korean Shamanism, series 4, no. 8.

King, Francis. 1975. Magic: The Western Tradition. London: Thames & Hudson.

———. 1990. Modern Ritual Magic: The Rise of Western Occultism. Bridport, Dorset: Prism.

King, Serge Kahili. 1990. Urban Shamanism. New York: Simon & Schuster.

Kinsley, David. 1993. Hinduism: A Cultural Perspective. 2d ed. Englewood Cliffs, NJ: Prentice-Hall.

Kister, Daniel A. 1997. Korean Shamanist Ritual: Symbols and Dramas of Transformation. Budapest: Akadémiai Kiadó.

Kitagawa, Joseph M. 1987. On Understanding Japanese Religion. Princeton, NJ: Princeton University Press.

Klostermaier, Klaus. 1994. A Survey of Hinduism. Albany: State University of New York Press.

Knott, Kim. 1998. Hinduism: A Very Short Introduction. Oxford: Oxford University Press.

Kohn, Livia. 2001. Daoism and Chinese Culture. Cambridge, MA: Three Pines Press.

Kornicki, Peter Francis, and Ian James McMullen, eds. 1996. Religion in Japan: Arrows to Heaven and Earth. Cambridge: Cambridge University Press.

Kraemer, Hendrik. 1960. World Cultures and World Religions: The Coming Dialogue. London: Lutterworth.

Krauss, Beatrice H. 1993. Plants in Hawaiian Culture. Honolulu: University of Hawaii Press.

Krickeberg, Walter. 1968. Pre-Columbian Mexican Religions. London: Weidenfeld & Nicholson.

Kroeber, Alfred Louis. [1925] 1976. Handbook of the Indians of California. New York: Dover, 1976. (First published in 1925 as Bulletin 78 of the Bureau of American Ethnology of the Smithsonian Institution.)

Ku Chieh-Kang. 1954. Ch'in-Han de Fang-shih yü Juei-shih [Proto-Taoists and Confucianists of the Ch'in-Han Period]. Shanghai: Chun-lien Press.

La Barre, Weston. 1938. The Peyote Cult. New Haven, CT: Yale University Publications in Anthropology, no. 13.

———. 1972. The Ghost Dance: The Origins of Religion. London: Allen & Unwin.

Laguerre, Michel. 1980. Voodoo Heritage. Beverly Hills, CA: Sage.

Lall, Kesar. 1991. Lore and Legend of Nepal. Jaipur: Nirala Publications.

Langdon, E. Jean Matteson, and Gerhard Baer, eds. 1992. Portals of Power: Shamanism in South America. Albuquerque: University of New Mexico Press.

Layton, Bentley. 1987. The Gnostic Scriptures. Garden City, NY: Doubleday.

LeFever, Harry G. 1996. "When the Saints Go Riding In: Santería in Cuba and the United States." Journal for the Scientific Study of Religion 35 (September): 318–30.

Lehtinen, Ildikó, ed. 1986. Traces of Central Asian Culture in the North: Finnish-Soviet Joint Symposium Held in Hanasaari, Espoo, 14–21 January 1985. Helsinki: Suomalais-ugrilaisen Seuran Toimituksia.

Lessa, William A., and Evon Z. Vogt, eds. 1979. Reader in Comparative Religion. 2d ed. New York: Harper & Row.

Lévi, Eliphas. [1913] 1982. The History of Magic. London: Rider.

Lewis, Ian M. 1989. Ecstatic Religion: A Study of Shamanism and Spirit Possession. 2d ed. New York: Routledge.

Lewis, James R. 1994. From the Ashes: Making Sense of Waco. Lanham, MD: Rowan & Littlefield.

Lienhardt, Godfrey. 1961. Divinity and Experience: The Religion of the Dinka. Oxford: Clarendon Press.

Lipner, Julius. 1994. Hindus: Their Religious Beliefs and Practices. London: Routledge.

Liu Chih-Wan. 1974. Chung-kuo Min-chien Hsinyang Lun-chi [A Treatise on Chinese Popular Religion]. Nanjing: Academia Sinica.

Liu, Da. 1979. The Tao and Chinese Culture. New York: Schocken Books.

Lowell, Percival. [1894] 1990. Occult Japan: Shinto, Shamanism and the Way of the Gods. Rochester, VT: Inner Traditions.

Luhrmann, Tanya M. 1989. Persuasions of the Witch's Craft: Ritual Magic in Contemporary England. Cambridge, MA: Harvard University Press.

MacGregor-Mathers, Samuel Liddell. 1948. The Book of the Sacred Magic of Abra-Melin the Mage. Reprint, Chicago: de Laurence.

Macquarrie, John. 1988. Twentieth-Century Religious Thought. 4th ed. London: SCM Press.

Mails, Thomas. 1979. Fools Crow. New York: Doubleday.

Majupuia, T. C., and Rohit Kumar. 1998. Gods and Goddesses: An Illustrated Account of Hindu, British, Tantric, Hybrid and Tibetan Deities. Laskar, India: Lalitipur Colony.

Malinowski, Bronislaw. 1982. Magic, Science and Religion and Other Essays. London: Souvenir Press.

Maraini, Fosco. 1952. Tibet Secret (Segreto Tibet), trans. Juliette Bertrand. Paris: B. Arthaud.

Martin, Bill. 1992. Matrix and Line: Derrida and the Possibilities of Postmodern Social Theory. Albany: State University of New York Press.

Martin, E. Osborn. 1972. The Gods of India: Their History, Character and Worship. Delhi/Varanasi: Indological Book House.

Mason, John, and Gary Edwards. 1985. Black Gods: Orisa Studies in the New World. New York: Yoruba Theological Archministry.

Maspero, Henri. 1978. China in Antiquity, trans. Frank A. Kierman Jr. Amherst: University of Massachusetts Press.

Mbiti, John S. 1969. African Religions and Philosophy. New York: Praeger.

McEwan, Colin, Christina Barreto, and Eduardo Neves, eds. 2001. Unknown Amazon: Culture in Nature in Ancient Brazil. London: British Museum Press.

McKenna, Terrance. 1992. Food of the Gods: The Search for the Original Tree of Knowledge: A Radical History of Plants, Drugs, and Human Evolution. London: Bantam.

Melton, J. Gordon. 1986. Encyclopedic Handbook of Cults in America. New York: Garland.

Melton, J. Gordon, Jerome Clark, and Aidan A. Kelly. 1991. New Age Almanac. New York: Visible Ink Press.

Menninger, Karl. 1969. Number Words and Number Symbols: A Cultural History of Numbers, trans. Paul Broneer. Cambridge, MA: MIT Press.

Metraux, Alfred. 1959. Voodoo in Haiti, trans. Hugo Charteris. New York: Oxford University Press.

Middleton, John. 1960. Lugbara Religion: Ritual and Authority among an East African People. Oxford: Oxford University Press.

Miller, Elliott, and Kenneth R. Samples. 1992. The Cult of the Virgin: Catholic Mariology and the Apparitions of Mary. Grand Rapids, MI: Baker Book House.

Mintz, Sidney W. 1972. Voodoo in Haiti. New York: Schocken Books.

Mohabir, Philip. 1992. Worlds within Reach: Cross-Cultural Witness. London: Hodder & Stoughton.

Mookerjee, Ajit. 1985. Ritual Art of India. London: Thames & Hudson.

Mooney, James. 1896. The Ghost Dance Religion of the Sioux Outbreak of 1890. Fourteenth annual report, part 7. Washington, DC: Bureau of American Ethnology.

Morgan, Lewis Henry. [1851] 1995. The League of the Iroquois. North Dighton, MA: JG Press.

Morphy, Howard. 1991. Ancestral Connections: Art and an Aboriginal System of Knowledge. Chicago: University of Chicago Press.

Morris, Jan. 1985. Feng Shui: Ancient Chinese Wisdom on Arranging a Harmonious Living Environment. London: Rider.

Mudrooroo. 1994. Aboriginal Mythology. London: Thorsons.

Muraoka Tsunetsugu. 1964. Studies in Shinto Thought, trans. Delmer M. Brown and James T. Araki. Tokyo: Ministry of Education.

Murphy, Joseph M. 1988. Santería: An African Religion in America. Boston: Beacon Press.

Murray, Margaret. 1921. The Witch-Cult in Western Europe: A Study in Anthropology. Oxford: Clarendon Press.

———. [1931] 1970.The God of the Witches. New York: Oxford University Press.

Nagel, Joane. 1996. American Indian Ethnic Renewal: Red Power and the Resurgence of Identity and Culture. New York: Oxford University Press.

Nakamura, Hajime. 1964. Ways of Thinking of Eastern Peoples: India-China-Tibet-Japan, trans. Philip P. Wiener. Honolulu: East-West Center, University of Hawaii.

Nelson, John K. 1996. A Year in the Life of a Shinto Shrine. Seattle: University of Washington Press.

Nicholson, Shirley, comp. 1987. Shamanism. London: Theosophical Publishing House.

Nigosian, Solomon A. 1994. World Faiths. New York: St. Martin's Press.

Noel, Daniel C. 1976. Seeing Castaneda: Reactions to the "Don Juan" Writings of Carlos Castaneda. New York: Putnam.

———. 1997. The Soul of Shamanism: Western Fantasies, Imaginal Realities. New York: Continuum.

O'Flaherty, Wendy Doniger. 1976. The Origins of Evil in Hindu Mythology. Berkeley and Los Angeles: University of California Press.

Olson, Carl, ed. 1990. The Book of the Goddess: Past and Present. New York: Crossroad.

Olupona, Jacob K., ed. 1991. African Traditional Religions in Contemporary Society. St. Paul: Paragon.

———, ed. 2000. African Spirituality: Forms, Meanings and Expressions. New York: Crossroad.

Osborne, Harold. 1968. South American Mythology. Feltham: Hamlyn.

O'Shea, Stephen. 2000. The Perfect Heresy: The Revolutionary Life and Death of the Medieval Cathars. New York: Walker.

Otto, T. 1963. Folklore in Japanese Life and Customs. Tokyo: Kokusai bunka shinkōkai.

Padmanabhan, Sivan Pillai. 1979. Temples of South India. Nagercoil: Kumaram Pathippagam.

Pal, Pratapaditya. 1981. Hindu Religion and Iconography: According to the Tantrasāra. Los Angeles: Vichitra Press.

Palmer, Martin, ed. and trans. 1986. T'ung Shu: The Ancient Chinese Almanac. London: Rider.

Park, Willard Z. 1938. Shamanism in Western North America. Evanston, IL: Northwestern University Press.

Parman, Donald L. 1994. Indians and the American West in the Twentieth Century. Bloomington: Indiana University Press.

Parrinder, Geoffrey. 1967. African Mythology. London: Hamlyn.

———. 1969. African Traditional Religion/Religion in Africa. Harmondsworth: Penguin.

Pearson, Joanne, Richard A. Roberts, and Geoffrey Samuel, eds. 1998. Nature Religion Today: The Pagan Alternative in the Modern World. Edinburgh: Edinburgh University Press.

Pentikäinen, Juha. 1998. Shamanism and Culture. Helsinki: Etnika.

———, ed. 2001. Shamanhood, Symbolism and Epic. Budapest: Akadémiai Kiadó.

Pérez Y Mena, Andrés I. 1998. "Cuban Santería, Haitian Vodun, Puerto Rican Spiritualism: A Multicultural Inquiry into Syncretism." Journal for the Scientific Study of Religion 37 (March): 15–27.

Peters, Larry G. 1978. "Psychotherapy in Tamang Shamanism." Ethos 6: 63–91.

———. 1981. Ecstasy and Healing in Nepal: An Ethnopsychiatric Study of Tamang Shamanism. Malibu, CA: Undena.

Pike, Sarah. 2001. Earthly Bodies, Magical Selves: Contemporary Pagans and the Search for Community. Berkeley and Los Angeles: University of California Press.

Powers, John. 2000. A Concise Encyclopedia of Buddhism. Oxford: Oneworld.

Powers, William K. 1987. "Lakota Religion." In The Encyclopedia of Religion, vol. 8, ed. Mircea Eliade. New York: Macmillan.

Preston, James J., ed. 1982. Mother Worship: Theme and Variations. Chapel Hill, NC: University of North Carolina Press.

Radin, Paul. 1956. The Trickster: A Study in American Indian Mythology. New York: Philosophical Library.

Ranger, Terence O., and Isario N. Kimambo. 1972. The Historical Study of African Religion, with Special Reference to East and Central Africa. London: Heinnemann.

Rao, T. A. Gopinatha. 1971. Elements of Hindu Iconography. Delhi/Varanasi: In-dological Book House.

Raphael, Melissa. 2000. Introducing Thealogy: Discourse on the Goddess. Cleveland: Pilgrim.

Rasmussen, Knud. 1930. Intellectual Culture of the Iglulik Eskimos, trans. William Worster. Copenhagen: Report of the Fifth Thule Expedition, vol. 7, part 1.

Ray, Benjamin C. 2000. African Religions. Upper Saddle River, NJ: Prentice-Hall.

Reader, Ian. 1998. The Simple Guide to Shinto. Folkstone: Global Books.

Regardie, Israel. 1969. The Tree of Life: A Study in Magic. 2d ed. New York: Samuel Weiser.

Reynolds, Valrae. 1978. Tibet, a Lost World: The Newark Museum Collection of Tibetan Art and Ethnography. New York: American Federation of Arts.

Rhie, Marylin M., and Robert A. F. Thurman. 1991. Wisdom and Compassion: The Sacred Art of Tibet. New York: Abrams.

Rippin, Andrew. 2000. Muslims: Their Religious Beliefs and Practices. London: Routledge.

Rose, Herbert J. 1926. Primitive Culture in Italy. London: Methuen.

Rosen, Barbara, ed. 1969. Witchcraft. Stratford-Upon-Avon Library no. 6. London: Arnold.

Rutherford, Ward. 1986. Shamanism: The Foundation of Magic. Wellingborough: Aquarian Press.

Ruthven, Malise. 1997. Islam: A Very Short Introduction. Oxford: Oxford University Press.

Sastri, H. Krishna. 1974. South-Indian Images of Gods and Goddesses. Varanasi: Bhartiya Publishing.

Saunders, Nicholas, Anja Saunders, and Michelle Pauli. 2000. In Search of the Ultimate High: Spiritual Experience through Psychoactives. London: Rider.

Scarboro, Allen, and Philip Andrew Luck. 1997. "The Goddess and Power: Witchcraft and Religion in America." Journal of Contemporary Religion 12 (January): 69–79.

Shattuck, Cybelle. 1999. Hinduism. London, Routledge.

Shilling, Chris, and Philip A. Mellor. 1998. "Durkheim, Morality and Modernity: Collective Effervesence, Homo duplex and the Sources of Moral Action." British Journal of Sociology 49 (June): 193–209.

Shirokogoroff, Sergei Mikhailovich. [1935] 1980. Psychomental Complex of the Tungus. New York: AMS.

Shorter, Aylward. 1975. Prayer in the Religious Traditions of Africa. New York: Oxford University Press.

Siikala, Anna-Leena. 1978. The Rite Technique of the Siberian Shaman. Helsinki: Folklore Fellows Communications no. 220.

Silko, Leslie Marmon. 1996. Yellow Woman and a Beauty of Spirit: Essays on Native American Life Today. New York: Simon & Schuster.

Simos, Miriam (Starhawk). 1979. The Spiral Dance: A Rebirth of the Ancient Religion of the Great Goddess. London: Harper & Row.

Simpson, George Eaton. 1978. Black Religions in the New World. New York: Columbia University Press.

Sjöö, Monica, and Barbara Mor. 1987. The Great Cosmic Mother: Rediscovering the Religion of the Earth. San Francisco: Harper & Row.

Skinner, Stephen. 1989. The Living Earth Manual of Feng-Shui: Chinese Geomancy. London/Harmondsworth: Arkana/Penguin.

Slotkin, James S. 1956. The Peyote Religion: A Study in Indian-White Relations. Glencoe, IL: Free Press.

Smart, Ninian. 1989. The World's Religions: Old Traditions and Modern Transformations. Cambridge: Cambridge University Press.

———. 1996. Dimensions of the Sacred: An Anatomy of the World's Beliefs. Berkeley and Los Angeles: University of California Press.

Smith, D. Howard. 1971. Chinese Religions. New York: Holt, Rinehart and Winston.

Smith, Edwin W., ed. 1950. African Ideas of God. London: Edinburgh House Press.

Somé, Malidoma Patrice. 1993. Ritual Power, Healing and Community. Portland, OR: Swan/Raven.

Somme, Deborah A. 1997. "Ritual and Sacrifice in Early Confucianism: Contacts with the Spirit World." Paper presented to the annual meeting of the American Academy of Religion, San Francisco, November 23.

Spence, Lewis. 1960. An Encyclopedia of Occultism. New Hyde Park, NY: University Books.

Stark, Rodney. 1999. "Atheism, Faith, and the Social Scientific Study of Religion." Journal of Contemporary Religion 14 (January): 41–62.

Steiger, Brad. 1982. Kahuna Magic. Rockport, MA: Para Research.

Stevens, Jay. 1989. Storming Heaven: LSD and the American Dream. London: Paladin.

Stevens, Keith. 1997. Chinese Gods: The Unseen World of Spirits and Demons. London: Collins and Brown.

Steward, Julian H., and Louis C. Faron. 1959. Native Peoples of South America. New York: McGraw-Hill.

Stutley, Margaret. 1985. The Illustrated Dictionary of Hindu Iconography. Boston: Routledge & Kegan Paul.

Sullivan, Bruce M. 1997. Historical Dictionary of Hinduism. Historical Dictionaries of Religions, Philosophies, and Movements no. 13. Lanham, MD: Scarecrow.

Sullivan, Lawrence E., ed. 2000. Native Religions and Cultures of North America: Anthropology of the Sacred. New York: Continuum.

———, ed. 2001. Native Religions and Cultures of South America: Anthropology of the Sacred. New York: Continuum.

Sun Bear. 1984. Sun Bear, the Path of Power: As Told to Wabun and to Barry Weinstock. Spokane, WA: Bear Tribe Publications.

Sutherland, Stewart, Leslie Holden, Peter Clarke, and Friedhelm Hardy, eds. 1988. The World's Religions. London: Routledge.

Swan, James A., ed. 1993. The Power of Place: Sacred Ground in Natural and Human Environments. Bath: Gateway Books.

Swatos, William H. Jr., and Luigi Tomasi, eds. 2002. Pilgrimage. London: Praeger.

Tagare, GaneshVasudeo. 1996. Saivism: Some Glimpses. New Delhi: D. K. Printworld.

Tambiah, Stanley Jeyaraja. 1970. Buddhism and the Spirit Cults in North-East Thailand. Cambridge: Cambridge University Press.

———. 1985. Culture, Thought and Social Action: An Anthropological Perspective. Cambridge, MA: Harvard University Press.

———. 1990. Magic, Science, Religion and the Scope of Rationality. Cambridge: Cambridge University Press.

Taussig, Michael T. 1980. The Devil and Commodity Fetishism in South America. Chapel Hill: University of North Carolina Press.

Taylor, Colin F., and William C. Sturtevant, consultants. 1996. The Native Americans: The Indigenous People of North America. New York: Salamander/Smithmark.

Taylor, John Vernon. 1963. The Primal Vision. London: SCM.

Tedlock, Dennis, trans. 1985. Popol Vuh: The Mayan Book of the Dawn of Life. New York: Touchstone.

Teixidor, Javier. 1977. The Pagan God: Popular Religion in the Greco-Roman Near East. Princeton, NJ: Princeton University Press.

Telesco, Patricia. 2000. Shaman in a 9 to 5 World. Freedom, CA: Crossing Press.

Thomas, Lawson E. 1985. Religions of Africa: Traditions in Transformation. San Francisco: Harper & Row.

Thomas, Nicholas. 1995. Oceanic Art. London: Thames & Hudson.

Thomas, P. 1971. Festivals and Holidays of India. Bombay: D. B. Taraporevala Sons.

Thompson, Lawrence G. 1979. The Chinese Religion: An Introduction. 3d ed. Belmont, CA: Wadsworth.

Thompson, Robert Farris. 1984. Flash of the Spirit. New York: Vintage Books.

———. 1993. Face of the Gods: Art and Altars of Africa and the African Americas. New York: Museum for African Art.

Tillich, Paul. 1963. Christianity and the Encounter of the World's Religions. New York: Columbia University Press.

Tipton, Steven M. 1982. Getting Saved from the Sixties. Berkeley and Los Angeles: University of California Press.

Treat, James, ed. 1996. Native and Christian: Indigenous Voices on Religious Identity in the United States and Canada. New York: Routledge.

Trowell, Margaret. 1954. Classical African Sculpture. London: Faber & Faber.

Turcan, Robert. 1996. The Cults of the Roman Empire, trans. Antonia Nevill. Cambridge, MA: Blackwell.

Turner, Victor W. 1957. Schism and Continuity in an African Society. Manchester: University Press.

———.1969. The Ritual Process: Structure and Anti-Structure. London: Routledge.

Tyberg, Judith M. 1970. The Language of the Gods. Los Angeles: East-West Cultural Center.

Underhill, Ruth M. 1965. Red Man's Religion: Beliefs and Practices of the Indians North of Mexico. Chicago: University of Chicago Press.

Valiente, Doreen. 1973. An ABC of Witchcraft Past and Present. New York: St. Martin's Press.

———. 1978. Witchcraft for Tomorrow. New York: St. Martin's Press.

Van Gennep, Arnold. 1989. Rites of Passage, trans. Monika B. Vizedom and Gabrielle L. Caffe. London: Routledge.

Vecsey, Christopher, ed. 1990. Religion in Native America. Moscow: University of Idaho Press.

Verger, Pierre Fátúmbí. 1954. Dieux d'Afrique: Culte des Orishas et Vodouns: À l'Ancienne Coté des esclaves en Afrique et à Bahia, la baie de tous les saints au Brésil. Paris: Paul Hartmann.

Vidyarthi, L. P., Makhan Jha, and B. N. Saraswati. 1979. The Sacred Complex of Kashi: A Microcosm of Indian Civilization. Delhi: Concept Publishing.

Vitebsky, Piers. 1995. The Shaman: Voyages of the Soul Trance, Ecstasy and Healing from Siberia to the Amazon. London: Macmillan.

Vogel, Virgil J. 1990. American Indian Medicine. Norman: University of Oklahoma Press.

Walters, Derek. 1995. The Feng Shui Handbook: A Practical Guide to Chinese Geomancy and Environmental Harmony. London: Thorsons.

Walton, Victor W. 1993. Islam: A Student's Approach to World Religions. London: Hodder & Stoughton.

Ware, James R., trans. 1955. The Sayings of Confucius. New York: New American Library/Mentor.

Watanabe Yasutada. 1974. Shinto Art: Ise and Izumo Shrines, trans. Robert Ricketts. New York: Weatherhill.

Waters, Frank. 1977. The Book of the Hopi. Harmondsworth: Penguin Books.

Watkins, Calvert. 1969. The American Heritage Dictionary of the English Language, ed. William Morris. Boston: Houghton Mifflin.

Watson, William, ed. 1981. The Great Japan Exhibition: Art of the Edo Period 1600–1868. London: Royal Academy of the Arts.

Watters, D. 1975. "Siberian Shamanistic Traditions among the Kham Magar of Nepal." Contributions to Nepalese Studies: Journal of the Institute of Nepal and Asian Studies 2: 123–68.

Welch, Holmes. 1965. Taoism: The Parting of the Way. Boston: Beacon Press.

Welch, Holmes, and Anna Seidel, eds. 1979. Facets of Taoism: Essays in Chinese Religion. New Haven, CT: Yale University Press.

Werner, E. T. C. [1922] 1984. Myths and Legends of China. London: Sinclair Browne.

Westwood, Jennifer. 1997. Sacred Journeys: Paths for the New Pilgrim. London: Gaia Books.

Weyler, Rex. 1992. Blood of the Land: The Government and Corporate War against First Nations. Philadelphia: New Society Publishers.

Wilber, Ken. 1996. A Brief History of Everything. Boston: Shambhala.

Willet, Frank. 1993. African Art. London: Thames & Hudson.

Williams, Paul. 1989. Mahayana Buddhism: The Doctrinal Foundations. London: Routledge.

————. 2000. Buddhist Thought: A Complete Introduction to the Indian Tradition. London: Routledge.

Willis, Roy. 1974. Man and Beast. London: Hart-Davis, MacGibbon.

Wilson, Brian. 1999. Christianity. London: Routledge.

Wilson, Bryan R. 1973. Magic and the Millennium. London: Heinemann.

Wilson, Monica. 1959. Communal Rituals of the Nyakyusa. Oxford: Oxford University Press.

Wolf, Arthur, ed. 1974. Religion and Ritual in Chinese Society. Stanford, CA: Stanford University Press.

Wu, Nelson I. 1964. Chinese and Indian Architecture: City of Man, the Mountain of God, and the Realm of the Immortals. London: Readers Union / Prentice-Hall International.

Yamamoto, Yukitaka. 1987. The Way of the Kami. Stockton, CA: Tsubaki America Publications.

Yamasaki, Taiko. 1988. Shingon: Japanese Esoteric Buddhism, trans. Richard and Cynthia Peterson. Boston: Shambhala Publications.

Yang, C. K. 1967. Religion in Chinese Society: A Study of Contemporary Social Functions of Religion and Some of Their Historical Factors. Berkeley and Los Angeles: University of California Press.

York, Michael. 1986. The Roman Festival Calendar of Numa Pompilius. New York: Peter Lang.

————. 1995a. The Divine versus the Asurian: An Interpretation of Indo-European Cult and Myth. Bethesda, MD: International Scholars Publications.

————. 1995b. The Emerging Network: A Sociology of the New Age and Neo-Pagan Movements. Lanham, MD: Rowman & Littlefield.

————. 1997. "New Age and the Late Twentieth Century." Journal of Contemporary Religion 12 (October): 401–19.

————. 1999. "Invented Culture / Invented Religion: The Fictional Origins of Contemporary Paganism." Nova Religio, September, 135–46.

———. 2001. "New Age Commodification and Appropriation of Spirituality." Journal of Contemporary Religion 16 (October): 361–72.

Young, William A. 1995. The World's Religions: Worldviews and Contemporary Issues. Englewood Cliffs, NJ: Prentice-Hall.

Yupho, Dhanit. 1970. The Custom and Rite of Paying Homage to Teachers of Khon, Lakon and Piphat. Thai Culture, new series 11. Bangkok: Fine Arts Department.

Yusa, Michiko. 2002. Japanese Religions. London: Routledge.

Zaehner, Robert Charles. 1957. Mysticism, Sacred and Profane. Oxford: Oxford University Press.

Zuesse, Evan M. 1979. Ritual Cosmos: The Sanctification of Life in African Religions. Athens: Ohio University Press.

Zwalf, W. 1981. Heritage of Tibet. London: British Museum Publications.

# Index

229

Quakerism, 66
Quechuas, 50–51

Rada, 59
Radicalism, spiritual, 167
Rama, 9, 91–92
Ramakrishna, 75
Raphael, Melissa, 187
Rationalism, 142; scientific, 9
Ray, Benjamin, 34, 37
Reenchantment, 144
Reid, David, 172–73
Reincarnation, 59, 102, 105, 109, 160
Religion(s), ix, 1, 48, 62, 65, 165; African tribal, 37; full range of, 166; no American designation, 46; pagan/gnostic divide, 158–59; paganism as the root of, 104, 167; religion and magic, 68–69; tribal 6, 10, 14, 32–38, 44, 175
*Rig-Veda* 78
Rites of nature, 150
Rites of passage, 23, 29, 34, 45, 57, 83, 148, 175; Hindu, 190
Ritual, 14, 149, 187; ritual circle, 187; ritualistic offerings, 147
Roman Catholic Church, 48, 50, 55, 59, 133–36, 141–42, 164, 170, 200; Roman Catholic elements, 53; Roman Catholic saints, 55
Roman, 144, 153; Empire, 11; *focus*, 156; most popular gods, 155
Rome, 22, 124, 203
Root-religion, viii, 167–68
Rutherford, Ward, 40–41

Sacredness of place, 13; sacred geography, 39
Saints, 56, 133, 137; Muslim, 140–41; Our Lady of Guadalupe, 134, 151; Our Lady of Guadalupe as Tontantzin, 199; St. Brighid, 134; St. Christopher, 148; St. Denis/Dennis, 134, 148; St. Expedite, 151; St. George, 77, 132, 134; St. John the Baptist, 135, 148; St. Jude, 151; St. Nicholas, 130; St. Vincent, 148
Salvation, 38
San Francisco, 150–51
Santería, 56–58, 60, 62–63, 134, 143, 152, 157, 184, 199. *See also* Lucumí; Ocha
Santero, 54

Sarasvati, 23
Saso, Michael, 40–41
Satanism, 162; Church of Satan, 203; Satan/Iblis, 201
Scientific empiricism, 142
Scientology, 165
Sectarianism, 3
Secular/secularism, 9, 47, 141–42, 202; secular religions, 166; secular West, 144
Secularization, 133, 142, 202
*Seiðr*, 61
Senecas' Handsome Lake movement, 52
Seven African Powers, the, 55
Shakti, 9, 93, 95, 192
Shaman, 21, 30, 34, 36–44, 49, 59, 121, 126, 128, 179; En-no-Gyoja, 172
Shamanism, 5–6, 10, 32, 37–44, 73, 141, 178; Amerindian shamanic practices/beliefs, 47, 50, 52; contrast with Afro-Latin practice, 56–57; core of, 144; Core Shamanism, 43; Mapuche, 51; Mongolian, 197; Neoshamanism, 43–44, 180, 185; shamanic trance, 46, 150–52; Shinto, 29; Siberian, 63; Tantric, 122, 125; Tibetan, 196
*Shang ti*, 16–19, 22
Shankaracharya, 158
*Shen*, 17, 171
*Shinden*, 25–26
*Shintai*, 25, 31
Shinto, 10, 14, 22–33, 36, 63, 73, 99, 115, 130, 132, 151, 157, 172–75; Ryōbu, Sannō and Yoshida, 24, 132; Sect, 23; Shrine, 23
*Shinbutsu shūgō*, 132
Shitala, 81, 88, 90, 95, 98
Shiva, 17, 80–84, 90–93, 103, 154, 190–92; iconic representation of, 75; iconographic antecedent to, 106; in Nepal, 119–20; in Thailand, 113; Lokesvara, 119, 122; relation to the *anima and animus*, 95; royal worship of, 109; Saivism, 9, 93, 193; son of, 115; supergod, 17; vehicle of, 100; wife of, 88. *See also* Lingam
*Shen*, 15, 171
Shrine, 36, 54, 73, 173, 177
Siberia, 38, 45; Siberian shamanism, 63
Sikhism, 10
Siklós, Bulcsu, 197

# About the Author

Michael York is principal lecturer for the Sophia Centre for the Study of Cultural Astronomy and Astrology at Bath Spa University College. He is director of the Bath Archive for Contemporary Religious Affairs, as well as codirector of the Academy for Cultural and Educational Studies in London and director of the Amsterdam Center for Eurindic Studies. His books include *The Roman Festival Calendar of Numa Pompilius, The Divine versus the Asurian: An Interpretation of Indo-European Cult and Myth*, and *The Emerging Network: A Sociology of the New Age and Neopagan Movements*.

*This work is dedicated to Chloë Myrth Dunscombe and Nathaniel John Pyke.*